HEALING
IS A
WAY OF LIFE

*'Therefore I tell you, whatever you ask for in prayer,
believe that you have received it, and it will be yours.'*

(Mark 11:24)

HEALING
IS A
WAY OF LIFE

PRACTICAL STEPS TO HEALING

Talks by Canon Jim Glennon

Compiled and Edited by Zillah Williams

❧

2009

Healing is a way of life: Practical steps to healing. Talks by Canon Jim Glennon. Editor: Zillah Williams.

All Scripture quotations, unless otherwise indicated, are taken from the *Holy Bible: New International Version®*. NIV®. Copyright © 1973, 1978, 1984 by International Bible Society. 1980 edition pub. by Hodder & Stoughton.

Scripture quotations marked (The Amplified Bible) are taken from The Amplified Bible, Copyright© 1954, 1958, 1962, 1964, 1965, 1987 by The Lockman Foundation.

Scripture quotations marked (KJV) are taken from The Holy Bible, King James Version.

Scripture quotations marked (Phillips) are taken from *Letters to young churches: a translation of the New Testament Epistles* by J. B. Phillips. Melbourne, E.C. Harris. Australian edition 1952.

Scripture quotations marked (RSV) are taken from the *Revised Standard Version of the Bible,* copyright 1946, 1952, 1971 by the Division of Christian Education of the National Council of Churches of Christ in the USA.

Scripture quotations marked (The Living Bible) are taken from the *The Living Bible Paraphrased* © 1971 by Tyndale House Publishers, Wheaton, Illinois 60187.

National Library of Australia Cataloguing-in-Publication entry

Author:	Glennon, Jim, 1920-2005.
Title:	Healing is a way of life : practical steps to healing : talks by Canon Jim Glennon / editor, Zillah Williams.
Edition:	1st ed.
ISBN:	9780646518626 (pbk.)
Subjects:	Glennon, Jim, 1920-2005--Sermons.
	Spiritual healing.
	Meditation--Christianity.
	Christian life.
Other Authors/Contributors:	Williams, Zillah, 1934-
Dewey Number:	234.131

Cover photograph:	Heather Chessell—road to Cradle Mountain, Tasmania.
Artwork:	Great Scott! art + design: www.greatscott.com.au

Published by Zillah Williams with the assistance of Love of Books Self Publishing Success: www.loveofbooks.com.au

Foreword

I warmly commend 'Healing is a Way of Life'. The helpful systematic layout, biblical focus and clear illustrations assist in shaping our view on wholeness and healing. This is a thoughtful and accessible volume that should be read widely and revisited regularly.

The Right Reverend Stuart Robinson
Bishop of Canberra and Goulburn

Dedication

This work is dedicated to the memory of Deaconess Gwyneth Hall whose ministry in producing the Sermon Notes has blessed so many people and made this book possible.

Testimony

Dear Reader,

I had the God-given privilege of attending the Healing Service in 1968 and sitting under the ministry of Canon Jim Glennon. It was through this ministry that I experienced healing. Since 1959 I had suffered with syringobulbia. The prognosis given by doctors was that it was incurable and would only deteriorate. God sent someone to direct us to Jim and his ministry of God's Word. It was through this ministry that God healed me. This was later confirmed by a number of physicians.

God was later to call my wife and I into Bible College, to the mission field, the Presbyterian ministry and to serve, firstly as chaplain in the army, then the navy, and to ministry in the church.

As you read this book of Jim's sermons and look deeply into the Bible, may God richly bless you. I know He will because He is FAITHFUL.

Yours in our Lord, Jesus Christ,

Ted Brooker

Acknowledgements

Many people have helped me with suggestions and comments during the preparation of this work. Special thanks are due to Mr Sid Eavis, the executor of Canon Glennon's estate, for lending me his collection of Canon Glennon's Sermon Notes; for permission to use the photograph of Canon Glennon on the back cover; and in so many other ways.

Thanks, also, to Peter Verco, former organist at the Healing Ministry, for his prayer support and encouragement, also to John Norfor for his helpful suggestions.

Mention must also be made of Sally Chambers who lives in Melbourne, Fl., USA. She has given support and encouragement from the inception of this project to its conclusion, along with valued editorial help and advice.

Canberra resident Helen Kahane's enthusiastic, personal use of the sermon material as it came into her hands for review, affirms the relevance of Canon Glennon's teaching for today's readers. Her dedicated help in the final stages of checking has been invaluable.

I would like to acknowledge the assistance of the 'Sisters of the Community of the Holy Name' in Cheltenham, Victoria (for information about Miss Eleanor Lindsay); Bronwyn Pryor, National Chair of 'Camps Farthest Out' (for information about Roland and Marcia Brown); and Professor Tom Frame, Director of St Mark's National Theological Centre, Canberra, who offered helpful guidance as to structure.

Last, but by no means least, thanks to Alan Williams, my husband, for his usual wise counsel.

Zillah Williams
Canberra

Preface

The Healing Ministry at St Andrew's Cathedral, Sydney, began in September 1960 under the leadership of Canon Jim Glennon (1920–2005).

Deaconess Gwyneth Hall (1914–2001), an Anglican who worked as a hospital chaplain, began attending the Healing Ministry services in 1961. She started making written notes of the sermons, sending carbon copies to interested friends. Demand for these grew and, in July 1963, the first duplicated Sermon Notes were produced. Canon Glennon dubbed the recipients of these: The Postal Congregation. As at 1984, 1000 copies were distributed to the congregation at the weekly services and another 4000 posted to people both within Australia and overseas.

The purpose of this book is to preserve Canon Jim Glennon's practical, biblical teaching on healing, as recorded in these Sermon Notes, and to make it available to as wide an audience as possible. It is presented in the form of a daily teaching over five days in the week.

The selected sermons cover the period from 1970 to 1988 but are not presented in chronological order.

Zillah Williams

Guidelines for Healing Today: Let the sick man call – 1

'Is any one of you sick? He should call the elders of the church'

—James 5:14

Scripture reading: James 5:13–16

Over the years I have had considerable experience in speaking to people about the Healing Ministry and hearing their questions. I think the question that has been asked more than any other is, 'Does the sick person need to have faith?' What does the Bible say? We find Jesus saying to a sick person, 'According to your faith be it unto you' (Matthew 9:29 KJV). This means that you will receive the answer to your prayer in proportion to your faith. On another occasion, when someone had been healed, he said, ' "your faith has healed you"' (Matthew 9:22). On yet another occasion, when someone wasn't healed, he said the reason was that those who had prayed for the sick person had 'little faith' (see Matthew 17:19–20). Matthew records that Jesus was unable to do many miracles in his home town because of people's lack of faith (see Matthew 13:58).

What all these texts are saying is that, the more faith the sick person has, the easier it is for him to draw on blessing from God. The less faith he has, the more difficult it is.

What the New Testament teaches is summed up by the words: 'Is any one of you sick? He should call' (James 5:14). In other words, the sick man may not have all the faith that is needed, but he must have enough faith to ask others to pray for him. He must believe that God exists, and that he 'rewards those who earnestly seek him' (Hebrews 11:6).

Key thought: If the person who is sick is too sick to call, then others can call on his behalf.

Thank you, Father, for your promise of healing and forgiveness as we call on the elders of the church to pray with us and for us. Amen.

Guidelines for Healing Today: Let the sick man call – 2

'He replied, "If you have faith as small as a mustard seed, you can say to this mulberry tree, 'Be uprooted and planted in the sea,' and it will obey you."'   —Luke 17:6

Scripture reading: Genesis 18:16–33

I want to make the point as clearly and as strongly as I can that someone who is sick needs to have faith enough to ask others to add their faith to his, and that he needs to continue to ask for prayer. This does not mean in an 'asking, asking, asking' way so much as in faith being added to faith — 'line upon line; here a little, and there a little' (Isaiah 28:10 KJV).

When the Healing Service in St Andrew's Cathedral first began, a woman had faith to come with a need and we prayed for her with the laying on of hands. There was no change that one could see, but she kept coming and kept receiving the laying on of hands. To my shame I said to myself, 'Oh we can't help her.' But she had faith to continue to come; faith enough to want other people to add their faith to hers; and faith enough to continue to draw upon the faith of other people—and she was wonderfully and completely healed.

Jesus said that, if we have faith like a grain of mustard seed, God will use it for our blessing. The mustard seeds in Palestine to which Jesus was referring can hardly be seen with the naked eye.

Key thought: However small your faith is to begin with, God wants to use it and give you a blessing. It might not be all you need, but that is how you can begin.

Our loving Father, we thank you for your Word. We would take it as our rule and guide. We would ask, and continue to ask, for prayer. In Jesus' name. Amen.

Guidelines for Healing Today: The elders of the church

'Is any one of you sick? He should call the elders of the church to pray over him and anoint him with oil in the name of the Lord.' — James 5:14

Scripture reading: 1 Timothy 5:17–21

The initiative for healing, James says, must be taken by the sick man, and the response must come from the elders of the church.

Who are the elders? Many would maintain that 'elders' means the ordained ministry. Some would interpret this a little more freely and say that it means the appointed representatives of the church. There would be general agreement that it means those who act for the church.

There are reasons why we need representatives of the church to pray over the man who has had faith to call. For example, it would be impractical for the whole church to go to a sickbed, so the few go on behalf of the many. They have considerable responsibility, because they not only go in their own right as members of the church, but they go on behalf of the church.

Dr. Broughton Knox, Principal of Moore Theological College in Sydney from 1959 to 1985, said that the inner meaning of the words 'call the elders of the church' is that it is the church itself which is really being called. However much the elders represent the church, it is the church which is to take the responsibility for praying for the sick man. It is the rank and file of the congregation who have been called and who have the responsibility to respond.

Key thought: Those who have been joined to Christ by repentance, faith and obedience and a work of the Holy Spirit are the real people who have the responsibility for praying for someone who has had faith to call for them.

We thank you, Father, for those who stand with us in faith and prayer. In Jesus' name. Amen.

Guidelines for Healing Today: The congregation is responsible

'"Brothers, choose seven men from among you who are known to be full of the Spirit and wisdom"' —Acts 6:3

Scripture reading: Acts 6:1–8

Philip and Stephen were not of the Twelve nor of the Seventy; they had not been commissioned—in the sense that they were not sent out to preach and heal. The only responsibilities that were laid upon them were that they should look after the cups of tea and other social requirements of the congregation. However, as we read of their ministry in the Acts of the Apostles, we see that they witnessed to Christ and laid hands on sick people for healing. Signs and wonders followed their ministry which was in no way behind that of the apostles in its effect. In saying this, I don't mean that everyone is to go around doing their own thing. What I do mean is that all of us are to assume our responsibility as members of the church in a corporate, team-like way, subject to leadership, and drawing upon the ministries of the Holy Spirit.

'Is any one of you sick? He should call the elders of the church' (James 5:14). What these words are saying is this: The man who calls for help is intended to be a member of the church; he calls the church in his need, and the church responds in a way that is meaningful. It is the leadership's responsibility to represent the church, and it is the responsibility of the church as a whole to minister to the sick man in an effective and ongoing way.

Key thought: The leadership should enable the congregation to accept the responsibility that the Bible says is theirs.

Our loving Father, we thank you for the provision of your Word and for this blueprint we have to follow. We would have faith and vision to act on these insights, which we do now. In Jesus' name. Amen.

Guidelines for Healing Today: Let them pray over him – 1

'And the prayer offered in faith will make the sick person well; the Lord will raise him up. If he has sinned, he will be forgiven.'　　—James 5:15

Scripture reading: Matthew 9:27–31

'Is any among you sick? Let him call for the elders of the church, and let them pray over him' (James 5:14 RSV). No-one who comes to the Healing Service in St Andrew's Cathedral, Sydney, is ever told, 'You don't have enough faith', because, if you have faith to come, you are doing your part. The responsibility to exercise faith is then on the shoulders of the elders, and the church. They are to 'pray over him'.

The church should remember three things when praying over the sick. They each begin with the letter 'P'.

Be Positive.

One aspect of faith is that prayer is to be made in a positive way. Having said this, I would add that I don't always pray for healing, even though healing is needed. Very often people come and ask for prayer for healing when they are, humanly speaking, in a terminal condition. We need to realise our limitations and know when we can pray in faith and when we can only relinquish the matter to God. I would rather not have to say this, but I do say it because it is what I act out in my ministry. To leave it out may lead one to promise more than one is able to perform.

But whether I am praying for healing or for some other appropriate blessing from God, my prayer is positive. When I am believing for a relevant promise of God in a pastoral situation, whether it be for myself or for someone else, I believe that I receive that promise. I make a decision and I affirm it by faith.

Key thought: The first requirement in praying over the sick person is to be positive.

Thank you, Father, that all your promises to us are 'yes' in Christ Jesus.

Guidelines for Healing Today: Let them pray over him – 2

'But if the Spirit of him that raised up Jesus from the dead dwell in you, he that raised up Christ from the dead shall also quicken your mortal bodies by his Spirit that dwelleth in you.'   —Romans 8:11 (KJV)

Scripture reading: 2 Timothy 1:1–7

Power – prayer should be powerful

It isn't enough for prayer to be positive; we also need the power of the Holy Spirit. The Bible says it is the Holy Spirit who quickens our mortal bodies. In the final analysis, it is the reality of the Holy Spirit which makes effective the promises of God. With this in mind, let us remember that we can 'grieve' the Spirit (Ephesians 4:30); we can 'quench' the Spirit (1 Thessalonians 5:19 KJV); we can 'stir up' the Spirit (2 Timothy 1:6 KJV) and we can be 'filled with the Spirit' (Ephesians 5:18). So, it is quite obvious that we are going to have varying degrees of the power of God in our lives and in our prayers. Sooner or later, in our prayer life, we have to be concerned with the power of the Holy Spirit, and to so live our lives that the Spirit is not grieved or quenched, but stirred up so that we are filled, and remain filled, with the Spirit.

Perseverance

The Bible says we are to 'pray without ceasing' (1 Thessalonians 5:17 KJV). I know what it is like to be affirming my faith for God's answer to prayer before I am out of bed in the morning, while I am cleaning my teeth, driving my car and, with a corner of my mind, during whatever else I am doing throughout the day.

Key thought: We are not heard for our much speaking, but we are heard for our continued faith.

Our loving Father, we believe for your blessing on our Healing Service and for ourselves personally. By your grace enable our prayer to be positive, powerful and persevering. For Jesus' sake. Amen.

Guidelines for Healing Today: Anointing him with oil – 1

'Samuel took the horn of oil and anointed him in the presence of his brothers, and from that day on the Spirit of the LORD came upon David in power.'
           — 1 Samuel 16:13

Scripture reading: Isaiah 61:1–3

What is the significance of the scriptural injunction that the person who calls for prayer for healing, and who is to be prayed over by the elders of the church with the Prayer of Faith, is to be anointed with oil?

There are many references in Scripture to being anointed. Oil was, among other things, an aspect of toilet preparation. It had a soothing and cleansing effect on the skin and was a relief from the hot, harsh desert sun. Anointing with oil was also a sign of hospitality. On one occasion Jesus commented that in the house he was visiting they had not anointed him with that intention, but that someone else had (see Luke 7:46).

Anointing with oil also had a medicinal quality. The 'Good Samaritan' poured on oil and wine — the oil for healing and the wine as an antiseptic (see Luke 10:34).

Anointing was also a religious act. The king was anointed with oil at his coronation as a sign that he was a sacred person. The anointing imparted a special enduement of the Holy Spirit. The person is being consecrated to God, and God is giving an outpouring of his Spirit. In the setting that we have in James 5:14,15 it is plainly being used in a religious sense. The elders of the church are praying and anointing. The person who is sick is calling for prayer for healing, but he is also coming to God and asking for spiritual blessing from God.

Key thought: One of the uses of oil in Scripture was to impart a special enduement of the Holy Spirit.

Thank you, Father, for your anointing with oil as an outward sign of our inward belief. In Jesus' name. Amen.

Guidelines for Healing Today: Anointing him with oil – 2

'If he has sinned, he will be forgiven'   —James 5:15

Scripture reading: John 9:1–7, 18–38

Folk often come to the Healing Service who have no Christian affiliation to begin with. Our concern is to bring Christ into focus for them as well as to minister healing.

The intention of the Healing Ministry is that people should progress from having their presenting need for healing met, to knowing Jesus as Lord. That is my main reason for being involved in this ministry because, more than in any other way, as far as my experience goes, it is a unique method of evangelism. We meet people at their point of need to begin with, but under the Holy Spirit the person ultimately comes to know the Lord Jesus Christ.

It is the Holy Spirit who quickens our mortal bodies and thereby gives healing, and the same Spirit takes of Christ and shows him to the person receiving the ministry. I have seen more people come to Christ in this way than in any other. Also, I have seen more people who were Christians to begin with, come into a deeper walk in the Spirit through the Healing Ministry than in any other way. This is the significance of anointing with oil. It is a sacramental sign—it has an outward form with an inward meaning. The outward form is the oil which has been blessed for a sacred purpose. The inward meaning is the important thing. It stands for the person's consecration to Christ and the imparting of the Holy Spirit.

Key thought: It is the Holy Spirit who quickens our mortal bodies and thereby gives healing, and the same Spirit takes of Christ and shows him to the person receiving the ministry.

Our loving Father, we thank you for these guidelines for healing today, and we thank you for the wonderful blessing there is in being anointed with oil, to the glory of Christ and the extension of your Kingdom. Amen.

Perfect Faith And Forgiveness – 1

'Forgive us our debts, as we also have forgiven our debtors'

—Matthew 6:12

Scripture reading: Matthew 6:5–15

People often ask me if there is something we can do to enable us to develop faith that does not doubt, faith that goes all the way and which can be applied in any and every situation. The answer is yes, there is something we can do, and it is directly inspired by the Word of God.

There is the well-known passage in Mark 11:22–24 in which Jesus speaks about praying in faith without doubting: '"Have faith in God," Jesus answered. "I tell you the truth, if anyone says to this mountain, 'Go, throw yourself into the sea,' and does not doubt in his heart but believes that what he says will happen, it will be done for him. Therefore I tell you, whatever you ask for in prayer, believe that you have received it, and it will be yours."'

His next words (v. 25) are: '"And when you stand praying, if you hold anything against anyone, forgive him, so that your Father in heaven may forgive you your sins."' It is significant that when Jesus is talking about 'faith that does not doubt' he links it at once, and intimately, with the need for us to forgive others who sin against us. That is not only so that our prayer can be answered, but also so that we can be forgiven by God! It can never be over-emphasised that we will not be forgiven by God for our sins if we do not, from our hearts, forgive everyone who has sinned against us.

Key thought: Forgiveness of others is of the utmost importance.

Thank you, Father, for your assurance of forgiveness. By your grace we freely forgive those who have wronged us. Through Christ, our Lord. Amen.

Perfect Faith and Forgiveness – 2

'"Do not judge, and you will not be judged. Do not condemn, and you will not be condemned. Forgive, and you will be forgiven."' —Luke 6:37

Scripture reading: Matthew 18:21–35

We are not saved because we forgive others; we are saved by our faith in Christ alone. But in a number of passages in the Bible it is made clear that God's forgiveness of us has to be followed by our forgiveness of others. I will venture to say that there is nothing that will lead to a greater release of faith in prayer for healing, or for any other of the promises of God, than to forgive others 'from our heart' for what they have done to us.

Notice that we are not to forgive just some, nor to forgive most. We are to forgive *all*. We are to forgive everyone and we are to forgive *from our hearts*. Isn't God a hard taskmaster in some respects? He is not satisfied with us making some token act. With God, it is all, or nothing at all. If we are to have faith that does not doubt, one of the requirements is that we forgive everyone, and forgive from our heart.

It is only as we forgive *everybody* from our heart that we are able to forgive in a complete way. It is only hard when we are seeking to do it in a 50–50 way. If we have the concept and reality of forgiving everyone from our heart, and that means all the way through, then, and then only, will it be possible.

Key thought: We are to forgive everyone who has wronged us.

Thank you, Father, that as we forgive all those who have hurt us we are free to exercise faith in prayer. We do that now. In Jesus' name. Amen.

Perfect Faith and Forgiveness – 3

"'For I will forgive their wickedness and will remember their sins no more.'"
— Jeremiah 31:34

Scripture reading: Luke 17:3,4; Matthew 18:21,22

You will have heard people say: 'Oh, I can forgive but I can't forget'. That's what happens when someone is making a gesture of forgiveness but it isn't from the heart. God doesn't say to us: 'I forgive you but I won't forget'.

There is no salvation in him remembering; the only salvation is in him forgetting, and it is that kind of forgiveness we are to extend to others.

It is not an optional extra. It is not something for those who can do it. It is something that we all have to do — beginning with me. We might well say that it is impossible — I won't disagree with that. Ultimately, it is only by the grace of God that it is possible to do these things.

I have been much blessed in my Christian walk by the example and the teaching of the Mary Sisters.[1] I stayed with them in Darmstadt some ten years ago.[2] Those who know the Mary Sisters well, especially those who have been there, know that there is a most extraordinary reality of Christian love, not only among the Sisters but shared among those who visit them.

The part about the Mary Sisters that is of special significance is that they look upon forgiveness as absolutely essential. This leads to a release of love and then of faith.

Key thought: What can we do to have complete faith? When you stand praying, forgive everyone from your heart.

O Father, we come to you, needing to forgive and to be forgiven. We would set our hearts to understand, so that you might give us your blessing and enable us to come to that perfect forgiveness of others. In Jesus' name. Amen.

[1] Evangelical Sisterhood of Mary.
[2] That is, in the late 1960s.

Why the Cross of Christ is Central to Healing – 1

'God forbid that I should glory, save in the cross of our Lord Jesus Christ'

—Galatians 6:14 (KJV)

Scripture reading: Galatians 6:11–18

When I began to be involved in the healing ministry, one of the first realisations that came to me was that I needed more of the power of the Holy Spirit than I had so far drawn on. So I went to Agnes Sanford[1], who was in Sydney at the time, and asked if she would pray with me that I might have a greater infilling of the Holy Spirit. She prayed for me on three occasions and, following the second occasion, on the Saturday of that week, I had a vision of the cross.

I could see Christ in the vision. He was grey with death and there was sweat on his face. But it wasn't Christ that occupied the vision but rather the cross. The wood of the upright part of the cross was like a tree trunk that had been in a fierce forest fire; it was black, broken and gnarled, and I reacted to it by saying: 'Oh! It's an awful cross. It's an awful cross. Oh! It's an awful cross'. And that was the only thing I said for the space of two hours—as long as the vision lasted.

At the time, I did not know why I should have had such a vision, but I believe it was because God wanted me to know that, if I wanted more of any blessing from him, I needed to know that it comes from the cross of Christ, because it was what Christ did on the cross that opens the way for us to the Father and enables us to draw on any and every blessing that God has for those who put their trust in Christ.

Key thought: It is what Christ has done for us on the cross which opens the way to the Father.

Thank you, Jesus, for what you suffered for us on the cross.

---

[1] Agnes Mary White Sanford (1897-1982) is considered to be one of the principal founders of the Inner Healing movement. She was the daughter of a Presbyterian missionary in China and the wife of an Episcopal priest. It was after reading her book *The Healing Light* that Jim Glennon asked the Dean of the Cathedral if he could start a service of divine healing at the Cathedral. The first service was held on September 28, 1960. Jim Glennon met Agnes Sanford at Easter in 1961 when she visited Australia. He held a Memorial Service for her at the Cathedral on 17th March, 1982.

Why the Cross of Christ is Central to Healing – 2

'with his stripes we are healed.'   —Isaiah 53:5 (KJV)

Scripture reading: 1 Peter 2:13–25

Peter tells us that what Jesus did in his body on the tree (that is, the cross), was to bear the sin of the world, including your sin and mine— sin in whatever form it takes—'He himself bore our sins in his body on the tree' (v.24).

Whether you think of sickness and infirmity as being part of the sin of the world, or whether you think in terms of Isaiah 53:5 'with his stripes we are healed', I affirm that what Jesus did on the cross was to provide freedom from sickness and infirmity. That is what the cross is all about.

Peter goes on to say that we are to 'die to sins'. This means that when we need healing we must keep in mind what Jesus has done, and reckon, or believe, that the problem has died with Christ. We are to react by affirming by faith—meaning, we are to believe it before we have it—that the problem has died with Christ. That is the theological understanding we need to have.

Jesus said that healing is part of the greater reality of the Kingdom of God. He said: "Heal the sick ... and tell them, 'The kingdom of God is near you'" (Luke 10:9). We are to be dead to sin and alive to righteousness. We are to be dead to those things that died on the cross and alive to healing which is a present sign of the Kingdom.

Key thought: Jesus has taken away both the sin of the world and our sickness and infirmity.

Our Loving Father, with great reverence and great awe, we look at the cross and we glory in it. For the Bible says, 'by his wounds we have been healed'. Father, teach us to understand this, deep down, all the way through—to affirm it by faith and to express it in what we do. Through Christ our Lord. Amen.

Three Main Themes in the Healing Ministry:

Seek God for himself – 1

'But Stephen, full of the Holy Spirit, looked up to heaven and saw the glory of God, and Jesus standing at the right hand of God.' — Acts 7:55

Scripture reading: 2 Corinthians 12:1–10

There is more than one way in which to pray. The usual basis for prayer is the belief that God is helping us with our problem. That is a perfectly valid way to pray, provided we are praying the Prayer of Faith as described in Mark 11:20–26.

The difficulty with this way of praying is that it focuses on the problem; it is as though God is behind us and we are facing our problem. I want to explain a different way to pray which involves turning around 180 degrees.

The problem is still there, but now it is behind us and we are facing towards God. Before, God was helping us with our problems. Now, our problems are helping us with God! That is the difference. It means that we are reacting to our permitted difficulties by moving closer to God and depending on God more—drawing closer to him, experiencing Father, Son and Holy Spirit. That is a very different way of praying.

Key thought: Turn around 180 degrees so that you are facing God, and your problems are behind you.

Father, we would react to our permitted difficulties by moving closer to you and depending upon you more. Through Jesus our Lord. Amen.

Three Main Themes in the Healing Ministry:

Seek God for himself – 2

'My heart says of you, "Seek his face!" Your face, LORD, I will seek.'

—Psalm 27:8

Scripture reading: Matthew 6:25–34

When Jesus said that we are to seek first the Kingdom of God and his righteousness, he meant that we are to seek God for himself, and not just so that things will be given to us. That is what the little word 'first' means. I am not saying this is easy to do; it requires patience and perseverance.

When we get this right—looking at God and not the problem, seeking him—we will know what it is to be filled with all his fullness, and we will have an experience of healing, an experience of 'our mountain being cast into the sea' (see Mark 11:23), an experience of answered prayer that far exceeds any other way of praying.

At an earlier time in my own life, before there was a Healing Ministry, and when I had broken down in health emotionally, I learned to pray this way. I know what it is like to get it right—not once, but day by day and time by time. This was the time in my life when I had, in my own small way, the abundance of revelation. God revealed himself to me, more and more. My problems, which had reached paralytic proportions, were—not all at once but, as it were spadeful by spadeful—cast into the sea. Those difficulties which had brought me to the end of my tether, I now not only do not have, but cannot recall ever having had.

Key thought: Turn around 180 degrees, so that your problems are behind you and you are facing towards God.

Our loving Father, we would depend on you more. We would react to our difficulties so that we seek you, and you only for yourself, and we do that now, more and more. Through Christ our Lord. Amen.

Three Main Themes in the Healing Ministry:

What you confess, you possess – 1

'Now faith is being sure of what we hope for and certain of what we do not see. This is what the ancients were commended for.'
—Hebrews 11:1, 2

Scripture reading: Matthew 12:33–37

One of the things fundamental to our Christian experience is to know what God has promised to provide and to exercise repentance, faith and obedience in order to draw upon this provision. This means that we accept the promised blessings of God in such a way as to believe we receive them, both for ourselves and for others—we are accepting the answer that God provides. We are confessing the answer that God provides with our words and in our hearts. Because we confess it, we possess it.

However, so often we confess and possess, not the answer which God provides, but the problem which has come from the sin of the world. Of course, the difficulty is that the problem is what we see. The problem is what we have. The problem is what gives rise to the anxiety, apprehension and fear. But a fundamental tenet of the Christian position is that we are to live, not by sight, but by faith (see 2 Corinthians 5:7). Faith is not what you see; it is what you hope for and what you believe you receive so that you do not doubt in your heart.

The point I want to make is that we are all confessing something, and we are all possessing something—whether we know it or not, whether we like it or not. And, so often, we are confessing and possessing the difficulties. What we are to confess and possess are the answers and the provision that God makes.

Key thought: You have what you accept.

Father, thank you that you have promised to provide for our every need. We accept your provision now. Through Jesus Christ, our Lord. Amen.

Three Main Themes in the Healing Ministry:

What you confess, you possess – 2

'"I tell you the truth, if anyone says to this mountain, 'Go, throw yourself into the sea,' and does not doubt in his heart but believes that what he says will happen, it will be done for him."' —Mark 11:23

Scripture reading: Acts 8:26–40

Jesus said that we are to believe we have received God's provision in such a way that we do not doubt in our hearts. It is not enough to confess, in a 50–50 way, the answer that God provides. Too often we have a foot in both camps, and this is why it doesn't work in the way that it needs to work. It will help us to be wholehearted in believing if we accept the provision of God in the same way as we accept Christ for salvation. If you keep this thought in mind, you will pray in a way you are already used to—that is, you will accept all the promises of God in the same way as you accept Christ, so that they are what you affirm by faith, and therefore in praise. As you affirm the promises of God by faith you will increasingly experience them by sight.

I can only say that, in my prayer activity, I am constantly seeking to switch over from confessing the problem to confessing the answer—for myself and for others.

Key thought: So often we find we are confessing and possessing the difficulties. What we are to confess and possess are the answers and the provision which God makes.

Our loving Father, we repent that, so often, we have a foot in both camps. We now accept your promises so that they are what we affirm by faith in an ongoing way until we experience them by sight. Amen.

Three Main Themes in the Healing Ministry:

What you confess, you possess – 3

'Elijah was a man just like us … he prayed, and the heavens gave rain, and the earth produced its crops.'   —James 5:17–18

Scripture reading: 1 Kings 18:42–46

Once, when I was conducting a mission in Gilgandra, a town in western NSW, I was asked to pray for rain. The area was in the grip of drought. I didn't immediately pray. The mission began on a Sunday and I didn't pray for rain until the following Thursday. I asked everyone to stand and I prayed along these lines: 'Lord, Jesus said whatsoever things you desire, when you pray, believe that you have received them so that you do not doubt, and they will be yours. We now accept rain for this locality. We confess it, and by faith we possess it, in Jesus' name'.

That was on Thursday. On Friday the skies were like brass. On Saturday, again the skies were like brass. On Sunday morning we came out from the church and I saw a small cloud in the sky and I praised God for that small cloud. We came to the mission service that night. Still no rain, but we were confessing rain by faith. After the service we locked up and were about to leave—when down came the rain! And it rained, and rained. The following day we left Gilgandra, only just getting out before the roads were closed. I shall never forget it! You see, the whole mission congregation was believing. They confessed it, and they possessed it. Faith gave way to sight.

I say again—what you confess, you possess.

Key thought: The whole congregation believed; the whole congregation confessed the answer.

Our loving Father, we would accept your blessings promised in your Word, for ourselves and for others, and we would so confess them that we possess them. In Jesus' name. Amen.

Three Main Themes in the Healing Ministry:

Moment-by-moment faith – 1

'For the earth bringeth forth fruit of herself; first the blade, then the ear, after that the full corn in the ear.' —Mark 4:28 (KJV)

Scripture reading: Isaiah 43:1–7

Let me begin by saying that the first principle of prayer is, I believe, to know the promises of God. That is what the New Testament is all about—the great and precious promises that God has made. The promises of God reveal the will of God, and the first thing to know is what God wants us to have.

The second principle of prayer is that we are to believe we have received the promises of God so that we do not doubt. Jesus said: "I tell you the truth, if anyone says to this mountain, 'Go, throw yourself into the sea,' and does not doubt in his heart but believes that what he says will happen, it will be done for him.'" (Mark 11:23).

Once you know the promises of God as revealed in the broad themes of the New Testament, and once you are believing that you have received these things so that you do not doubt in your heart, there is the need for ongoing, moment-by-moment faith. I never tire of saying that when I accepted the promise of salvation and by faith believed on Christ, nothing happened. So I went back to my rector and said, 'Rector, it's not working', and he said to me, 'You have to have moment-by-moment faith'. I remember how I went away and disciplined my mind by affirming God's blessing in my life in a moment-by-moment way.

Key thought: We need to discipline our minds until we have developed a moment-by-moment faith.

Loving Father, your promises are ours by faith. We would discipline our minds to appropriate all your blessing this day, in a moment-by-moment way. In Jesus' name. Amen.

Three Main Themes in the Healing Ministry:

Moment-by-moment faith – 2

'The man who approaches God must have faith in two things, first that God exists and secondly that it is worth a man's while to try to find God.'

—Hebrews 11:6 (Phillips)

Scripture reading: Hebrews 11:6–12

The Bible says that faith is what you hope for; it is not what you have (see Hebrews 11:1), and that 'without faith it is impossible to please God' (Hebrews 11:6). This means that there has to be a time when we are thanking God for his blessing before we have it in reality. But, if you get it right so that you are affirming the promise of God by faith in a moment-by-moment way, you will increasingly find that, as in my conversion experience, faith gives way to sight— 'first the stalk, then the ear' (Mark 4:28).

That is how you exercise faith for all the promises of God. You believe you have received them. Almost always this has to be followed by a moment-by-moment faith affirmation until faith gives way to sight.

Part of what I now want to say in this connection concerns fasting. The purpose of fasting is to provide a moment-by-moment reminder to be affirming the blessing of God by faith. This is also what is meant by sacrificial prayer; a sacrifice is being made—you are creating circumstances that, rightly understood and rightly reacted to, will give you moment-by-moment faith. Would to God we all knew much more about fasting and ministering before the Lord (see Acts 13:2). We would have much more blessing from God than we have at present.

Key thought: We must affirm the promise of God moment by moment, until faith gives way to sight.

Father, we thank you for your blessing and believe we have received it so that we do not doubt in our heart, and we continue to affirm it by faith until we see it by sight. Amen.

Three Main Themes in the Healing Ministry:

Moment-by-moment faith – 3

'the testing of your faith develops perseverance.'   —James 1:3

Scripture reading: 1 Peter 5:6–12

I used to have an eye complaint called 'iritis'. It is a very painful condition and requires skilled and immediate medical help. I know what it is like to be out of action for weeks at a time when I've had these attacks. As time went by, I decided that I would exercise faith for healing.

I noticed that I got iritis in October. Because it had happened in previous Octobers, I believed it would happen in following Octobers. The Bible says: 'What I feared has come upon me' (Job 3:25). Be that as it may, I came to the point where I believed God had made a promise to raise me up as far as this was concerned (see James 5:14,15), and then I believed I was receiving this healing. Nothing happened, but I began to discipline my mind with moment-by-moment faith.

I disciplined myself to react to the pain by affirming, in faith, that God was healing me. Because the pain continued, I had a moment-by-moment reason to believe, and I continued to believe until the pain and the iritis went away. When it returned at a later time I again accepted healing. On this occasion the pain went away more quickly. As I continued to react to the pain and the alarming symptoms by knowing the promise that God would raise me up, and by exercising faith in this moment-by-moment way, I reached the point where the iritis never came back again.

Key thought: As you exercise moment-by-moment faith in a cumulative way, the blessing is there.

Our loving Father, we would have moment-by-moment faith in the promises of God. We would react to our difficulties so they provide that moment-by-moment reminder to be believing God. Thank you, Father, we do that now, in Jesus' name, and for Jesus' sake. Amen.

Healing is a Way of Life – 1

'He satisfies my desires with good things, so that my youth is renewed like the eagle's.'   —Psalm 103: 5

Scripture reading: James 1:1–8

Healing is not something you draw on by waving a magic wand, nor is it something which can be dispensed in an automatic way.

Let me explain. I have often discussed this point with medical practitioners and I am interested to find that so many of them agree with what I say. I maintain that all sickness begins with overstrain—in one way or another, one time or another—either through a series of circumstances or by something in particular. It may well be caused by something which is not the person's fault, but, in principle, all sickness, all breakdown, begins with overstrain. It follows that an intelligent ministry of healing helps the individual to see the area of overstrain, so that he, or she, will understand where they have gone wrong and will repent.

We all have our limits, and it is only being intelligent and Christian to realise what those limits are. If there had been a proper understanding of this to begin with, it is very likely that there would have been a 'fence at the top of the cliff', rather than the need for 'an ambulance at the bottom'[1]. If ministry is going to be effective in enabling the sick person to draw on wholeness for the future, he needs to know the area of overstrain where he has been tempting providence, and he needs to repent of it so that he has a way of life which lies within the limits of his strength or endurance, and sometimes the limits of his faith.

Key thought: In principle, all sickness, all breakdown, begins with overstrain.

Heavenly Father, we would turn away from those things that have contributed to our illness, and this we do now. In Jesus' name. Amen.

---

[1]Reference to a poem by Joseph Malins, *A Fence or an Ambulance*, 1895. The poem argues that preventing accidents by erecting a fence at the top of a cliff is better than merely providing the means to rescue people once they had fallen over the edge.

Healing is a Way of Life – 2

'So do not throw away your confidence; it will be richly rewarded. You need to persevere so that when you have done the will of God, you will receive what he has promised.' —Hebrews 10:35,36

Scripture reading: Philippians 3:12–16

So often, a Prayer of Faith is prayed by the minister, by the person seeking healing and by the congregation, but afterwards—and I am as much to blame as anyone else—we allow our thoughts to be dominated by doubt, fear and anxiety. If faith is to be effective, we have to pray the Prayer of Faith in a meaningful way and ensure that our ongoing thoughts are of the same kind.

More and more I see the importance of the Healing Service and ask those who approach me for ministry if they will come to the Healing Service first and join the congregation. It is not because I want to swell the numbers. My reason is that, if a person will meaningfully and consistently belong to our fellowship, they will find how to make healing a way of life. They will find that the supportive fellowship, the help they will draw on from the ministry of all believers, the person-to-person contact day in and day out—all these will help them reach the goal of developing a new way of life. I have no hesitation in saying that the Healing Service and the healing congregation, and all that they mean, are the most important ingredients we have to enable people to draw on healing from God.

Key thought: The Prayer of Faith for healing must issue in our ongoing thoughts being an expression and extension of that Prayer of Faith.

Father, we would confess that we have our shortcomings in these things. Bless us so that healing will become 'a way of life'. This is our prayer of confession, of repentance, of faith and of praise. In Jesus' name. Amen.

More Light on Faith: There is no risk in faith – 1

'"Have faith in God," Jesus answered.'   — Mark 11:22

Scripture reading: Mark 11:12–14, 20–25

When I was at a conference in Suva recently,[1] a Roman Catholic priest said to me how much his own prayers were more and more the prayers of faith. God was guiding him in this direction. Then he said something like this: 'I have been asking myself, is there any risk in exercising faith? Do you go out on a limb, where there is a risk involved in praying the Prayer of Faith?' adding, 'I have come to the conclusion that there is no risk in faith'. He didn't say why he had come to that conclusion, and I'm glad he didn't, because, as I thought about what he had said, I decided upon the reasons I would give in making such a statement.

In the latest edition of the Revised Standard Version of the Bible, Mark 11:24, a verse we have used a lot in the Healing Service, is translated: 'Therefore I tell you, whatever you ask in prayer, believe that you have received it, and it will be yours'. Earlier editions had: '… believe that you receive …'. The explanation is that the best of the Greek manuscripts have the expression in what is called the aorist tense. The aorist tense refers to a past occurrence which has a continuing significance.

When we pray that God will make one of his promises effective in our lives, we might use words like this: 'Father, we know that we can receive your promise' or 'Father, we know that we will receive your provision' or even, 'Father, we know that we are receiving your provision'. But what we are to say and think is, 'Father, I believe I *have received* your promise.'

Key thought: We can know that there is no risk in faith, because Jesus said we are to affirm that we have received the blessing.

Father, we affirm that we have received the provision we have asked for. Through Christ our Lord. Amen.

[1] Prior to August 1976.

More Light on Faith: There is no risk in faith – 2

'Now faith means putting our full confidence in the things we hope for, it means being certain of things we cannot see.'—Hebrews 11:1 (Phillips)

Scripture reading: 1 Thessalonians 5:12–24

We are to believe that we have received our request so that we do not doubt in our heart. That is faith in prayer. When we believe that we have received the promise of God so that we are completely sure—obviously there is no room for doubt, or risk, or reservation.

The Prayer of Faith means that we believe we have received God's blessing so that we do not doubt in our heart—before we see it. That is faith as Jesus described it, and that is faith as we have to get it right in our prayer, and in our thinking. Do you see the point this Roman Catholic priest made—that, when we pray in faith like this, there is no risk?

It follows that, if in drawing on the promises of God we believe that we have received them so that we're sure, our reaction is praise and thanksgiving!

There is no risk in faith, because we first of all know what the promise of God is; we believe we have received it; we do not doubt in our heart; we affirm it by faith, and there is ongoing praise whenever the matter comes to mind.

Key thought: Faith is thanking God before you see it.

Our loving Father, we thank you that, as your word comes through to us with increasing clarity, we can see what the path of faith is for us. We rejoice that there is no risk in faith because we can be completely committed to that which you have promised to give; we believe that we have received it so that we do not doubt in our heart, and we affirm it by faith. Father, we praise your name for these things. Through Christ our Lord. Amen.

More Light on Faith: 'In God's time', true or false? – 1

'Then Jesus answered, "Woman, you have great faith! Your request is granted." And her daughter was healed from that very hour.'
—Matthew 15:28

Scripture reading: Mark 7:24–30

A very common saying is: 'It will happen in God's time'. People who pray the Prayer of Faith and who accept the healing ministry of the Church also say this—especially if they have prayed the Prayer of Faith and the healing is not yet there. It has become part and parcel of our prayer-thought, and prayer-language. But, as with a good deal of our 'Christian' understanding, it has no foundation in Scripture. The Bible does not use that expression at all in regard to healing.

The testimony of the Gospels and the Acts of the Apostles is that healing is related to the faith that is exercised, both as to the time of the blessing and the extent of the blessing. In Matthew chapter eight Jesus said that the centurion's servant would be healed according to the centurion's faith—and he was healed at once. Likewise, the woman in Mark chapter seven.

This means that, if our faith is equal to the mountain to be moved, we can expect healing to follow as a matter of course. That is what the New Testament says and that is what we have to face up to, even though it may make us feel uncomfortable. If there is an absence of blessing, we must face up to the fact that Jesus says that, where the blessing is not there, it is because faith has not been exercised in the way, and to the degree, that is necessary for those particular circumstances.

Key thought: The expression: 'In God's time' has no foundation in Scripture.

Our loving Father, we would face up to what is revealed in Scripture and so believe your Word that we may experience the fullness of your blessing. Through Christ our Lord. Amen.

More Light on Faith: 'In God's time', true or false? – 2

'"Why couldn't we drive it out?"' —Matthew 17:19.

Scripture reading: Matthew 17:14–20

In the well-known story from Matthew chapter seventeen, the disciples failed to heal a boy brought to them by his father. When they asked Jesus why they had failed, he told them it was because they had so little faith.

With this particular mountain there had to be a greater release of the Holy Spirit because there was a bigger problem to overcome. The disease was more advanced—there were other complications, and so forth.

However, no-one should think that, if the mountain is big and their faith is small, nothing can happen until their faith increases. As soon as we exercise what faith we have, even if it is as small as a grain of mustard seed, the healing Spirit of God will begin to flow. Because our faith is not equal to the mountain to be moved, there may be no outward sign of healing at first. But, if we continue to exercise what faith we have, the Spirit of God will continue to work so that we will find signs of healing as time goes by— 'first the blade' (Mark 4:28 KJV).

God's time? God's time is now! God's time is when you believe and in proportion to your faith.

Key thought: When we have accepted God's blessing for any of his promises, the Holy Spirit is at work to bring about the blessing.

Our loving Father, we come to you as pilgrims, saying: 'I believe, help my unbelief'. Father, so bless us that we will use what belief we've got, and know your blessing is there in proportion. Father, bless us that we will grow in faith, and bless us that our faith will be used more and more, that your Kingdom will be extended, and the name of Jesus will be glorified. Amen.

Make Your Prayers More Effective: The release of faith – 1

'he has given us his very great and precious promises'   —2 Peter 1:4

Scripture reading: 2 Corinthians 1:8–11

If we are going to make our prayers more effective, there are certain basic things we must always keep in mind. It is good to keep a notebook so that you can more easily bring to mind the things you have learned from instruction you have received, Scriptures you have read, and pastoral experience you have gained.

The first requirement for effective prayer is that we must know what God has provided and what he wants us to have. Our responsibility and our opportunity as Bible-reading Christians, is to search the Scriptures to see what are 'the very great and precious promises' God has made. We need to know them and have them at our fingertips so that we can draw on the promise which is appropriate to the particular need we may have.

The second requirement for effective prayer is that we appropriate the promises of God and live out our faith in the way Christ has taught. He says: 'whatever you ask for in prayer, believe that you have received it, and it will be yours' (Mark 11:24).

The third requirement for effective prayer is that we affirm our acceptance of the promise by faith. Faith means we are thanking God before we have the blessing. There will be times when our faith is put to the test. We have to avoid thinking, and saying, 'But it's not working'. Rather, we need to discipline our minds so that, by faith we say, 'Praise God, praise God, praise God'.

Key thought: Know God's promises; accept them; affirm them by faith.

Thank you, Father, for these foundational truths which enable us to grow in our understanding of effective prayer.

Make Your Prayers More Effective: The release of faith – 2

'And we know that in all things God works for the good of those who love him'
—Romans 8:28

Scripture reading: Proverbs 3:1–12

When we are drawing upon a promise of God and believing that we receive it, so that we do not doubt in our hearts (see Mark 11:23), and when we are affirming it by faith, we also need to include the words of Jacob in our ongoing prayer: '"I will not let you go unless you bless me." ' (Genesis 32:26). We have to nail our faith-colours to the mast, because when the mountain is big and faith is small—and this is often the case—we need a 'release of faith'. It is another way of referring to prevailing, or sacrificial, prayer.

If there is going to be the release of the faith we need, we have to hold on to what we are affirming—come what may! You will frequently find that you are brought to the end of your tether. In 2 Corinthians 1, Paul said: 'We were under great pressure, far beyond our ability to endure' (v.8); he went on to say: 'But this happened that we might not rely on ourselves but on God' (v.9).

God wants us to come to the point where we are not trusting in ourselves but in him. He brings us to the end of our self-dependence so that we will trust in him alone.

Key thought: God will bring you to the point where you are trusting, not in yourself, but in him.

Thank you, Father, that when we are at the end of our tether, we have come to a place where we are depending on you more.

Make Your Prayers More Effective: The release of faith – 3

'And as for us, why do we endanger ourselves every hour? I die every day' —1 Corinthians 15:30,31

Scripture reading: Psalm 56

We will not come to the point of trusting, not in ourselves but in God, unless we know the basics that I have referred to, and unless we are also saying, 'I will not let you go unless you bless me'. It is not easy; it is not pleasant. Paul and his companions told themselves, 'This is the end'. They thought it was all over, until they realised that their difficulties were to enable them to trust in God alone.

That is the 'release of faith'. It is what God does. It is the grace of God. It might be that we have to go through this a number of times. It might not be a 'once only' experience. Paul said, 'I die every day'.

There are no short cuts but, if we have this understanding, God can enable us to come through to the release of faith, and then our prayers are effective in a way that otherwise they cannot be. I repeat—where the mountain is big and faith is small, this is where you need the 'release of faith'.

How to make your prayers more effective? Know the promise of God; accept it, like you accept Christ for salvation; affirm it by faith, and it might well be that you have to say, 'I will not let you go unless you bless me'.

Key thought: When you come to the point where you are trusting, not in yourself, but in God—that is the 'release of faith'.

Our loving Father, we thank you that we can come into a deeper experience of prayer and faith and of the mountain being moved. We set our hearts to understand and to chasten ourselves before the Lord our God, that you might enable us to have that experience, through Christ our Lord. Amen.

Make Your Prayers More Effective: 'Will' never comes – 1

'they received the message with great eagerness and examined the Scriptures every day to see if what Paul said was true.' —Acts 17:11

Scripture reading: Acts 17:1–15

The Bible says that God 'has given us his very great and precious promises' (2 Peter 1:4) and that 'no matter how many promises God has made, they are "Yes" in Christ' (2 Corinthians 1:20), meaning that God wants us to have what he has promised.

It cannot be said too often that we need to search the Scriptures; we must have the promises of God at our fingertips in order to draw upon the resource of God which is appropriate to our need, or the need of someone else.

In saying this, I do not mean that I simply go ahead, irrespective of the circumstances, and believe for the promise in this situation or that, because we know that often the mountain is big and faith is small. Sometimes, what faith we have is mingled with fear, so that we are hoping for the best and fearing the worst. For example, I would seldom, if ever, pray that someone in the terminal stages of some, humanly-speaking, lethal illness be raised up.

We need to exercise discernment in a given situation as to whether it is appropriate to draw upon a particular promise of God, or whether there are other promises of God which would be more appropriate. I don't want to give the impression that one goes in 'boots and all', irrespective of the circumstances; we need to know the promise of God for our situation.

Key thought: Before we pray in any situation we need to discern what is the appropriate promise of God to draw on.

Loving Father, you have provided everything we need for life and godliness. We praise you, and thank you, and humbly accept your provision for our need. Through Jesus Christ our Lord. Amen.

Make Your Prayers More Effective: 'Will' never comes – 2

'"whatever you ask for in prayer, believe that you have received it, and it will be yours."'   —Mark 11:24

Scripture reading: Romans 8:28–39

Once we know the promise of God, we are to believe that we have received it. This is what we do when we pray for conversion, and this is how we are to think and pray about any promise of God. We are to believe we have received it, as Jesus said, and to the point where we do not doubt in our heart. But what happens in practice is that we go on 'asking' for things to happen, to the point where it is all we ever do. There is nothing wrong with asking—'"Ask and it will be given to you"' (Matthew 7:7)—but it is not the 'asking' that makes the promise effective. It is believing that we have received it so that we do not doubt, which enables God to make the promise a reality in our lives.

What would you think of a person who was believing for the promise of conversion but who, in prayer said, 'Lord, I believe I will be saved'? The person would be lovingly corrected and told: 'You are to believe you have received God's promise so that you affirm it is now your possession. And if, after having prayed and thought like this, there is no change, remember that you are affirming it by faith, and faith is thanking God before you have the blessing by sight—to the point where you do not doubt in your heart'.

Key thought: Sometimes in prayer we say we believe something will come to pass. Instead, we should believe we have received God's promise so that we affirm it is now our possession.

Thank you Father, that you have assured us that we only have to ask and you meet our needs. We accept that and believe it now, by faith. Thank you Father, thank you Jesus, thank you Holy Spirit. Amen.

Make Your Prayers More Effective: 'Will' never comes – 3

'"If you believe, you will receive whatever you ask for in prayer."'

—Matthew 21:22

Scripture reading: 1 John 5:1–15

One of the things I feel convinced about is that we have to get it right 'the Jesus way', which means we have to get prayer right 'the Jesus way' and act out our prayer in the way that our Lord has taught.

In my own prayer life, if there is a promise of God for my need, I accept it so that I make a decision; then I discipline my mind to affirm that this is what I have now accepted and what I believe I have received.

This is the prayer I would pray at the time when I am accepting the promise: 'Father, thank you for the promise to provide for my material needs (for example). I now accept that provision. This is my decision. From here on out I thank you by faith for your blessing. Through Christ our Lord. Amen.'

If the answer comes at once, I can thank God 'by sight'. However, it might well be that there is no answer at all to begin with. This is where I have to discipline myself so that I don't say, 'It's not working', but, as in conversion, to affirm it by faith. I then choose a phrase that means something to me and continue to affirm it: 'Thank you Father, you are providing for my needs'.

Key thought: Keep on with a simple prayer of affirmation so that you are thanking God by faith for the promise you have accepted and are believing for.

Our loving Father, we believe that, by your grace, you are enabling us to pray more effectively about that which you have provided for us. We believe that you are helping us in this. Through Christ our Lord and for his sake. Amen.

Your 'Quiet Time': Start the day right

'"When you pray, go into your room, close the door and pray to your Father"'   —Matthew 6:6

Scripture reading: Luke 6:12–19

We should set aside a time in the day, preferably in the morning and as early as practicable, when we have what we call a Quiet Time. This is a prayer time, a time of reading the Bible, of waiting on God. I suggest that it is good to have our daily Quiet Time in the same place, and at the same time, day by day. I believe it needs an hour given to it to enable us to cover, in sufficient depth, the various matters which ought to be brought under the umbrella of prayer.

One of the requirements of faith is that we should instinctively react to a problem so we affirm the answer. For example, if I were to drop my watch, I must grab it the moment it leaves my fingers or it will fall to the ground and be damaged. It would be no good dropping it and thinking that some time later I can recover it so that damage is avoided. In the same way, if we are to have blessing, we must react to problems in that immediate and instinctive manner and affirm the answer by faith.

This will apply if, before we're out of bed, something comes to mind causing anxiety, or resentment, or to do with some sickness in ourselves or in others. If this happens, it is then that we have to begin our Quiet Time for the day. It will take the form of affirming the blessing of God for that day and in those particular circumstances: 'Thank you Father, that you are helping me now'.

Key thought: One of the requirements of faith is that we should instinctively react to the problem so that we affirm the answer.

Help us, Father, so that we will immediately react to today's problems by faith, affirming the answer. Through Christ our Lord. Amen.

Your 'Quiet Time': Continue the day right

'And whatever you do, whether in word or deed, do it all in the name of the Lord Jesus, giving thanks to God the Father through him.'

—Colossians 3:17

Scripture reading: 1 Thessalonians 5:1–11

We need to practise the presence of God in our ongoing daily activity. This will be with what I refer to as 'arrow prayers'. By an arrow prayer I mean a one-sentence petition that is directed to God: 'Thank you Father, for your blessings … Glory be to the Father, and to the Son, and to the Holy Spirit … Thank you Jesus, that you're with me now…Thank you God, for your healing …', etc. You can say an arrow prayer in any spare moment you have; when you are doing the washing up, while waiting at traffic lights, when in your office, or wherever your daily duty takes you. The point is that there is the need to remind ourselves moment by moment of God's presence, and to practise that presence wherever we are.

Brother Lawrence, a Roman Catholic lay brother, wrote the well-known and well-loved classic *The Practice of the Presence of God*. He found it wasn't enough to go to the great services in the monastery chapel where they worshipped God in a beautiful and elaborate way. If God was going to be with him during the day, he had to practise the presence of God when he was scrubbing the pots and pans. And this is what we all will have to do.

Key thought: We need to remind ourselves, moment by moment, of God's presence, and to practise that presence wherever we are.

We praise you, Father, that you are with us every moment of the day and night. Amen.

Your 'Quiet Time': Conclude the day right

'may the lifting up of my hands be like the evening sacrifice'
—Psalm 141:2

Scripture reading: Luke 17:11–19

The last thing I want to share with you about our Quiet Time is how we might have our evening prayer. I believe it is of the utmost value to have a time of prayer when we look back over the day we have just experienced and allow the Holy Spirit to reveal to us the blessings that have come to us from God during the day. In this evening prayer time I only concentrate on the blessings. It is a time of returning thanks. Jesus said to the leper who was healed and who returned to thank him: '"Were not all ten cleansed? Where are the other nine?... Then he said to him, "Rise and go; your faith has made you well." ' (Luke 17:17,19).

You will be surprised to find how many things there are for which to give thanks at the end of the day. Let the Holy Spirit show you something to thank God for and then praise him for it. Then you will find the Holy Spirit will show you something else, and again you will return thanks. Then he will show you something more, and so on. It is a beautiful and effective way to conclude your day with God.

Not infrequently, it is the people who are the busiest who can find the most time for prayer. The busier John Wesley was, the earlier he got up, because he maintained that, the busier he became, the more necessary it was to have time with God in prayer.

Key thought: I believe God would have us discipline ourselves so that, just as Jesus prayed all night, there will be a real sense in which we pray all day.

Our loving Father, we thank you with full hearts for the resource of prayer, and we would believe for your blessing so that our prayers are made more effective, for your glory and the increase of your Kingdom in our lives. For Jesus' sake. Amen.

Your 'Quiet Time': God has many answers – 1

'I thank my God every time I remember you. In all my prayers for all of you, I always pray with joy'
— Philippians 1:3,4

Scripture reading: Philippians 4:1–7

By the expression 'God has many answers' I mean that there are a number of ways in which we can pray and, in our Quiet Time, we should draw on those different ways of praying so that we are praying appropriately for each and every situation.

There are two ways in which you can begin your Quiet Time and be enabled to concentrate in prayer. Bring to mind the things you are already believing for and, as you praise God, it will help you come into the deeper reaches of prayer. Then let God bring to your mind some urgent matter for which you have to depend on him, either for yourself or for someone else, and you will find that this, too, will help you concentrate in prayer.

Sometimes when I am saying my prayers the phone rings and, as it is by my elbow, I answer it. My first reaction very often is: 'Oh dear me! there is a disturbance to my Quiet Time'. However, I frequently find that it is someone with a prayer request, and I sense the urgency and the importance of the need, so that when I have finished the conversation I have an urgency in my mind and spirit to pray for this particular matter. I believe that God permits such phone calls to help me concentrate in my praying, because the urgency and the relevancy of the need give me no alternative but to believe God for this person at this time.

Key thought: Begin by praising God for things you are already believing for.

Father, thank you for the blessings which we have accepted by faith; thank you, too, for enabling us to depend on you more for those things where faith is our only resource. In Christ Jesus. Amen.

Your 'Quiet Time':   God has many answers – 2

'My soul yearns for you in the night; in the morning my spirit longs for you.'   —Isaiah 26:9

Scripture reading: 1 Timothy 2:1–8

As you continue in prayer, the Holy Spirit will remind you of things for which you haven't yet accepted his blessing—things you are worrying about which are still problems. You should use your Quiet Time to bring these things into focus so that you accept God's blessing like you accept Christ for salvation: 'Father thank you for your promise of healing, I now accept wholeness in this particular situation. This is my decision and I now thank you by faith'. You pray that through until you get it right—switching from the problem to the answer so that the answer is what you have now accepted.

There is another way to pray which should always be part of our daily prayer time. In this way of praying we allow the problem to be our reason for depending on God more. As well as accepting God's answer for our need, so that it is what we accept and what we affirm, we should discipline our minds so the problem helps us draw closer to God and, ultimately, to seek God for himself. It is what we should do every day in our Quiet Time. It is sometimes called contemplative prayer. You contemplate the reality of God. You are being filled with all the fullness of God.

Key thought: The Holy Spirit will bring to our minds the different ways in which we can pray.

O Father, thank you that there are so many wonderful things we can do in our Quiet Time. Bring them to our remembrance day by day, more and more—these things and other things, that we may draw upon the many answers that you provide, the many promises and the many ways of prayer; for your glory, for our blessing and the extension of your Kingdom. Amen.

Your 'Quiet Time': God has many answers – 3

'Don't you know that you yourselves are God's temple and that God's Spirit lives in you?'
— 1 Corinthians 3:16

Scripture reading: Ephesians 3:14–21

In your Quiet Time remember that your body is the temple of the Holy Spirit. Allow your prayer to come to the point where you are contemplating your temple being filled with all the fullness of God. You will then have a reality of God within you; you will have a way of prayer; you will have a blessing you will not be able to contain.

You often hear people say: 'Oh, I feel guilty about praying for myself but I am alright when I am praying for other people'. Absolute nonsense! I spend a lot of time praying about myself, not just for selfish reasons but that I may be a channel of blessing for other people. Therefore, in your Quiet Time, react to every need—your own and that of others—so that you come into the presence of the Spirit of God and think of your physical frame, your temple, being filled with the Spirit of Christ.

If you have time (I am very serious), spend an hour just meditating on the reality of God in your temple and you will not only be communing with God but, as a result, God can use you for the blessing of others. One of the things I learned from Agnes Sanford was just that. Before she ministered to people she would take an hour just to meditate on the reality of God in herself so that she was filled with the Spirit and so that the Spirit might then flow out in rivers of living water for the blessing of others.

Key thought: When we are filled with the Spirit we can be a blessing to others.

Thank you, Father, for the gift of your Holy Spirit. So fill us now that you can use us to bless others.

Practising Healing – 1

'faith by itself, if it is not accompanied by action, is dead' —James 2:17

Scripture reading: James 2:14–26

Faith must issue in what we do, otherwise it is mere hot air. How, then, can we act out the faith we are exercising in order to have answers from God?

The Prayer of Faith which we have prayed in our Quiet Time must determine our ongoing thought activity. We must consciously discipline our minds so that this is how we think about the subject we have prayed about—not only on that day but on other days—and perhaps, when the mountain is big and faith is small, over a long period of time.

Frequently, we get this right to begin with. The Prayer of Faith, either our own or the faith of other people added to ours, makes a great impression on us—we receive such a blessing of the Holy Spirit that we do react in that positive way for a time but, later, we return to an acceptance of the problem rather than accepting the answer. This is not altogether a criticism because the problem is what we see; it has a certain gravitational pull so that we have a bias towards thinking like that.

The reason why healing sometimes begins and then stops is because we begin in faith and then we return to affirming the problem. We are no longer walking by faith; we are now reacting in terms of what we see by sight. This will mean that the blessing stops and the problem continues.

Key thought: The faith we exercise in our Quiet Time must issue in our ongoing thought activity.

Father, forgive us that often our faith has not issued in our works. Bless us so that our faith will issue in our thoughts and in what we do. Amen.

Practising Healing – 2

'Taking him by the right hand, he helped him up, and instantly the man's feet and ankles became strong.'
                                                                —Acts 3:7

Scripture reading: Acts 3:1–10

Faith must issue in what you do and there is a special emphasis about the 'doing' that I want to share with you now. I remember learning this lesson at St John's Darlinghurst. I was about to speak at a meeting in the parish hall and, in the hymn before the address, the Rector came up to me and said that someone in the front row had a migraine headache; he asked if I would come and pray for her. I thought it was an extraordinary time to choose to pray for someone but I couldn't avoid it—and didn't wish to. I went with the Rector to this young woman who was sitting down, obviously distressed. The Rector and I prayed for her the Prayer of Faith: 'Thank you Father, for your promise of healing; we accept it, we have made a decision; we affirm it by faith through Christ our Lord'. I said this meaningfully, and then looked down at her; she was obviously no different—her face still showed she was in pain.

I remembered that wonderful story in the Acts of the Apostles where Peter and John prayed for a man at the Beautiful Gate. They not only prayed the Prayer of Faith but they put their faith into action so that Peter took the man by the hand and lifted him up and he was healed. I had prayed the Prayer of Faith about this girl and she was obviously still the same, so I bent down and took her hand and said: 'Stand, and sing the hymn'. She obeyed my request and told me, later, that her headache went in that moment.

Key thought: Faith has got to issue in what you do.

Bless us, loving Father, so that we act upon our faith. Through Jesus, our Lord. Amen.

Practising Healing – 3

'When he saw them, he said, "Go, show yourselves to the priests." And as they went, they were cleansed.'   —Luke 17:14

Scripture reading: Luke 8:40–48

Is your Prayer of Faith being answered about this or that? If the answer is 'no', then look around for something you can do to put your faith on the line. Now, don't misunderstand me. The reason why you are sick is almost certainly because you have been overdoing it—your resistance has been lowered and sickness has come in. This means that if you get off that bed of sickness and try to do all that you should not have been doing in the first place, you will have a relapse and I take no responsibility for it!

We do not want a person lying down and saying: 'I'm sick, I'm sick, I'm sick'—but neither do we want them acting foolishly by doing too much, too quickly, and making more problems than they solve. We do not want either extreme.

If you put your faith into action—let us say you get up and do something—you may well be troubled by your illness. If this is so, you must learn to react in a positive and informed way. For, if you should react to any sickness symptoms by saying: 'Oh dear me, I am sick', what will happen?' etc., it would be better to stay in bed and enjoy the perks of being sick! This is when you have to know what to do, and do it. You must react to the sickness symptoms by affirming something like this: 'Thank you Father, you are healing me now'. You don't ignore the problem—that is foolish; you react to the problem in a positive way by affirming the healing for which you are believing.

Key thought: Think, talk and act in terms of healing.

Father, enable us to react to our symptoms so that we affirm the answer we are believing for. Through Christ our Lord. Amen.

Practising Healing – 4

'that is how you should stand firm in the Lord, dear friends!'
—Philippians 4:1

Scripture reading: 2 Thessalonians 2:13–17; 3:1–5

Affirming healing has to be done in three ways, if it is to succeed:

First—it must be done at once. If you are going to put your faith into action, you must react to the sickness symptoms by instantly affirming: 'I thank you Father; you are healing me now'. It is no good doing it after you have had a fear reaction; it must be the way you react, so that it is your reaction.

Second—you must consistently react in this way. It is no good instantly reacting in a positive way for half the time, and instantly reacting in a negative way for the other half of the time. You must do it all the time.

Third—you must react in this positive way until the blessing is there by sight, "'I will not let you go unless you bless me.'" (Genesis 32:26) gives the clue.

This story explains what I mean: One of our number was stricken with a migraine headache when she was driving from the country to her home in Sydney. For some reason she needed to press on, so she had no alternative but to affirm God's blessing; she just had to react to the searing pain by affirming every time: 'Thank you Father, you are enabling me to get home. Thank you Father, you are healing me now!'. She reacted instantly and consistently—until the headache lessened, so that she arrived home safely, completely healed.

Key thought: We must put our faith into action at once, consistently and until we have the blessing by sight.

Dear Father, help us to so discipline ourselves that we affirm your blessing by faith until it is ours by sight. Amen.

Is Healing for Today? – 1

'Dear friends, do not believe every spirit, but test the spirits to see whether they are from God, because many false prophets have gone out into the world.'   —1 John 4:1

Scripture reading: 1 Corinthians 12:4–11

I recently heard a distinguished theologian say, as though there were no other point of view, that healing was only for the time of Christ and not intended to be an ongoing resource in the Church. As you can imagine, I listened with the utmost attention to what was, to me, a quite extraordinary statement!

He said that, because the references to healing were almost entirely in the Gospels and the Acts of the Apostles, and because there was no great emphasis on healing in the epistles—which refer to a later time—that this showed that healing was in decline when the epistles were written. The implication of this, he said, was that healing was not intended to last after the time of Christ, and certainly was not intended for us today.

When you hear that kind of argument from a distinguished scholar it makes you think! But, if you do think, you will find that exactly the same thing could be said about Baptism and Holy Communion, but no-one deduces from this that the sacraments of Baptism and Holy Communion were in decline when the epistles were written, and that this implies they were not intended for us!

Question everything! You can see how superficial, how prejudiced, how misleading were that theologian's words. For, obviously, if you can't say about Baptism and Holy Communion that they were only for the early church because they are referred to less frequently in the epistles, you can't say it about healing.

Key thought: Search the Scriptures. Have a reason for the hope that is in you.

Father, thank you that your Word assures us that healing, and all your provision is for us today just as much as it was in the early Church. Amen.

Is Healing for Today? – 2

'He called his twelve disciples to him and gave them authority to drive out evil spirits and to heal every disease and sickness.' —Matthew 10:1

Scripture reading: Matthew 4:23–25

What are the positive reasons for affirming that healing is for today?

First of all there is the commission given, not only to the apostles, but also to the general group of the disciples; and also to the deacons, who were not commissioned to preach or heal, but had a healing ministry like that of the apostles.

When the Archbishop of Sydney, Dr Marcus Loane, spoke from this pulpit on the tenth anniversary of the Healing Service,[1] he said: 'Our Lord came to preach the gospel and to heal the sick. That was also the work he sent his followers to do, and that is the ongoing ministry which his servants are still called to fulfil in his name and for his sake'.

As well as the general commission to preach and heal, we have the fact that part of the ministry given to the ongoing Church is the gift, or gifts, of healing (see 1 Corinthians 12:9). There is also the great statement in James which sets out how the healing ministry is to be exercised in a church context: 'Is any one of you sick? He should call the elders of the church to pray over him and anoint him with oil in the name of the Lord. And the prayer offered in faith will make the sick person well; the Lord will raise him up. If he has sinned, he will be forgiven' (James 5:14,15).

So we have positive, consistent statements in Scripture that healing is a continuing resource in the Church and is available today in response to faith.

Key thought: Scripture affirms that healing is for today.

Thank you, Father, for the assurance we have from your Word that healing is your provision for us today. Our prayer is praise. Through Jesus Christ, our Lord and Saviour. Amen.

---

[1] 30th September 1970.

Is Healing for Today? – 3

'All Scripture is God-breathed'   —2 Timothy 3:16

Scripture reading: 2 Timothy 4:1–8

I like to hear what God is saying today, and so when all the bishops of the Anglican Church worldwide assemble at Lambeth, as they did in August last year [1978], I listen to what God says through our leaders. Resolution 8 of the Conference, under the heading 'The Church's Ministry of Healing' states:

> The Conference praises God for the renewal of the ministry of healing within the Churches in recent times and reaffirms:
> 1. that the healing of the sick in his name is as much a part of the proclamation of the Kingdom as the preaching of the good news of Jesus Christ;
> 2. that to neglect this aspect of ministry is to diminish our part in Christ's total redemptive activity;
> 3. that the ministry to the sick should be an essential element in any revision of the liturgy (see the Report of the Lambeth Conference of 1958, p.2.92).

At the Cathedral we have found the healing ministry to be valid, relevant, effective and needful. Linked with the preaching of the Good News, it restores the full dynamic of what God has provided for his people. We know, on the basis of what we have experienced time and time again, that God heals today in the same way as he healed in the days of Christ's earthly ministry, using faith—yours and mine, and ours.

Key thought: Linked with the preaching of the Good News, the ministry of healing restores the full dynamic of what God has provided for his people.

Our Loving Father, we do not need to be persuaded; we have the testimony in our lives that you heal today, and we would honour your name by affirming this now. We think and speak in love of those who have a different point of view, and would only pray that the Spirit will guide them so that they will interpret the Bible consistently and in a balanced way.

Is Healing for Everyone? – 1

'"For God so loved the world that he gave his one and only Son, that whoever believes in him shall not perish but have eternal life."'

—John 3:16

Scripture reading: Philippians 2:25–30

Given that healing is for today, the next logical question to ask, and answer is, 'Is healing for everyone?'. There are those who ask, 'What assurance have I that God will heal me?'

In Philippians 2:25–27 we read of one early Christian brother, Epaphroditus, who 'was ill, and almost died'. In 2 Timothy 4:20 we read of Trophimus who was 'sick in Miletus'. Again, in 1 Timothy 5:23 we learn of Timothy's 'frequent illnesses'. People refer to these three men in the Bible and ask, if God meant everyone to be healed, why didn't he heal these men? He may well have healed Epaphroditus (Philippians 2:27) but what about Trophimus and Timothy?

What balanced answer can we give? What answer can be drawn from the Scriptures? Let us first look at it in the area of conversion.

If it were said that Judas Iscariot was not saved, and that Alexander the Coppersmith was unconverted (see 2 Timothy 4:14–15), would we deduce from this that it might not be God's will that someone be saved? Anyone with ten cents worth of theological understanding would answer the question on the grounds of whether or not there was a promise of God concerning salvation—not by referring to two men who were not saved. We would not compromise the clear promise of Scripture that it is God's will that all men be saved, simply because there were some who did not appropriate that salvation! Their fault and failure does not compromise the availability of God's blessing.

Key thought: God's will for us is revealed in Scripture.

Father, thank you that your will for us is Kingdom Perfection in forgiveness, salvation and healing. In Jesus' name. Amen.

Is Healing for Everyone? – 2

'For God did not send his Son into the world to condemn the world, but to save the world through him.' —John 3:17

Scripture reading: John 1:1–14

There is a clear promise of healing in the New Testament: 'And the prayer offered in faith will make the sick person well; the Lord will raise him up. If he has sinned, he will be forgiven' (James 5:15). This is a promise as clear and uncompromising as any other promise in the New Testament! We would therefore deduce that there was some failure on the part of those mentioned in the New Testament who were sick—or of those who were their spiritual advisers—which would account for the fact that, at the time of writing (we do not know what may have happened later) they had not appropriated the blessing God had provided.

Often the 'mountain' is big and faith is small. This is something which we have to consider, both when we seek to understand the Bible reports of those who were not healed, and when we hear of people who are not healed in our day and generation.

I suggest to you that, just as we have this understanding about the promise of conversion, and that it is not compromised or lessened by those who have not appropriated it, so, too, we should not compromise the promise of healing because there were two or three who were sick.

Just as there is a promise of conversion which applies to all and is available in response to faith, we would also say, in principle, that there is a promise of healing which is made operative through the exercise of faith, and is available to all who will appropriate it.

Key thought: The clear promise of Scripture is healing in response to faith.

Loving Father, we would keep our eyes of faith on your promise of healing. Through Christ, our Lord. Amen.

Is Healing for Everyone? – 3

'" One thing I do know. I was blind but now I see!"'   —John 9:25

Scripture reading: Numbers 21: 4–9; John 3:14

Is healing for everyone? It might surprise some people to be told that you don't have to be a Christian to be healed! Our Lord frequently ministered healing without prefacing it, or following it, by the forgiveness of sins. People often became followers of Christ because of healing, but no-one was refused healing because they were not believers in Christ. Indeed, I venture to say that our Lord used healing as a way of touching people where they were at, so that he was able to provide good news for them, and then lead them on to the deeper things of faith as time went by.

However, while healing is available for all in response to faith, it needs to be said that the time must come for everyone to stand before the judgement seat of God. We come to the point where we die, and that means we are not healed. We need to know that there is a time to pray for healing and a time when we ought not to pray for healing.

There is a time when the appropriate ministry is to relinquish the person to God in the grace of Christ and in the comfort of the Holy Spirit. I say this because it is important for us to have a balanced approach when thinking about any Christian matter, including that of Christian healing.

However, while that is true and is part of the whole, it doesn't negate the fact that, in principle, healing is for everyone.

Key thought: It is important to maintain a balance when thinking about any Christian matter, including Christian healing.

Our loving Father, we believe that you will clarify in our minds that you have made a promise of healing and that it is therefore your will and provision that this be available for everyone. Father, we thank you for this and praise your name. Through Christ our Lord. Amen.

Can we Dictate to God? – 1

'Jesus answered, "My teaching is not my own. It comes from him who sent me."'   —John 7:16

Scripture reading: 2 Corinthians 1:15–22

A Christian minister once said to me: 'I believe God can and does heal, but can we dictate to God?'. He was saying that he believed in healing but that we cannot demand that God heal. I don't know whether the question was deliberately phrased in this way so that a certain answer had to be given—because no-one, either inside or outside of the Healing Ministry, would think for one moment that we can dictate to God.

What is the right way to approach God so as to have his blessing, whether it be for healing or for anything else? It is by understanding the promises he has made to us. There was the old agreement, or promise— the Old Testament. These were the promises made by God to mankind through the words of the prophets and other teachers. These promises looked forward to the New Testament, or the new promises that would be made by Christ, sealed by his blood and forever available to those who will turn to God in repentance, faith and obedience.

I sometimes think that we could search the New Testament all our born days and forever be coming to fresh aspects of the promises God has made to his children. This is why informed Bible study is essential for our Christian walk and our prayer life, for we must know what God has provided. Christianity is not man reaching up to God; it is not man working out what God ought to give him. Christianity is understanding what God has revealed; what God has shown us; what God has said, primarily through Christ, and recorded in the New Testament.

Key thought: We search the Scriptures to find the promises God has made to his children.

We praise and thank you, Father, for the blessings you have provided. Through Jesus, our Lord. Amen.

Can We Dictate to God? – 2

'"You know with all your heart and soul that not one of all the good promises the LORD your God gave you has failed. Every promise has been fulfilled; not one has failed."'   —Joshua 23:14

Scripture reading: 1 Kings 8:54–61

We search the Scriptures to see what are the great and precious promises that God has made us.

There is the promise of forgiveness. If we confess our sins, God is faithful to forgive us, both now and for eternity (see 1 John 1:9). That is a very basic promise and provision of God but it is only one of the promises God has made.

There is the promise of healing. The Prayer of Faith will raise up the person who is sick; this is consistent with all that Jesus taught, and with all else that is in the New Testament (see James 5:14,15).

Another of the promises of God is that he will fill us with his Spirit so that we have power for our Christian walk and will be witnesses of the Lord Jesus (see John 14:16,17).

It is a promise of God that we are to be equipped to do the work of God (see Ephesians 4:11–13).

Another promise is that God will provide for our material needs—the things we eat and the things we wear. Jesus said that if we seek the Kingdom of God and his righteousness these things would be given to us as well (see Matthew 6:31–33).

Once we know what promises God has made to us; once we know what the New Testament says, then we go on to draw upon those promises by faith.

Key thought: We can count on God to keep his promises.

Thank you, Father, for making your will known to us. We draw upon your promise for our need today.

Can We Dictate to God? – 3

'Always be prepared to give an answer to everyone who asks you to give the reason for the hope that you have.'   — 1 Peter 3:15

Scripture reading: 2 Thessalonians 1:3–12

I once ministered to a boy who was grievously ill and, when I had been to the home a number of times, I asked his mother, 'Do you believe God is healing John?'. She said to me, in a perfectly agreeable and straightforward way, 'I will believe it when I see it'. I am not criticising her, but that is not faith. Faith is accepting a promise, affirming it in an ongoing way and saying in our spirit: '"I will not let you go unless you bless me."' (Genesis 32:26).

You can see why I am profoundly ill at ease with the way my friend and colleague put his question— 'Can we dictate to God?'. I repeat: the answer we receive depends on the way we ask the question. No, of course we can't dictate to God, but that is a false question. That is not the issue; the issue is, what has God promised us? Once we know that, then we can draw on it by faith, for we are exercising faith about what is God's will for us to have.

Think through these things; search the Scriptures for yourself so that you know where you stand and are able to share these things with others—both those who want to draw on blessing from God and those who misunderstand how we are to approach God.

Key thought: We are not dictating to God when we draw upon the blessings he has promised to give us.

Help us, Holy Spirit, to be ready to answer those who question us about our faith.

Can We Dictate to God? – 4

'"Everything is possible for him who believes."'　　　　　—Mark 9:23

Scripture reading: Matthew 7:7–11

One of the most beautiful experiences I have had of healing was with Ted Brooker, now the Reverend Ted Brooker. Ted had syringobulbia —a degenerative condition of the nerve system which leads to the brain. There is no medical cure. He came with his wife to see me a number of times and I talked about the problem first in one way and then in another. But none of this helped him until the Holy Spirit guided me to take off my watch and hold it out to him saying, 'I am offering you my watch. I want you to have it. What must you do for it to be yours?' He said, 'I must take it.' So I asked him to take it, adding, 'What do you say?' And he said, 'Thank you.' 'Are you sure you've got it?', I asked. 'Yes,' he replied. Then I said, 'God has made you a promise of healing. He is offering it to you as a gift. You must have faith. That means that you must take it. Are you sure you've got it now?' And he said, 'Yes.'

Later, I invited him to come up the spiral staircase into the Cathedral Bell Tower to watch the bells being rung at the weekly practice. I didn't know that, because of his disease, he couldn't turn round without falling over. He walked up the spiral staircase—and down the spiral staircase—without a tremor. Subsequent exhaustive tests at Sydney Hospital showed no trace of the illness. He had been cured in a moment, and cured permanently.

Key thought: God offers healing to us as a gift.

Our loving Father, we praise you that all the promises of God find their 'Yes' in Christ. We praise you for the promises you have made, including that of healing and we would have faith for your provision and accept it now. Through Christ our Lord. Amen.

Healing and Suffering in the World – 1

'God saw all that he had made, and it was very good.' — Genesis 1:31

Scripture reading: 1 Peter 3:8–16

On one occasion, after I had preached at an evening church service, I was approached by a man who asked: 'How can you believe in healing when you see all the suffering in the world?'

As Christians we need to know the answer to this question. It is a good question. I did not mind it being asked. I welcomed it, and gave the man my answer.

When God made things in the beginning, the Bible says he saw all that he had made and it was very good. God made everything perfect; man was perfect, the creation was perfect; the problems, tragedies and suffering which we now take for granted were unknown. All suffering, all tragedy, all sickness and all pain is contrary to God's will and design.

God did not make man to be a 'robot'—a 'puppet on a string'. The Bible says that God made man in his own likeness and image (Genesis 1:26,27), which means that Adam had the power of choice. The tragedy is that Adam chose to step outside the limits God had placed around him— he chose to do what was wrong. He was disobedient to God, and the Bible says all sickness, all disaster and all sin stems from that disobedience.

We all do many wrong things—big things or small things. We are all involved in what we call the 'sin of the world'. We inherit it, we are tainted by it, we are influenced by it. It isn't just my sin (though it includes my sin); it is the sin of us all, the sin of the race, the sin of mankind.

In the fullness of time Christ came to die on the cross so that by his sacrificial death he might take away the sin of the world.

Key thought: All sickness and suffering is due to the 'sin of the world'.

Dear Father, we praise you for the wonders of your creation, and for your plan and purpose to restore the Kingdom to us through the sacrifice of Christ our Lord. Amen.

Healing and Suffering in the World – 2

'The next day John saw Jesus coming towards him and said, "Look, the Lamb of God, who takes away the sin of the world!"' —John 1:29

Scripture reading: John 19:25–30

Jesus took the sin of the world upon himself; he became the 'scapegoat'. He fulfilled all that had been foretold in the Old Testament, so that he was a sacrifice and offering for the root cause of all suffering, and so that he himself could say, 'It is finished'.

This means that, if we accept what Christ has done on our behalf, we are forgiven our part in the sin of the world, and so we speak about Christ as being our 'Saviour'. It also means that a full circle has been turned— we are forgiven, we are reconciled to the Father and the Kingdom has been restored to us. It means that healing is available to us.

It is our opportunity and our responsibility to accept this blessing for ourselves and for others, and to say that it is available for the whole wide world.

So, how can you believe in healing when you see all the suffering in the world? You can believe in it because healing is the answer for the suffering of the world. That's what the healing ministry of the Church is all about. This should be the reason for the hope that is in us.

A full circle has been turned; the perfect resource is available and we can draw on it with faith which does not doubt.

Key thought: You can believe in healing because healing is the answer for the suffering of the world.

Our loving Father, bless us as we work through these things so that we come to understand the reason for the hope that is in us and realise that your healing is the answer for the suffering of the world. We draw on it now, by faith, more and more. In Jesus' name and for Jesus' sake. Amen.

Stress is the Killer – 1

'Cast thy burden upon the LORD, and he shall sustain thee: he shall never suffer the righteous to be moved.'   —Psalm 55:22 (KJV)

Scripture reading: Philippians 4:4–9

When I was in the United States recently[1] I was given the book, *Inner Balance*[2]. It is written, in the main, by medical specialists and it is interesting to learn what the top men in the medical profession in the United States are saying about stress.

Professor Hans Selye, one of the contributors to the book, puts it like this: 'Innumerable studies of disease processes have shown that stress, more than any other factor, determines whether there is a proper balance in our lives. Most of us are born healthy, but if the harmful stresses resulting from improper perception, personal misbehavior, and environmental conditions tip the balance, we slide down the slope from health to disease.' He goes on to say: 'The goal of medicine should therefore be to understand the patient as a person: to establish the circumstances that precipitated his illness—the underlying conflicts, hostilities and griefs; in short, the bruised nature of his emotional state' (pp.29, 47).

Stress, more than any other factor, is the underlying cause of physical ailments. It follows that it is stress which needs to be prevented if physical illness is to be avoided; where there is illness, it is stress which needs to be healed, if healing is to be drawn upon in depth. We are, of course, not ignoring the presenting symptoms, but we are saying—or rather, people like Professor Selye are saying—that the underlying causes have to be understood and treated, if a cure is to be effected.

Key thought: We must avoid getting stressed.

Help us, Father, to recognise stressful situations and, with your Holy Spirit's help, to deal with them.

---

[1] September, 1980.

[2] Elliott M. Goldway, ed. *Inner Balance: the Power of Holistic Healing.* New Jersey, Prentice-Hall, 1979.

Stress is the Killer – 2

'When I kept silent, my bones wasted away through my groaning all day long.'
—Psalm 32:3

Scripture reading: Psalm 139:1–18

Stress is the killer. In case you think that only ulcers are being talked about, let me read from another paper in the book, *Inner Balance*. Dr Simonton of the Cancer Counseling and Research Center, Fort Worth, Texas, writes: 'We believe that cancer is often an indication of problems elsewhere in an individual's life, problems aggravated or compounded by a series of stresses six to eighteen months prior to the onset of cancer' (p. 121).

Speaking as a medical layman, I think this is the most encouraging sign I have seen coming out of modern medicine, and I thank God it is on the increase.

What so often happens is that a person is in a situation which creates a serious problem for them in personal relationships at work or at home—you name it. They take it out on themselves and it gnaws a hole in their minds and emotions. Stress has a cumulative effect, and what these eminent medical authorities are saying is that this stress, more than any other single factor, is the underlying cause of physical illness.

I once ministered to a woman in this position and she said, 'But what can I do?'. I answered, perhaps rather naively, 'Well, you can cast your burden upon the Lord'. She was an informed and prayerful Christian, and her reply was, 'I do that, but I keep taking it back'. I helped her by believing with her, so that our combined faith enabled her to truly and meaningfully cast her burden upon the Lord so that he sustained her in her real-life situation.

Key thought: We need to cast our burden of stress upon the Lord and leave it there.

Loving Father, show us what stressful event in our past needs to be brought out into the open and dealt with. In Jesus' name. Amen.

Stress is the Killer – 3

'"Come with me by yourselves to a quiet place and get some rest."'

—Mark 6:31

Scripture reading: Mark 6:7–13; 30–32.

When I was in the United States[1], I had a most interesting experience when visiting the Good Samaritan Episcopal Hospital in Portland; there I saw the most advanced hospital chaplaincy work I have ever come across.

I was told by one of the lay workers who, under supervision, visited the hospital and made pastoral calls on behalf of the chaplain that, before she left the hospital, she would have a debriefing session. The chaplain would talk things through with her, correcting her where necessary, give his support, and pray with her for the pastoral calls she had made. These sessions served to further instruct her in the work she was doing. In addition, she told me that this debriefing, which the chaplain so expertly handled, had the effect of her leaving her problems at the hospital, which meant that she never took them home. In other words, the problems did not result in her becoming stressed.

I like the Living Bible translation of Philippians 4:6,7b: 'Don't worry about anything; instead, pray about everything; tell God your needs ...' and 'His peace will keep your thoughts and your hearts quiet and at rest as you trust in Christ Jesus'. It underlines the point that this is what God wants us to do—that is, not to be anxious but to pray and let his peace give quiet to our minds and hearts because of our trust in Christ. If we understand the need for this, and develop our capacity to put it into practice, we will be taking a major step forward to retaining our health—or regaining it, should we be sick at present.

Key thought: Whatever our work, or situation, we need the opportunity to debrief.

Thank you, heavenly Father, for those with whom we can share the events of the day and the burden of ministry.

---

[1] In June and July of 1980. A report of the trip was given to the Healing Ministry congregation in a sermon on 9th July 1980.

Stress is the Killer – 4

'"Be still, and know that I am God; I will be exalted among the nations, I will be exalted in the earth."'
— Psalm 46:10

Scripture reading: Psalm 46

When I was in Melbourne last week,[1] I had contact with Miss Eleanor Lindsay,[2] a lady who is exercising a remarkable healing ministry; she has a licence from the Archbishop of Melbourne to extend that ministry in his diocese. I had an hour-long talk with her during which she kindly explained to me how she went about her work. I was very interested to be told that she does not pray for the presenting problem the person has; her concern is to identify the stress factors which have contributed to the person's illness. She then seeks to draw upon the appropriate blessing of God for the healing of those stress factors, after which, she says, it is a comparatively easy thing to draw on help and healing for the presenting symptoms. I think she is, in a courageous and effective way, acting upon the precepts of Professor Selye and others. Stress is the killer. We must be concerned, in a preventive way, as well as in a remedial way, to come to grips with it, for it is the great problem behind illness.

Key thought: Factors which have caused stress in people's lives should be identified when ministering healing.

Our loving Father, we are all in degree the victims of stress. We would so come before you now that we cast our burden upon the Lord Jesus and have peace in our mind and heart. We believe this both now and in an ongoing way. Amen.

---

[1] September 1980.
[2] Miss Eleanor Lindsay was brought from Scotland by Archbishop Woods and commissioned by him to conduct a healing ministry within the Anglican Church. In 1975 she took up residence in Cameron Cottage in the grounds of the Retreat House of the Community of the Holy Name in Cheltenham, Victoria. Many people came to her for prayer and healing.

God Wants You to Have These Blessings:

Power over sinful habits – 1

'Search me, O God, and know my heart; test me and know my anxious thoughts. See if there is any offensive way in me, and lead me in the way everlasting.'   —Psalm 139:23,24

Scripture reading: 1 John 1:5–10

It is important to have power over sinful habits because they grieve and quench the Holy Spirit. I am not only referring to habits that are obviously sinful but also to those we rather take for granted and do not think are sinful. When we remember that St Paul said: 'everything that does not come from faith is sin' (Romans 14:23), we will realise we can have habits that don't shock us perhaps, but which, nevertheless, can grieve and quench the Spirit.

One example of a sinful habit is a complaining attitude or the practice of criticising other people. It is a sinful habit which we have every reason to overcome, for to be critical of others is not only in itself an act of unfaith (we could, instead of criticising, be believing God to change the situation for good), but it also contributes to a spirit of dissatisfaction and disunity amongst a wider group of people.

Another sinful habit is unforgiveness. Again, we take it for granted but there is nothing that can grieve and quench the Spirit more than unforgiveness.

In a nutshell, sinful habits are anything less than, and different from, the standards of Christ. Who among us, beginning with myself, does not have sinful habits? We all need the power and grace of God to overcome them.

Key thought: It is important to have power over sinful habits because they grieve and quench the Holy Spirit.

Holy Spirit of God, show us those sinful habits which hinder our oneness with the Father. We would repent of them and be cleansed. Through Jesus Christ, our Lord. Amen.

God Wants You to Have These Blessings:

Power over sinful habits – 2

'If we confess our sins, he is faithful and just and will forgive us our sins and purify us from all unrighteousness.'
— 1 John 1:9

Scripture reading: Psalm 51

With nearly every sin there is a satisfaction—a tendency to want to return to it because of the satisfaction there is in having that habit. It means that we don't want to overcome it; there are reasons why we'd prefer to keep it.

If we are to turn from our sinful habits, it will be by God's grace. To make us draw on God's grace things have sometimes to get worse before they get better. Sometimes God has to permit the difficulties to bring us to the end of our tether, and only then, when our fallen self-nature is flattened, is he able to come through with his grace and enable us to want to leave the problem behind.

I like the words of 1 John 1:9 where it says that if we confess our sins—our sinful habits—God is faithful and just to forgive us and to cleanse us from all unrighteousness. We accept the first part of the verse but neglect the second. We know what is meant by 'forgiveness' but are not as clear about 'cleansing'. The word 'cleanse' means that God takes away the sin itself. That is what God wants; he doesn't forgive so that we can go on sinning. That borders on hypocrisy. He forgives that he might cleanse, and that means taking away the sinful habit so we no longer have it. So we need to confess our sinful habit and believe, not only for forgiveness, but also for cleansing.

Key thought: It is by the grace of God that we are brought to the point of wanting to be rid of our sinful habits.

Father, we repent of our sinful habits—our criticism of others and our unforgiveness—please forgive us. Thank you that we are made clean through the blood of your Son, Jesus Christ, our Lord. Amen.

God Wants You to Have These Blessings:

Power over sinful habits – 3

'Blessed is he whose transgressions are forgiven, whose sins are covered.'   —Psalm 32:1

Scripture reading: Romans 12:9–21

If we are to draw upon God's blessing in order to have power over a sinful habit, we may need to say in our prayer: '"I will not let you go unless you bless me."' (Genesis 32:26). Some of our sinful habits are deeply entrenched and, if we are to be free of them, we will have to continue to believe—not asking, asking, asking, but believing, believing, believing—thanking God by faith and continuing to thank God by faith. We may need to continue in prayer and persevere in prayer, adding faith to faith, finding that the sinful habit is taken away like the growth of a plant: 'first the blade, then the ear' (Mark 4:28 KJV). That is the idea of continuing in prayer, or of the mountain being moved gradually and progressively.

It might well be a great help to have others adding their faith to ours. As I say to people who come to me for counselling: 'I am not involved in your problem. I can believe for you with some degree of being objective'.

I once had a difference with someone which went very deep and it became a sinful habit to reflect on this disagreement. I finally overcame it by God's grace—but this is the point I want to make: it was beginning to draw upon God's help that was the hard part. Once I began, God enabled me to go further until I was completely free of the sin of unforgiveness.

Key thought: We may need to persevere in order to overcome a sin which has become a habit.

Thank you, Father, for your grace which enables us to persevere in overcoming those things in our lives which grieve your Holy Spirit. Amen.

God Wants You to Have These Blessings:

Joy and peace every day – 1

'May the God of hope fill you with all joy and peace as you trust in him, so that you may overflow with hope by the power of the Holy Spirit.'

—Romans 15:13

Scripture reading: Romans 15:1–14

There is a connection between drawing on God's power to overcome sinful habits, and having the joy and peace which God means us to have every day. I don't think I am exaggerating when I say that the Christians I have met who have the greatest joy and peace in their lives are the Mary Sisters—members of the Evangelical Sisterhood of Mary, whose home base is in Darmstadt, West Germany. Their experience of joy and peace stems from their concentration on having power over sinful habits. They have a phrase: 'repentance, the joy-filled life'. Their point is that when we turn from sin we are enabled to draw on joy and peace.

You cannot have joy and peace as a kind of 'positive thinking' activity, but when we have power over sinful habits it is a logical consequence that we will draw on those blessings from God.

We need to know that joy and peace are characteristics of the Christian experience, and, assuming that we are actively and meaningfully drawing upon, not only forgiveness but cleansing, we need to consciously appropriate that experience.

Dr John Schindler of the United States wrote a book called *How to Live 365 Days a Year* in which he claimed that, if he could get his patients to lift their thoughts into pure joy and peace every day for ten minutes, and leave behind all hate, fear and conflict, he could get them well, keep them well and help them to live a long and useful life.

Key thought: Confession of sin, and cleansing from sin, brings joy and peace.

Thank you, heavenly Father, for the peace you give us through the cleansing blood of Jesus, our Lord and Saviour. Amen.

God Wants You to Have These Blessings:

Joy and peace every day – 2

'A cheerful heart is good medicine'   —Proverbs 17:22

Scripture reading: Isaiah 12

In his own way, what Dr Schindler was saying in his book is that you have to overcome the sinful habits of hate, resentment and conflict, and then you can lift your thoughts into the pure joy and pure peace that God gives. If you do that, he says, you can get well, you can stay well and you can live a long and fulfilled life.

It would be wrong and misleading to think that you could have ten minutes of joy and peace, then live the rest of the day in any way you wanted to, and that it would still work out. Obviously, Dr Schindler didn't mean that, and I want to make it clear that I don't mean that either. I would add to what the doctor has written by saying that the ten minutes a day is just a way to enable all our thoughts for that day to be filled with joy and peace.

To have God's joy and peace in a continuing way requires an ongoing discipline, but it is a positive one. We are training our minds to appropriate these blessings from God—moment by moment, thought by thought and circumstance by circumstance, all day long. I like the text from Proverbs which says: 'A merry heart doeth good like a medicine' (Proverbs 17:22 KJV).' It does good to the person who has a merry heart, and it does good to those who have contact with him. Where there is joy from God there is peace, and where there is peace from God there is joy. Put the two together and it will lead to healing and a long and worthwhile life.

Key thought: We need to understand what God has provided; then we need to consciously appropriate it.

Enable us, Father, to be disciplined in repentance, faith and obedience, so that we can daily draw on your blessings of joy and peace. In Jesus' name. Amen.

God Wants You to Have These Blessings:

Joy and peace every day – 3

'"Do not let your hearts be troubled. Trust in God; trust also in me ..."'

—John 14:1

Scripture reading: John 14:15–27

We are so used to our lot in life that very often it never so much as crosses our minds that we could be different, and that God wants us to be different.

When I was a young clergyman I was struck by the comment of a parishioner who said, 'The minister always says what we should be, but never says how we can have it'.

How are we to have joy and peace in believing? The answer is that we draw on all the blessings of God by repentance, by faith and by ongoing obedience. Obedience means we have to walk the Christian way, otherwise we will grieve the Spirit and lose our blessing. The point I want to make is that, provided you are turning from sin, you should then exercise faith for these gifts from God. Know they are available; accept them like you accept Christ for salvation; make a decision so that you know it is something you have done, and then affirm it in an ongoing way by faith—and that means praise.

There is no reason why everyone who reads these words—whoever you are, whatever background difficulty you may have and wherever you may live—there is no reason why you cannot have joy and peace in believing.

Key thought: We draw on all the blessings of God by repentance, faith and obedience.

Father, we draw upon your joy and peace. We believe for it through Christ, and by faith we affirm that you are giving it to us now. Thank you, Father. Amen.

God Wants You to Have These Blessings:

Practical help in every situation – 1

'"So do not worry, saying, 'What shall we eat?' or 'What shall we drink?' or 'What shall we wear?' … seek first his kingdom and his righteousness, and all these things will be given to you as well."' —Matthew 6: 31–33

Scripture reading: Mark 6:34–44

Archbishop William Temple, a former Archbishop of Canterbury, once said, 'Christianity is the most materialistic of all religions'. The Archbishop had a knack of putting things in a way that made people think. What he meant was that, more than any other religion, Christianity is concerned with material things as well as spiritual. You need only to read Matthew chapter six and the words of Jesus where he says in effect: 'Don't worry about your material needs; God knows you have to provide for what you wear and what you drink and what you eat. God will look after you and provide these things for you'. You can't be more materialistic than to be concerned with what you eat and drink and wear.

Jesus said that God is so concerned about looking after this kind of need that he even knows how many hairs are on our heads (see Matthew 10:30). We think we become preoccupied with these things, especially when a parent is looking after a child and providing for his or her future, but any such preoccupation is nothing compared with the concern that God has for us. God knows that we need these things, and Jesus expressly states that if we will seek the Kingdom of God and the righteousness of God, our material needs will be added to us in a detailed way.

Key thought: God has promised to look after us, if we put him first.

Father, we seek to put you first in our lives; to seek to love and obey you in all things.

God Wants You to Have These Blessings:

Practical help in every situation – 2

'"Ask and it will be given to you; seek and you will find; knock and the door will be opened to you."'
—Luke 11:9

Scripture reading: Luke 11:1–13

We all have material needs and we would be very unrealistic if we said we hadn't. I believe that part of our Christian understanding, part of our prayer activity, part of what we mean by the Prayer of Faith, is to believe that God is concerned about providing for each need. We are more important than the sparrows and the crops, all of which God looks after perfectly. If he looks after these things perfectly, he will look after us in even greater perfection.

In the Third Epistle of John we read: 'I wish above all things that thou mayest prosper and be in health, even as thy soul prospereth' (3 John 2 KJV). It is this kind of balance I want to bring into focus—to encourage us all to bring every need under the umbrella of faith and believe God for his provision. If you have a need for your soul, then believe for it in prayer. If you have a need for health, then believe for it in prayer. And, if you have a need of a material nature, believe for that in prayer—and God will meet all your needs out of his bounty.

Key thought: God is concerned about providing for our every need.

Our loving Father, we believe today for material provision, so you will make our hearts glad, your name glorified and your Kingdom extended. Lord, you know the needs we all have and we believe for those needs being met now, in Christ our Lord. Amen.

All or Nothing at All – 1

'Immediately the boy's father exclaimed, "I do believe; help me overcome my unbelief!"'   —Mark 9:24

Scripture reading: Psalm 116

If there is one subject I teach on more than any other, it is the subject of faith. I make no apology for this because faith is the great requirement, the essential requirement, if we are going to have God's blessing, including the blessing of healing. I don't say that faith is the only requirement—there are three things needed if you are going to draw on God's blessing:

- you have to repent—that is, you have to turn from your old life;
- you have to believe—you pray the Prayer of Faith;
- you have to obey God, not only now but in an ongoing way.

However, it was Jesus who said that the central requirement was that of faith. He said we have to believe so we do not doubt in our hearts. But what do we so often do? We hope for the best and fear the worst! It is as though we've got two horses pulling a cart—one representing faith, and the other representing doubt and fear. We go through the motions of faith, and we do it sincerely; we might even know that the outcome will depend on our prayer, but at the same time we are haunted by being in bondage to the problem. The Bible says we are to walk by faith (2 Corinthians 5:7) so that it becomes our lifestyle.

I say to people who come to me for counselling: 'Prayer is not just this' (as I hold my hands together in an attitude of prayer), 'Prayer is this' (pointing to my forehead, implying that it is the way we think).

Key thought: Faith is the essential requirement in order to draw on God's blessing.

Father, we want to believe your Word without doubting, but sometimes we are under attack; help us with our unbelief. For Jesus' sake. Amen.

All or Nothing at All – 2

'But when he asks, he must believe and not doubt, because he who doubts is like a wave of the sea, blown and tossed by the wind.'　　—James 1:6

Scripture reading: Job 23:1–12

I have come to realise, in my walk of faith, that if we've got two horses—Faith and Fear—pulling the one cart, we will find that, as time goes by, Fear wins out. We can be going through the motions of faith meaningfully, sincerely, effectively—holding on for dear life, if you like—but, because our thoughts are partly given over to negativity, not only will that negativity continue, but it will grow and ultimately become dominant. When that happens, your prayer life is a burden and a heartache. You don't know where to turn. Your problems increase until people can see it in your face and it is reflected in your conversation— until you are filled with despair so that you wonder whether prayer is a waste of time. One mightn't even realise what is really happening, and even if one does, it becomes a situation from which there is no escape.

Now, strangely enough, it is precisely when we come to the end of our tether that things begin to happen. I like that expression 'the end of our tether'. It's in the J. B. Phillips version of 2 Corinthians 1:8 where Paul said: ' … we believe now that we had this experience of coming to the end of our tether that we might learn to trust, not in ourselves, but in God who can raise the dead'.

What really happens is that we come to the end of our self-dependence. The result is joy and peace in believing. And, because you're believing so you do not doubt, God is doing the work.

Key thought: When we come to the end of our self-dependence, we come to faith.

Loving Father, help us to be like Jesus, and to depend upon you more. In Jesus' name. Amen.

All or Nothing at All – 3

'The LORD is good, a refuge in times of trouble. He cares for those who trust in him'   —Nahum 1:7

Scripture reading: Mark 8:34–38

When we come to understand that we have to put all our eggs into the 'faith basket', we realise that we need to discipline our prayer reactions and our thought reactions so that, from here on, we do believe in a complete kind of way. It is a case of 'all, or nothing at all' if it is going to work with God.

I can only say, since working through this myself, what a great relief and blessing it has been to me in my thinking and praying about the healing ministry.

There's only one way to pray so that your prayer takes off with wings—you've got to go all the way in faith. If you don't, sooner or later you're going to be brought to the end of your tether and the negative side is going to win. But that's not the end, for perhaps it is only then that we are enabled to come to faith which does not doubt. And while it might be an ongoing cycle, we can at least give ourselves, through discipline and prayer, to getting it right—for we learn to pray, and we learn how to have faith.

Key thought: It is a case of 'all, or nothing at all' if it is going to work with God.

O Father, we're only ordinary people, and I'm very ordinary. But we are those who would give ourselves to you, that you would teach us how to pray. Teach us how to have faith which does not doubt. And so bless us all, each one, that all our faith eggs will be in one basket. In Jesus' name, and in the power of the Holy Spirit. Amen.

Teach and Encourage – 1

"'I have set you an example that you should do as I have done for you."'
　　　　　　　　　　　　　　　　　　　　—John 13:15

Scripture reading: Luke 10:17–24

One of the features of the ministry of our Lord Jesus Christ was the way in which he taught his disciples. He exercised the full range of his ministry in front of them, and with them. He preached the gospel; he healed the sick; he ministered to people in a variety of circumstances, mainly to exercise his own ministry, but also so that he might send out his followers to do what he had done.

It is no less important to see the encouragement which Jesus gave his disciples. After they had been sent out to do what he had taught them to do, they returned and gave their report. Our Lord listened with approval, and told them, 'I have given you authority … to overcome all the power of the enemy' (Luke 10:19). What an encouragement it must have been to the disciples that the Lord should be approving of their ministry and give them ongoing authority.

When Agnes Sanford came to this country for the first time, she conducted a teaching mission here at St Andrew's Cathedral, on the healing ministry. The Cathedral was packed night after night as this remarkable woman taught from the Word of God. She was someone who was motivated to teach. She also conducted daily healing seminars, inviting people to offer themselves for prayer. She would pray for them but would invite other people at the seminar to share in the ministry and lay hands on the person for healing. So people were not only being taught what to do, but were also being encouraged to do it themselves.

Key thought: Jesus taught his disciples by his own example, and he encouraged them in their ministry.

Father, equip us to teach your truth to those who look to us, and to encourage them in the way Jesus has shown us. In Jesus' name. Amen.

Teach and Encourage −2

*'Whatever you have learned or received or heard from me, or seen in me—
put it into practice. And the God of peace will be with you.'*—Philippians 4:9

Scripture reading: Luke 10:1–9

When I first went to Moore Theological College—I'm sorry to have to
admit this, but confession is good for the soul—I said to myself: 'I only
need the finishing touches'. I was appointed as catechist in a multichurch
parish (more than one church in the parish) where I served for twelve
months. My next appointment was again as a catechist in a multichurch
parish where I remained for two years. So, for three years in all, I was on
my own. The minister was in one church and I would be in the other, and
I thought it was all fine. However, in my fourth year I went as catechist to
a single-church parish where I was with the rector all the time, and I came
to realise that, up until then, all I had been doing was perpetuating my
ignorance! What a valuable twelve months I had, sitting at this rector's
feet, being instructed and sometimes being corrected.

I think my experience might not be dissimilar to that of other people.
Until we are taught, until we are instructed, until we have the Word of
God opened to us and see it worked out in other people's lives, it may be
that all we are doing is perpetuating our own ignorance.

When people come to see me for counselling I almost always suggest
that they come to the Wednesday night Healing Service. This is because
one of the prime purposes of this ministry is to provide instruction and
to offer correction, so that participants can learn the principles of divine
healing from both teaching and example. Sometimes, I have to say—as
it has been said to me—'You're on the wrong track'. Sometimes they
will persist—and then I have to say, 'STOP!' because, until you act in an
informed way, you are only going to perpetuate your own difficulty.

Key thought: We need to be prepared to learn from those God has put
in authority over us.

*Dear Father, help us to listen to what you want us to learn. Through the
power of your Holy Spirit. Amen.*

Teach and Encourage – 3

'Then Samuel said, "Speak, for your servant is listening."'

—1 Samuel 3:10

Scripture reading: 1 Timothy 4:1–16

The Healing Service provides encouragement as well as instruction. Everyone needs to be encouraged. You know, I think that the characteristic which makes a great leader is the ability to encourage other people so that they are motivated to act effectively. There is no ministry more needed (and which complements the ministry of instruction) than one which encourages people in their Christian walk.

After I had been ordained and had served as curate in two Sydney parishes, I went to England as a curate under Canon Bryan Green at St Martin in the Bull Ring, in the Diocese of Birmingham. Having started off at Moore College thinking I knew everything, I arrived in Birmingham thinking I knew nothing!

St Martin in the Bull Ring was one of the premier churches in England; our Sunday night congregation was always 1,300 and the parish life and activity was in proportion. I was overwhelmed. The rector could see that I was very insecure and hardly knew what to do, and he might have been entitled to think: 'Well, he's a dud'. But he was one of those great leaders, and when he had to go to a school council meeting in the north of England for three days, taking his wife and secretary, he invited me to go with them. I'm sure it was only to encourage me—and that is what those three days meant for me. Being close to the rector and others, being able to share personal conversation and asides, gave me the encouragement which I needed. He brought out my positive strengths and helped me to put them into practice—and I never looked back.

Key thought: A good leader will be an encourager.

Thank you, Father, for those who bless us by their encouragement. Amen.

Teach and Encourage – 4

*'Joseph, a Levite from Cyprus, whom the apostles called Barnabas (which
means Son of Encouragement)'*   —Acts 4:36

Scripture reading: Acts 15:22–35

Some time ago we had a visiting American psychiatrist come to this
country. She was referred to in the press as the 'Leading American
Psychiatrist'. I was incredulous when I heard what she said were the
principles she followed in her psychiatric practice. The principles of
psychiatry are that you look backwards to the causative factors in
people's problem situations and help them see why they behave as they
do. You help them make adjustments, essentially looking at weaknesses
so they can be remedied. But this woman psychiatrist said: 'I do not
worry about the weaknesses. I help people develop their strengths.
When I do that, I find that the weaknesses are brought under control
and kept in their right perspective'. Well, that's revolutionary as far as
psychiatric practice is concerned. But it's jolly good common sense,
and I said 'amen', because it is so like the ethos of my own ministry.

We need instruction in order to know what is the appropriate thing
to do. We need encouragement, which often means that our strengths
are discerned so that we are helped to stand on our own feet, and do our
own thing, under God.

We all need to be taught, we all need to be encouraged and we all
need to teach and we all need to encourage one another. Isn't that right?
I feel it so deeply in my spirit. I invite you to respond.

Key thought: Helping people recognise their strengths is better than
pointing out their weaknesses.

*Father, help us to be encouragers and help others grow in the gifts and
abilities you have given them so that they will, in your strength, overcome
their weaknesses. For your glory. Amen.*

Accepting Christ for Other People – 1

'When Jesus saw their faith, he said to the paralytic, "Son, your sins are forgiven."'
—Mark 2:5

Scripture reading: Mark 2:1–12

The account in Mark's Gospel of the healing of the paralytic man is of great interest because it gives a clear-cut illustration from the ministry of Jesus Christ of the faith of other people being used so that the sins of someone else could be forgiven.

About three years ago I met a couple in the Cathedral grounds—a man and wife whom I knew well. As they greeted me I could see they were distressed. They told me they were very worried about their daughter, Helen,[1] who, as far as they could tell, was not a Christian. They asked me if I would pray for Helen, and I said I would.

I held this couple in the highest regard as practising Christians and they had opened their hearts to me, so I felt a special responsibility to respond. When I prayed about the matter, I did something I had never done before—I prayed like this:

> Father, I thank you that Jesus has died that we might be forgiven. I thank you that it is your will that all men be saved and come to the knowledge of the truth, and I thank you for that story in the Bible which says that, when Jesus saw the faith of four men, he said to someone else, 'Your sins are forgiven'. So now I accept Christ as Helen's Saviour; I believe on Jesus on her behalf. I stand in the breach with my faith, that you will see my faith in Christ for her and say to her, 'Your sins are forgiven'. This is my Prayer of Faith. In Jesus' name. Amen.

Key thought: We have a scriptural precedent for exercising the Prayer of Faith for the conversion of other people.

Thank you, Father, for this encouragement to pray in faith for others. Amen.

[1] Name has been changed.

Accepting Christ for Other People – 2

'I have been reminded of your sincere faith, which first lived in your grandmother Lois and in your mother Eunice and, I am persuaded, now lives in you also.'   —2 Timothy 1:5

Scripture reading: Matthew 9:1–8

I so accepted Christ for Helen that, when she came to mind, my immediate reaction was to say: 'Oh, thank you Father for Helen's salvation. Thank you, Father, that she is in Christ because I believe for her'. I didn't pray about her every day, but when the Lord brought her to my mind, that is how I reacted.

About twelve months later I again met Helen's parents. They spoke to me along these lines: 'You remember we asked you to pray for Helen?—well, she has joined the church. Previously she never entered its doors; and now she is in charge of all the youth work in the parish. She is a member of the Parish Council, and the rector told us only a week or so ago, what a wonderful influence for Christ she is in the whole congregation'.

I have followed up the matter since then, and I know Helen is increasingly active in her parish church. My faith, and the faith of her parents (for they had faith to ask for other faith to be added to theirs), had so availed for Helen that she had come to faith herself.

Do not misunderstand me. I am not saying our faith is in place of the other person's faith when we accept Christ for them. What I am saying is that our faith on their behalf so enables the Holy Spirit to bless them and lead them into all truth that they come to faith in Christ themselves.

Key thought: Our faith enables God to work in the lives of others.

Help us, Father, to understand these things so we can believe for others to be saved and healed. In Jesus' name. Amen.

Accepting Christ for Other People – 3

'"with God all things are possible."' —Matthew 19:26

Scripture reading: 1 Corinthians 7:12–17

I received a letter from a lady in the country, with the question: 'Surely there is a limit for what you can believe for other people?'. I wrote back and said: 'Why? There is no limit at all; the only limit is your vision and your faith'. She has since written me a charming letter in which she said: 'Oh, this has transformed my life. My friend and I have accepted Christ for her husband and he has already come to Christ, so he is exercising faith for his own salvation'.

Another lady told me that her minister heard a taped address that I had given at a mission in Victoria. In it I had said that you can believe on Christ for someone else's salvation. Her minister straightway believed on Christ for his son's salvation—and his son came to Christ. Hearing this, the lady decided to believe for her husband's salvation. As a result he came to Christ; then she believed that he be filled with the Holy Spirit. And now, she told me, he is in theological college training for the ministry.

Dear brethren, stop wringing your hands about those who are unconverted, and pray for them. But praying for them means to have faith for them; and that means to accept Christ on their behalf. If you do that so that you do not doubt, then it will enable them to have faith in Christ for themselves. Praise God!

Key thought: There is no limit to what you can believe for other people; the only limit is your vision and your faith.

Thank you, Father, for the hope you have given us in Christ Jesus, that our believing prayer for others is effective for their salvation and blessing. Amen.

Moving the Bigger Mountains:

Faith affirms that you 'have received' – 1

'So then, brothers, stand firm and hold to the teachings we passed on to you, whether by word of mouth or by letter.'   —2 Thessalonians 2:15

Scripture reading: Hebrews 6:13–20

The bigger the mountain to be moved—that is, the bigger the problem we have, the more developed our sickness, the more complex our circumstances—the more we have to be concerned with exercising faith in the way the Bible describes, the way our Lord Jesus Christ taught.

I am amazed at how people make up their own ideas of what is meant by faith; one person will say one thing and another will say something else. It doesn't matter a scrap what I say or what anyone else says. The only thing that is important is what Christ has said. Make sure that what you explain to yourself and to others is the direct teaching of our Lord Jesus Christ, because God does not change to suit us; with him there is 'no variableness, neither shadow of turning' (James 1:17 KJV). We have to get things right the Jesus way. When we do, it works, and until we do, it doesn't!

What then did our Lord Jesus Christ say about faith? Mark 11:24 sets out what Jesus taught about faith, and is consistent with what the New Testament says in other places about faith in prayer. Our Lord said: 'whatever you ask for in prayer, believe that you have received it, and it will be yours', and in the previous verse he says that our believing should be to the point where we do not doubt in our heart. You are to believe you have received the answer to your prayer.

Key thought: Faith affirms that we have received.

Our loving Father, we affirm we have received your blessing, and by faith we praise your name. Through Christ our Lord, Amen.

Moving the Bigger Mountains:

Faith affirms that you 'have received' – 2

'But we are ... of those who believe and are saved.'　—Hebrews 10:39

Scripture reading: Ephesians 1:3–14

Believing we have received the answer to our prayer shouldn't surprise Christians because, when we act out faith for conversion we say we are saved. We don't say: 'I believe I could be saved' or 'I will be saved', or even 'I am being saved'. We say that we are saved, referring to it as something that is finished and complete.

I have earlier referred to my experience of conversion. When I was a late teenager I accepted Christ as my Saviour at a mission at St Luke's Clovelly. I said as a result—because that is what we were taught to do—'I am saved', but I didn't experience any change. I had no witness of the Spirit that Christ was in my life. I was saying, 'I am saved, but nothing has happened'. After a few weeks I went back to the rector and told him, 'Rector, I have been affirming I am saved, but nothing has happened'. I have always remembered him saying to me, 'Jim, you have to affirm it by faith!'. He explained that faith is not what you see; it is not how you feel. He said that faith meant thanking God before you have the blessing by sight, and affirming this in your mind. I understood that and stopped saying, 'I am saved but it's not working!' and started to say, 'I am saved and I'm affirming it by faith. Praise God!' and I disciplined my mind to continue to make that affirmation. It wasn't what I saw. It wasn't what I felt. It was believing something before I had it, to the point where I was praising God.

Key thought: We do not affirm what we see. We affirm the answer.

Father, we continue to affirm we have the blessing you have promised.

Moving the Bigger Mountains:

Faith affirms that you 'have received' – 3

'You will keep in perfect peace him whose mind is steadfast, because he trusts in you.'   —Isaiah 26:3

Scripture reading: Psalm 33

I am continually dismayed by people who foolishly discontinue their medical treatment because they are making some faith affirmation. The healing ministry of the Christian church seeks to work in the closest association with the medical profession, and I earnestly advise you to continue receiving your medical treatment and continue to take your medication. The doctor is not affirming something by faith; he is reacting to what he sees, and it is right that you draw upon the medical resource. Do what your doctor says and do it with a good conscience. Both approaches are valid, both are necessary. Then you have balance.

I want to tell you a story. Once, I found on my face a noticeable mark of skin cancer. My reaction was to be appalled and shocked. I began praying in faith but I kept on rubbing my finger over the spot and thinking, 'Is it better yet?'. It never seemed to improve. Then I got it right. I believed I had received the blessing so that I was praising God. As a result, I lost interest in poking at the mark with my finger or looking at it in the mirror, because I wasn't concentrating on what I had. I was affirming something by faith, and in the long run I had to drive myself to look in the mirror to see how it was getting on and, when I finally looked, it had gone.

'Moving the bigger mountain!'. Faith affirms that you have received, so praise God with a full heart. And keep on with your medical treatment.

Key thought: Faith equals praise.

Let us pray: Our loving Father, we thank you that by faith we affirm we have received your blessing, and by faith we praise your name. Through Christ our Lord. Amen.

Moving the Bigger Mountains:

Persevere in prayer – 1

'men ought always to pray, and not to faint'   —Luke 18:1 (KJV)

Scripture reading: Luke 18:1–8

Who among us hasn't got a bigger mountain in our lives that needs to be moved? I have said that faith affirms that we have received the answer to our prayer, and now I want to say that we are to persevere in prayer.

Luke 18:1–8 is the story of the Unjust Judge. More importantly, it is the story of the woman who would not take 'no' for an answer, but kept on knocking until the judge responded and met her need. Christ used the story to illustrate how we should pray. We are to keep on asking, we are to keep on believing. It finds an echo in the Old Testament story of Jacob who was led to the point of saying to God, '"I will not let you go unless you bless me"' (Genesis 32:26).

When we have a bigger mountain to move, we may well need to persevere in exercising faith and to continue to praise God by faith. As we continue to affirm 'faith in praise' we are enabling the Holy Spirit to minister to us the reality of what God has promised to give.

As far as healing is concerned, we are drawing upon the Holy Spirit who quickens our mortal body—that is, healing. When we continue to affirm 'faith in praise' we are enabling the Holy Spirit to flow at that time and so healing comes to us. When we are persevering in praise we are enabling God to cast our mountain of sickness into the sea, spadeful by spadeful.

Key thought: Persevering in prayer to move the bigger mountains means to continue to praise God by faith.

Thank you, Father, that you are enabling us to persevere in prayer and the mountain is being moved, spadeful by spadeful. Through Jesus Christ our Lord. Amen.

Moving the Bigger Mountains:

Persevere in prayer – 2

'One of those days Jesus went out into the hills to pray, and spent the night praying to God.'   —Luke 6:12

Scripture reading: Romans 8:5–11

If you have time on your side you can continue in prayer in a leisurely way. There is nothing wrong with that, but many people haven't got time on their side. They will need to persevere in 'faith and praise' in a more intensive way.

Many years ago, before I was actively involved in the Healing Ministry, I was very ill with emotional problems. I didn't have time on my side. My need was urgent. It had to be dealt with now! I remember (and this is why I can speak about this with insight and emphasis) how I had to continue in 'faith and praise' for every moment of the day— before I was out of bed in the morning, while I was brushing my teeth, driving my car, and with a corner of my mind in whatever else I was doing during the day. I had to. I didn't have time for more leisurely prayer. There was no virtue in this on my part, or on the part of anybody else who does that. They get it right because they have to—yet they choose to. It is what is meant by sacrificial prayer.

I have said before that, when our Lord had to move a bigger mountain, he prayed all night. When we have to move a bigger mountain we may need to pray all day. That is persevering in prayer. The Healing Ministry is not shallow water fishing. It is out with the big ones. You soon know what separates the men from the boys when it comes to persevering in prayer.

Key thought: A bigger mountain needs continual prayer.

We praise you, loving Father, for the power of your Holy Spirit which brings life to our mortal bodies.

Moving the Bigger Mountains:

Persevere in prayer – 3

'A cord of three strands is not quickly broken'   —Ecclesiastes 4:12

Scripture reading: Psalm 103

One of our number had an urgent problem, a 'bigger mountain', and he felt the need for others to persevere in prayer and faith with him. So he gathered half a dozen like-minded men and women who, he knew, would stand with him; he told them his need, so that they did it together.

Perhaps you can break one stick with your hands or over your knee, but put together six such sticks or more and they will not break, because there is strength in numbers. And there is strength in numbers in prayer and persevering prayer.

If you have to move a bigger mountain, get others to do it with you, but make sure they have faith that does not doubt. Keep them up-to-date with what is happening because, when people pray, they need to be encouraged and they need to pray in a relevant way. So keep the communication lines open. That is very important.

Key thought: Ask others to pray with you.

Our loving Father, we thank you for the encouragement we have from the words of Christ that we are to keep on asking, keep on believing, and to keep on praising God. We do that now, for ourselves and for one another. In Jesus' name. Amen.

Moving the Bigger Mountains:

Complete, lacking in nothing – 1

'And let steadfastness have its full effect, that you may be perfect and complete, lacking in nothing.'   —James 1:4 (RSV)

Scripture reading: Acts 16:16–18

If we are going to pray effectively, we must first of all understand what God provides—what the New Testament reveals, not just in any isolated text, but as the broad themes of Scripture.

The first thing that increased my understanding of what God provided, was something said to me by a couple whose hunchbacked child had been healed. When I asked them to explain how it had happened, they said, 'The perfection is within you'. I didn't know what they meant. Later on, I found it was a reference to the words of our Lord Jesus Christ when he said, 'the kingdom of God is within you' (Luke 17:21). Then I understood what was meant by the Kingdom of God—it is God's perfect blessing, which includes healing. That is what he meant when he said: 'Heal the sick who are there and tell them, "The kingdom of God is near you"' (Luke 10:9).

The second thing that helped me was our Lord's words to his disciples: 'I have given you authority ... to overcome all the power of the enemy' and 'nothing will harm you' (Luke 10:19). That insight has stood me in good stead over the years and in many different circumstances. God provides his perfect blessing, his perfect provision, so that nothing will hurt us—in other words, he gives us power over material things.

I believe God provides this perfect resource so that we might draw upon it. We may draw upon it imperfectly, we may dilute it in one way or another; but when we pray in repentance, faith and obedience, that is what is available to us.

Key thought: God provides his perfect blessing; his perfect provision.

Thank you, Father, for your perfect provision for all our needs.

Moving the Bigger Mountains:

Complete, lacking in nothing – 2

'"Go," said Jesus, "your faith has healed you."'　　　　—Mark 10:52

Scripture reading: Mark 10:46–52

I sometimes say that you need to continue to come to the Healing Service until you know what to do, and then in your real-life setting you need to sweat it out until you get it right, and then it will work for you.

A number of years ago a man brought his wife to see me. The wife, poor dear, was a chronic epileptic. She was so heavily medicated to control her 'fitting' that I can only describe her as a walking zombie. She was absolutely unable to relate to anyone or anything and I couldn't get through to her at all. Her husband was German and had grown up in a Nazi home where they didn't even believe in God, and so it wasn't very easy to speak to him either.

I saw them a number of times but it was very hard going and, after a while, they didn't come any more. They had an appointment but it wasn't kept. I really thought the wife may have died.

About six months later they returned. The man explained that he hadn't been able to keep the appointment because there had been a change in his work circumstances. So they were left on their own. He told me how he remembered what had been said at our counselling sessions and how, as he travelled to and from work on the bus, he would strive to get it right in his mind and accept healing for his wife. He got it right because he had to. He had believed for his wife and she had been healed!

Key thought: When we know what to do, we should do it.

Our loving Father we praise you that we can move the bigger mountains. We praise you that you provide that we may be complete, lacking in nothing. We accept that now and affirm it. In Jesus' name. Amen.

A Fence at the Top – 1

'He who did not spare his own Son, but gave him up for us all—how will he not also, along with him, graciously give us all things?' — Romans 8:32

Scripture reading: John 1:19–34

We are intended to be people who wholly believe for God's blessing in our daily walk. We are to discipline ourselves to react to any area of strain, any symptoms of sickness, by affirming the perfect blessing of God. We are not to react in terms of what we see by sight, but in terms of what we accept and affirm by faith.

Not all Christians have this understanding. We should ask ourselves what it is that, as Christians, we can draw upon by faith. I maintain, and it is an absolutely central point of my own platform and of my teaching ministry, that God's perfect Kingdom blessing is available for us all, now.

The Bible says that the whole point of our Lord Jesus Christ's coming to earth was to take away the sin of the world. Now, have you ever asked yourself why, if our Lord has taken away the root cause of all our problems, we have so many troubles? I used to ask this question when I first started to study theology, and no-one gave me the answer. Christ has taken away the sin of the world so that, when we put our trust in him, we can be reconciled to the Father and be made one with God; and, because of this, God restores his Kingdom to us. The full circle has been turned—do you see? That is why we affirm that God has provided his perfect blessing for us.

Key thought: We are not to react in terms of what we see by sight, but we are to react in terms of what we accept and affirm by faith.

Thank you, Father, for restoring your Kingdom to us. Thank you, Jesus, for taking away the sin of the world, which includes our separation from God, our fallen human nature and our sickness and infirmities. Amen.

A Fence at the Top – 2

'Fear not, little flock; for it is your Father's good pleasure to give you the kingdom.'
　　　　　　　　　　　　　　　　　　　—Luke 12:32 (KJV)

Scripture reading: Luke 15:25–32

Do you know that God's perfect blessing doesn't even have to be asked for? When I hear people in prayer saying: 'Lord, we ask this ... and we ask that ... ', I really wonder what their understanding of God's provision is. There's nothing wrong with asking—the Bible says we're to ask—but asking does not enable the blessing to be received. What enables the blessing to be received is believing that you have received it. It doesn't have to be asked for because we, as Christians, already have it. The Kingdom of God, God's perfect blessing, is within you. I've said many times—why ask for what you've got? The Kingdom of God, God's perfect provision, is within you now.

When I first heard, from a layman, that God had provided his perfect blessing so that it didn't even need to be asked for, quite frankly, I did not understand. I had been so used to the idea that, here we are in this mess and, if God gives us any help, it's help to put up with our problems. Then he told me: 'You will wake up one morning, and you will know it is true'. Now, I didn't 'wake up one morning and know it was true', but the point of what he said was abundantly fulfilled in a gradual, progressive way. I certainly did come to the point of having this inward conviction that God's perfect blessing was available—and it didn't even have to be asked for. All I had to do was to accept it.

Key thought: The Kingdom of God, God's perfect blessing, is within you.

Father, thank you that we have your perfect blessing so that it doesn't even have to be asked for. We affirm this now, by faith. Through Christ our Lord. Amen.

A Fence at the Top – 3

'I have given you authority to trample on snakes and scorpions and to overcome all the power of the enemy; nothing will harm you.' —Luke 10:19

Scripture reading: Deuteronomy 34

Someone once said to me: 'I haven't got your conviction of faith'. I replied: 'If you would have a conviction of faith, you must first know for sure what God has provided for you'. This is step one! There isn't anything to which you can give your heart, mind, prayer and spiritual searching that is more rewarding than this—that you will know, in your heart of hearts, either all at once or in a progressive way, that his perfect provision, his perfect blessing, his perfect healing, his perfect help in anything and everything, is your possession; it only has to be accepted for it to be effective. That is the touchstone of my whole activity in the Healing Ministry.

A consequence of what I have said is this: you shouldn't get sick in the first place. We need to draw on this wholeness of blessing, this perfection of blessing, in a preventive way. For, if the perfection of blessing is available as an ambulance at the bottom of the cliff, it must be there to be drawn on as a fence at the top! Think about it! We should be so living our lives in the reality of God's wholeness, in the reality of God's Kingdom, that we remain in health.

I'm going to say it again and again. Jesus said that NOTHING ... NOTHING ... NOTHING shall by any means hurt you. That's what Jesus said, and that is what I am talking about.

Key thought: To accept God's perfect blessing means that we can remain in a state of health, which is God's will for us.

Thank you, Father, that it is your will for us to be whole and remain well. We accept your provision by faith, and in Jesus' name. Amen.

A Fence at the Top – 4

'I shall yet praise him, who is the health of my countenance, and my God.'
—Psalm 42:11 (KJV)

Scripture reading: Psalm 42

I've got a feeling that there are people in the Healing Service who delight in the Healing Ministry as an ambulance at the bottom of the cliff, but are none too pleased to think it might be a fence at the top. A fence at the top would require them to face up to certain things in their lives which they are unwilling to face up to.

I maintain that to accept God's perfect blessing means we can remain in a state of health, and that this is God's will for us. It is what God's perfect blessing is all about, in a preventive way.

It is high time that all of us, myself as much as anybody else, took this seriously—we've got nothing to lose except our problems. I believe this is what the Bible says and what the Bible means when taken to its logical conclusion. If his perfect blessing is available at the bottom of the cliff, it's available at the top! The reason why we affirm this is because the sin of the world has been taken away; it is because the Kingdom has been given to us; and it is because Jesus said: 'nothing shall hurt you'. What a glorious challenge! What a glorious inspiration. What a changing, transforming thought!

Key thought: We should face the challenge of 'the fence at the top'.

O Father, we feel excited when we realise something more of all that you have for us. We would have a fence at the top. We would have a glorious vision of the Kingdom of God coming to us through Christ in the power of the Holy Spirit. And this is what we would give you thanks for, and so draw on your blessing that we will wake up one morning and know that it is true. Amen ... Amen ... Amen.

How to Believe for Health – 1

'His divine power has given us everything we need for life and godliness'   —2 Peter 1:3

Scripture reading: Ephesians 6:10–17

God provides for continued health, meaning that you stay well. Now, if we are going to experience this as a blessed reality, there are at least three things that we must keep in mind.

First of all, we must know that this blessing is available. In Ephesians 6:16 Paul says: '... take up the shield of faith, with which you can extinguish all the flaming arrows of the evil one'.

The Bible also says: 'Where there is no vision, the people perish' (Proverbs 29:18 KJV), and 'how shall they hear without a preacher?' (Romans 10:14 KJV). The preacher's job, first of all, is to say what God has provided.

There is a beautifully structured theological basis for having this vision or understanding that God provides for our health. It can't be repeated too often that, when God made things, he saw that they were good. Then came temptation and sin. All the problems in the world, including sickness and infirmity, come from the sin of the world.

The central theme of the Christian faith is that Jesus came and took away the sin of the world. It has been done! God has taken away the root cause of all sickness. He said, 'It is finished' (John 19:30). God has restored his Kingdom, his perfect blessing to us, and part of that perfect blessing is that he has given us health.

Key thought: God has taken away the root cause of all sickness.

We praise you, loving God, that you have dealt with sin and sickness and restored to us your Kingdom through the cross of Jesus Christ, your Son. Amen.

How to Believe for Health – 2

'Jesus said, "It is finished." With that, he bowed his head and gave up his spirit.'
—John 19:30

Scripture reading: Matthew 27:50–56

The second thing to remember in seeking God's provision of continued health is that we must accept it; that is, we must pray the Prayer of Faith. We must accept health. Remember, we accept all of God's blessings in the same way as we accept Christ for salvation. That is how we pray the Prayer of Faith. This means we have to come to the point where we pray like this:

> Father, I thank you that Jesus has taken away the sin of the world; I thank you that you have provided for me my Kingdom health, and I now accept it. I accept it so that it is what I have by faith. This is my decision. Thank you Father; this is now the real me, by grace. Thank you Father, thank you Jesus, thank you Holy Spirit.

You so pray that this is your decision and what you really accept. It is the real and new you; you affirm it in an ongoing, thought-by-thought, and circumstance-by-circumstance way. As in conversion, so in believing for God's health—we know it is available, then we accept it so that it is what we accept. We make our decision, and this is where we now stand.

Key thought: God has restored to us his perfect blessing, and part of that perfect blessing is that he has given us health.

Father, you have given us your Holy Spirit to lead us into all truth. Help us now as we apply our minds to understanding these things. In Jesus' name. Amen.

How to Believe for Health – 3

'In addition to all this, take up the shield of faith, with which you can extinguish all the flaming arrows of the evil one.' —Ephesians 6:16

Scripture reading: Matthew 4:1–11

The third thing to have in mind when drawing upon God's provision of health is that we must affirm it by faith day by day. We must daily bring into focus what we have already accepted at his hand. Speaking for myself, I frequently come to my Quiet Time in anything but that frame of mind. I set myself to pray, therefore, until I come to that desirable state of heart, mind and spirit whereby I am affirming by faith what I am believing for from God. That is what our Quiet Time is for. It might well be for other things, but that is the point I am wanting to make now.

Because the devil does throw his flaming darts at us we might be attacked by him so that symptoms of sickness appear. That is when we need to take up, more than anything else, the shield of faith, wherewith we quench all the fiery darts of the evil one. And so, if you feel those darts coming, do not react by putting the wrong label on yourself— 'Oh dear me, I've got the flu'—react by putting up the shield of faith. Having faith means that the fiery darts of the evil one are being put out. Hold on to that until they fall away.

Over all the years of my involvement with the Healing Ministry, I have spent much time just 'nutting things out'—taking things to their logical conclusion, getting it right and learning from my mistakes. Now, we all have to do this, so read your Bible; employ the mind that God has given you and come to your own conclusion as to what God provides.

Key thought: Raise the shield of faith against the devil.

Help us, Holy Spirit, to diligently search the Scriptures and learn to trust, not in ourselves, but in God.

How to Believe for Health – 4

'pray in the Spirit on all occasions with all kinds of prayers and requests.'
—Ephesians 6:18

Scripture reading: Galatians 2:11–21

I remember a lady, a trained nurse, who was believing for health and, to her concern, would sometimes feel really serious migraine headaches coming on. Although she was a medical worker (and sometimes it is the medical people who find most difficulty doing this) she would not accept the idea that she was getting a migraine. She told me that, wherever she was working, she would put up the shield of faith. She would affirm that God, because of Jesus, and through the power of the Holy Spirit, was quenching the fiery darts of the wicked one which were manifesting themselves in this form. She said she affirmed this, phrase by phrase, thought by thought, until the headaches fell away.

However, the devil didn't stop. Again and again he came back. It would have been so easy for anyone to say: 'Oh dear me! I must be reasonable, I do have a migraine', but this valiant Christian continued to put up the shield of faith and affirm healing so that she did not doubt in her heart. She affirmed it so that she did not let God's promise go—until the fiery darts were again quenched. As she continued to act this out, the migraines came back less frequently, were less severe, were easier to overcome, until finally they did not come back again. Her health has been preserved in that area.

Thank God for the ambulance at the bottom of the cliff—we're not minimising that—but I say again, let us so live that we have a fence at the top. Know that God has provided health for us; accept it and affirm it day by day, until more and more it is blessed reality.

Key thought: Accept health and affirm it, day by day.

Loving Father, I accept your promises as reality in my life. Thank you Father, thank you Jesus, thank you Holy Spirit. Amen.

Living on the Kingdom Plane – 1

'"The kingdom of God does not come visibly, nor will people say, 'Here it is,' or 'There it is,' because the kingdom of God is within [1] you."'
—Luke 17:20,21

Scripture reading: Mark 4:26–32

The expression 'Living on the Kingdom Plane' was coined by Pastor Roland Brown who, with his wife Marcia, for many years conducted 'Camps Farthest Out'[2] around the world. Roland Brown went from conference to conference, month after month, country after country and year after year. Despite this tremendous load of responsibility, constant travel and outgoing ministry, he was always relaxed and happy. He had an effective ministry, both in preaching and the laying on of hands for healing. Nothing wore him out, nothing frustrated him. When asked how he managed to keep up the pace he would simply say, 'I am living on the Kingdom plane'.

What did he mean by this? He meant that God provides the Christian with the Kingdom resource and blessing. God provides his perfection of blessing in any and every situation in which the Christian finds himself. He means us to draw upon the perfection of blessing so that it is the way we live and move and have our being. We are to live on the 'Kingdom plane'.

You see, God in Christ has taken away the sin of the world, which is the root cause of all disease and all disharmony, whether it be personal or corporate, national or cosmic. Because of that, if we put our trust in Christ and what he has done on the cross, we are forgiven our part in the sin of the world and we are reconciled to the Father, both now and for eternity. Because we have been reconciled, the Father has restored to us his Kingdom.

Key thought: We are to live on 'the Kingdom plane'.

We praise and thank you, Father, that you have restored the Kingdom to us and we would live in that reality now. Through Christ our Lord. Amen.

---

[1] Or, *among*
[2] 'Camps Farthest Out' was a ministry begun by Glenn Clark in the 1930s in America and brought to Australia in 1959/60 by Baptist pastor Roland Brown and his wife, Marcia.

Living on the Kingdom Plane – 2

'I can do everything through him who gives me strength.'

—Philippians 4:13

Scripture reading: Matthew 13:24–30

I am fond of saying that you don't have to ask for God's perfect blessing, because it has been given to you. Why ask for what you already have? It only needs to be known, accepted, and affirmed by faith for you to draw upon its reality.

Jesus said, 'Heal the sick ... and tell them, 'The kingdom of God is near you' (Luke 10:9). He is saying that healing is 'a sign' of the Kingdom. This means that the reality of healing is one of those blessings that can be drawn on and experienced because it is part of the Kingdom which is within you. I have no hesitation in saying that the understanding of the Kingdom of God which Roland Brown had, and which I have, is the most important insight I have drawn on in the course of my Christian life and ministry.

The Kingdom has been given. Why, then, don't we experience it? Assuming we know we need to have a vision of what is available, and that we accept it and affirm it by faith, we also need to know that unrepented sin will prevent us from drawing on Kingdom blessing. As we turn from sin we draw on Kingdom perfection in our daily lives.

If you will apply yourself to understand this reality and draw upon it in practice, I believe you, too, would have (if you have not already) the same testimony—that this is what can transform your prayer life and your daily experience of God's blessing.

Key thought: To repent of known sin enables us to draw on God's provision of Kingdom blessing.

Our loving Father, we thank you for Jesus' words, 'the Kingdom of God is within you'. Because of this we thank you that we can live on the 'Kingdom Plane', now and always. Amen.

Appoint a Day for Your Blessing – 1

'Simon Peter answered him, "Lord, to whom shall we go? You have the words of eternal life."'   —John 6:68

Scripture reading: John 4:43–54

Captain Kevin Cullen of the Church Army[1] once spoke of a mission he had conducted in a city in Queensland. The minister of a local church told him that he had reached a point in his ministry where there had to be blessing from God; the things in the Bible had to come true. If they didn't, he would leave the ministry. This was not a negative statement— at least, I do not interpret it in that way; rather it was positive. It had to happen now. It was now or never!

In other words, the circumstances in which the minister felt himself placed had brought him to the end of his tether. He was in the position where God had to pour out his blessing. This had the effect of enabling both the minister and Kevin Cullen to depend on God in a totally meaningful way.

The point I want to make is that, when that happens—when we are in the place where we totally depend upon God—there is a release of faith and praise, and a consequent release of the Holy Spirit. That is what happened in this particular parish. There was a reality of blessing that reminded them of what the Bible speaks about in the infant Church. People were converted, filled with the Spirit and healed, sometimes without any outward ministry. When the Holy Spirit is poured out he is his own minister and does his own work.

Key thought: Coming to the end of our own resources means we are in the position where God can pour out his blessing.

We praise you, Father, that as we learn to depend upon you more, your Holy Spirit powerfully works in us, for your glory. Amen.

---

[1] The Church Army, an Anglican institution committed to evangelism, was established in Australia in 1934.

Appoint a Day for Your Blessing – 2

'But he said to me, "My grace is sufficient for you, for my power is made perfect in weakness."'
                                        —2 Corinthians 12:9a

Scripture reading: Isaiah 58:1–9

We need to understand what I will call the dynamic of how we can draw upon God's blessings—the scripturally-based factors we need to know about, link together and make operative, so that we can have God's blessing. Surely it isn't something reserved for a minister at the end of his tether. It is something God wants to provide for *all his children*, wherever they are and whatever their need.

We could be in a similar position to this minister whereby we cry out, 'I must have God's blessing'. Like him, this could bring us through to faith and praise and the outpouring of the Holy Spirit. That would be one way we could have a similar blessing in our own lives.

I also need to say that I believe we can, by fasting, create the circumstances that will bring about this blessing. Fasting creates the circumstances whereby we depend on God more. This is the meaning of fasting. The dynamic of fasting is that we choose to react to the sensation of being without food so that we depend upon God more.

I well remember the late Fr John Hope[1] of Christ Church St Laurence [Sydney] who chose this artificially created circumstance of fasting. The church's weekly healing service was held every Wednesday and he would fast from early morning until the service was over so that he might be enabled to depend upon God more.

Key thought: God wants to provide his blessing for all his children, wherever they are and whatever their need.

Father, we are in the place where we must have your blessing. We depend on you, more and more, and praise you for the answer to our need. Through Jesus Christ, our Lord and Saviour. Amen.

[1] Fr John Hope (1891–1971). Anglican clergyman in the Anglo-Catholic tradition; a vigorous advocate of social justice who believed in the healing ministry of the Church and introduced the Order of St Luke to Australia.

Appoint a Day for Your Blessing – 3

'Therefore I will boast all the more gladly about my weaknesses, so that Christ's power may rest on me.' —2 Corinthians 12:9b

Scripture reading: Joshua 5:13–15, 6:1–6

Kathryn Kuhlman used to say: 'Appoint a day for your blessing'. If you wrote to her and asked her to pray for your healing, she would nominate a day when she was going to particularly believe for that blessing.

I am talking now about the whole range of God's promised blessings. Whatever the promised blessing of God is, you can appoint a day to receive it. By that I mean you are led to appoint a day when you are committed to believe, so that you do not doubt in your heart that the blessing will be there. So that you will not misunderstand me—because it will only work when you get it right—it means you are putting all your eggs in the one basket. 'I will not let you go unless you bless me', is your inner conviction.

If you do this in the way I am describing, I believe it is an expression of what St Paul said: 'I die daily' (1 Corinthians 15:31 KJV). You are saying on one particular day, 'I come to the end of my tether; today I depend upon God only and completely'. If you act this out in this fully committed way, you will find when you come to that point of inner and wholehearted commitment, that there will be a release of faith and praise, which is what you have to have if God's blessing is to be poured out. You come to the point where you are sure and you are thanking God with a light and full heart, and you will find there is blessing from God.

Key thought: We can make a decision to die daily to self and rely completely on God.

Father, you are worthy of our trust. We trust you now, fully and completely. In Jesus' name. Amen.

Appoint a Day for Your Blessing – 4

'By faith the walls of Jericho fell, after the people had marched around them for seven days.'
—Hebrews 11:30

Scripture reading: Joshua 6:8–20

Because so often the mountain is big and our faith is small, we may have to appoint a day for our blessing in a repeated and cumulative way. That is how the Mary Sisters acquired their remarkable and wonderful 'Canaan' property in West Germany. They believed God had given them this property but, humanly speaking, it was quite impossible for it to come into their hands. So they would appoint a day when they would be wholly committed to be believing for it: 'Thank you Father, you are doing it now'. They would go in procession around the perimeter as though they were going around the walls of Jericho, calling on the Lord. They were committed to it, like God's people were when they encircled Jericho.

Every time they appointed a day for their blessing, the walls came down in degree. They kept on doing it, over a number of years, until finally the property came into their sole possession.

You need to have a reverent sense of experimentation in doing these things. You might not get it right to begin with. You might need help, but can I ask you to at least have the open-mindedness to try. And let us seek to do that, for our own need and the need of the Healing Service and for whatever blessing God lays upon our hearts for which we need to believe.

Key thought: You can appoint a day when you are committed to believe that the blessing will be there.

Our loving Father, we want to die daily. We would be in the position where we trust, not in ourselves, but in God; and, as we do this, we thank you for the release of faith and praise and Holy Spirit blessing, making real the promises of God. For Jesus' sake. Amen.

Stay Well: How to avoid overstrain – 1

'"For my yoke is easy and my burden is light."'   —Matthew 11:30

Scripture reading: Matthew 11:25–30

I would describe strain as when people are carrying more burdens than they are safely able to bear. It would be foolish to think we could go through life, even as a Christian, without stress.

It is my considered judgement that nearly all sickness is caused, directly or indirectly, by overstrain or stress. Many doctors affirm that between sixty and seventy percent of physical problems are emotionally caused, and more than one medical authority affirms the figure to be more like ninety percent.

Dr. Griffith Evans MD, FRCS, an eminent Welsh physician, maintained that there was a two-year gap between a person becoming emotionally stressed and the onset of physical malfunction.

Some time ago a lady came to me and said she had a lump in her side; she asked that I would pray the Prayer of Faith that she be healed. I asked her to think back to about two years before the lump appeared—in case anything had happened that could be described as emotional stress. She said that, two years before, her son had been divorced and had subsequently remarried. She went on: 'I am a Christian woman, Canon Glennon, and to me marriage is something that is "until death us do part". It is a constant heartache and deep hurt to me that my son should be divorced'. I said to her: 'Well, I can see your point completely, but it is no good reacting to it so that it becomes overstrain—which could be the cause of your problem'.

Key thought: Doctors agree that stress is the root cause of most physical illnesses.

We thank you, Holy Spirit, for showing us the stress factors which are the root cause of our sicknesses and that Jesus has dealt with them through the cross.

Stay Well: How to avoid overstrain – 2

'Cast all your anxiety on him because he cares for you.'   — 1 Peter 5:7

Scripture reading: 1 John 4:7–21

I told the lady who was stressed because of her son's divorce that the Bible says we are to cast our anxiety upon the Lord.

'Well, I've tried to do that,' she replied, 'but I find that it isn't long before I'm worrying about it again. I take it back again.'

I prayed the Prayer of Faith with her, both for the healing of the emotional overstrain and the healing of the physical malfunctioning. The emotional overstrain was handled quite easily, but the physical problem—the lump in the side—did not alter. After she had been coming for about a fortnight I told her I thought it unwise to delay things any further if she was not healed, as far as the Prayer of Faith was concerned, and that she should go to a surgeon. She agreed, and I arranged for her to see a Christian surgeon. He was on holiday and it was another fortnight before she was able to meet him. I continued to pray with her, both for the emotional overstrain and the physical problem. When, finally, she went to the surgeon, he couldn't find the lump in her side and, to her embarrassment, she couldn't find it either. She had been healed and has remained healed since.

This is an illustration—and I think there would be plenty more if we only understood these things better—to show that, in this case, overstrain was a cause of physical illness. Sometimes, of course, it's the cause of emotional illness.

Key thought: If we are going to stay well, we have to avoid stress.

Father, we cast the burden of our anxiety and emotional hurt on Jesus, and in its place we accept your Kingdom perfection healing. Praise you, Father. In Jesus' name. Amen.

Stay Well: How to avoid overstrain – 3

'Carry each other's burdens, and in this way you will fulfil the law of
Christ.'   —Galatians 6:2

Scripture reading: Deuteronomy 5:12–15

It stands to reason that, if we are going to stay well, we have to avoid overstrain, both physical and emotional.

We must first learn that there is a limit to the burdens we can bear. In other words, we are to know when to stop. When we are young we don't seem to realise this; when we get older it is forcibly presented to us. We go past the point where we should have stopped—we get sick as a result of the overstrain—and then we realise we have done the wrong thing. We only learn things the hard way but, would to God we did learn them! It's not wrong to make a mistake if we learn from it.

Once we have suffered from the effects of stress we should be able to recognise the symptoms on subsequent occasions and should have enough sense, enough maturity, to pull back and alter our way of doing things.

Secondly, if we are to avoid stress, we should have a day of rest every week. We can stand up to great strain, great burdens, for six days of the week if, on the seventh, we rest from those responsibilities. Your day of rest need not be Sunday which, for one reason or another, might be a very active day. But I can only say that we should have one day, whichever the day happens to be, when we are resting, and not working or carrying our burdens.

Key thought: We should learn from our mistakes and know when to stop.

Father, we confess that we often go beyond our physical and emotional limits. We would obey your Word and rest as you have commanded. Thank you for your love and healing power. Amen.

Stay Well: How to avoid overstrain – 4

'Two are better than one … If one falls down, his friend can help him up.'
—Ecclesiastes 4:9,10

Scripture reading: Psalm 84

I have already referred to the third way whereby we can avoid overstrain but I want to develop it a little more. When the lady who had the lump in her side told me she was unable to cast her burden on the Lord and leave it there, I told her *I would believe for her.* After all, it was easier for me. I wasn't involved in her particular problem. At the end of the fortnight she said she was not burdened with the emotional problem to do with her son any longer.

I still have contact with this lady and happen to know that the blessing has remained secure in the ensuing years. She entered into that blessing because someone else had faith with her, and for her, that she was being enabled to do this. So, if you find you cannot cast your overstrain on the Lord, seek out some trusted Christian friend who knows how to pray the Prayer of Faith and ask him to add his faith to yours.

How to avoid overstrain: realise that we all have our tolerance, past which we cannot go with safety. If we have learned this the hard way—which will apply to virtually everybody—at least profit from it so that you will recognise the symptoms of strain later on and will, with God's help, not go past that point. Have regular rest, daily and weekly—essential if overstrain is to be avoided. Finally, remember the beautiful New Testament direction—that we are to avoid overstrain by casting our burdens upon the Lord.

Key thought: We can ask others to add their faith to ours.

Dear Father, we would be among those who learn from our mistakes. Thank you that you provide us with wisdom to understand our physical limitations as we learn to depend on you more. In Jesus' name. Amen.

Stay Well: How to avoid depression – 1

'So do not fear, for I am with you; do not be dismayed, for I am your God. I will strengthen you and help you; I will uphold you with my righteous right hand.' —Isaiah 41:10

Scripture reading: Ephesians 5:8–20

May I make it clear that I am not talking about the *healing* of depression. I am speaking in a preventive way, so it is 'How to *avoid* depression'.

First, a word as to how depression comes. It is an over-simplification, but what I am saying is quite right in principle. Some depression is inherited; some depression is acquired. It comes because the person is surrounded by difficulties and they become so used to their problem situations that they take them for granted. People become depressed, in varying degrees, by reacting negatively to conditions of stress.

For most of my life, including years as a minister in the church, I had no idea that my difficult, negative, stressful circumstances could be improved or changed. If God gave me any help, he gave me help to put up with things in the 'My grace is sufficient for you' kind of way.

Then I learned something, which is the first of two things we have to know if we are to avoid depression. It is this: God has provided his perfect blessing for his children. This is what is meant by Jesus' words: 'the kingdom of God is within you' (Luke 17:21). The Kingdom of God is God's perfect blessing.

I realised that I didn't have to put up with all those difficulties which had increasingly dogged my steps during my whole life up until then, and that the same truth applied to other people as well.

Key thought: A person becomes depressed when he, or she, reacts to negative circumstances in a negative way.

Thank you, Father, for the reality of your Kingdom perfection. Thank you that Jesus told us that the Kingdom of God is within us and we have received your perfect blessing. Amen.

Stay Well: How to avoid depression – 2

'Therefore, if anyone is in Christ, he is a new creation; the old has gone, the new has come!'
—2 Corinthians 5:17

Scripture reading: Matthew 21:18–22

In one sentence—people become depressed when they react to negative circumstances in a negative way.

How to avoid depression? First of all, we recognise that the same negative difficult personal circumstances are still there—at home, at work, at church. The point I want to make is that it is *how we react to them* that will determine whether or not we avoid depression.

If you would avoid depression—if you would have God's blessing rather than difficulties—you must, first of all, know that the perfection of blessing is available and that *it is within you.* You don't have to ask for it, you only have to accept it and believe so that you do not doubt in your heart. It is perfection.

The second thing you need to do to avoid depression is to pray the Prayer of Faith and draw on this perfection in your particular circumstances so it is that which you accept, rather than the difficulty.

Nine tenths of the trouble is that we accept the problem and not the answer! What you have will depend on what label you put on it. So often the label spells 'problem', 'sickness' or 'depression', and people wonder why they can't break free. They can't break free because they are in bondage to what they have accepted. But, if you put on the label which is the Kingdom perfection, then that is what you have and that is what will grow, so old things pass away and all, ALL, things become new.

Key thought: Accept Kingdom perfection. You have what you accept.

Dear Father. We thank and praise you that the perfection of your Kingdom is within us. We affirm it and accept it now, by faith and moment by moment. Through Jesus our Lord. Amen.

Stay Well: How to avoid depression – 3

'"Ask and it will be given to you; seek and you will find; knock and the door will be opened to you."' —Matthew 7:7

Scripture reading: Psalm 146

If you know the perfect blessing of God is available, and you have accepted it in your circumstances, you do not react in depression but you react in praise—praise by faith. When you get it right by faith, you then get it right by sight. But you won't get it right until you know what is available, and it won't work even then until you accept it, so that it is what you accept—and you accept it by faith.

Paul says: 'give thanks in all circumstances, for this is God's will for you in Christ Jesus' (1 Thessalonians 5:18). You cannot be depressed if you give thanks in everything, and you give thanks in everything because the perfection is available: once you accept it, that is what you've got and that is what God is bringing about, more and more. If what I've said lacks any kind of clarity I can communicate it in one sentence: You have what you accept. Think about it.

Key thought: When you know what is available and have accepted it in your circumstances, you react in praise.

Our loving Heavenly Father, we hear your words saying to us that you want us to be complete, lacking nothing. O Father, we confess what is no less than sin, in that we have reacted in less than faith in your perfect blessings. O Father, we repent and we would so become aware of the perfection that is available that we accept it in more and more circumstances of our lives so that it is what we accept. Bless us now that this will be your ministry to us. For Jesus' sake. Amen.

Faith for Bondage – 1

'Then Jacob prayed, "... Save me, I pray, from the hand of my brother Esau ..."'
—Genesis 32:9,11

Scripture reading: Genesis 12:10–20

Many people are in bondage to a particular problem. It might be that they are in bondage to more than one problem but, one or more, there are those problems which always have them beat!

The particular problem to which people are in bondage can vary tremendously. It may be something personal, known only to that person and God. It might be in relation to others, e.g. the parent might be in bondage to a difficulty the child is in. It might be the prospect of a husband coming home drunk. It might be the reality of a sickness or of temptation.

It could be that you have a social engagement next week, and you are petrified of social engagements in general, or of this one in particular. You will probably be in an agony of anticipation and it will be your anticipation of what will happen which will determine the outcome. Because you are fearing the worst, you will not be surprised when the worst happens. How are you to pray?

If we are to overcome our fear of a future event (it might be today, it could be tomorrow, it could be every day) there is only one way forward, as far as my experience goes, and it is this: there has to be in-depth prayer until faith comes in anticipation of that situation.

Key thought: Do not wait for the 'crisis point'. Make time to pray, well before the problem arrives.

Loving Father, you know the area in which we need to be set free from anxiety and worry about a coming event. We affirm your blessing now for that which has held us in bondage. We affirm that you have gone before us and that it has been dealt with. We believe this by faith. In Jesus' name. Amen.

Faith for Bondage – 2

'So Peter was kept in prison, but the church was earnestly praying to God for him.'   —Acts 12:5

Scripture reading: Psalm 57

Part of the difficulty is that when we fail in a certain area we are afraid it will happen again and, as I have said many times, fear brings about that which we fear, in exactly the same way as faith brings about that for which we have faith: ' ... the thing which I greatly feared is come upon me' (Job 3:25 KJV). Sometimes we can be hoping for the best yet fearing the worst, which describes the situation in which many people find themselves.

Let us assume that the problem occurs when your boy or girl comes home from school, or when your husband comes home from work, or when your wife gets up in the morning. Whatever the problem is that has got you beat, you must have effective prayer in anticipation. Do not wait for the time when it happens. When the crisis is upon you, you've had it! There must be prayer when you have the opportunity to pray in a quiet and reasoned manner and with sufficient time for it to be effective.

For the sake of illustration, let us say you have got a crisis coming in the afternoon. Have a time of prayer in the morning that is truly meaningful.

Prayer concerning a coming crisis, or stressful situation, should be prayer in depth; prayer until you come to the conviction of faith and until there is a release of the Spirit; prayer until you're on the Kingdom plane—and this could be more time-consuming than we might sometimes think.

Key thought: Plan to pray well before 'crunch' time.

Thank you, Father, that when we bring those things that are troubling us to you, you are able to solve the problems before we have to deal with them.

Faith for Bondage – 3

'I have set the LORD always before me. Because he is at my right hand, I shall not be shaken.'
—Psalm 16:8

Scripture reading: Psalm 71

Is there an area where you suffer defeat, not only in yourself but, perhaps, concerning someone near to you? If you will pray in depth — true depth — until there is a heart conviction of faith and the blessing of God before you have to face the problem, you will find that the circumstances have been marvellously altered by the power of God.

When you come to faith concerning your problem, it will mean that your ongoing thoughts will be those of 'joy and peace in believing' (see Romans 15:13 KJV), and you will find that the sting has been taken away. However, you may well have to come to the point of prayer and ongoing faith the next day, too. If you don't, you may find that the sting has returned and, again, you are left flat on your back! But if you will set aside enough time for prayer *before* you come to the problem event, or situation in a day-by-day way (if that is the cycle involved), you will find, perhaps surprisingly quickly, that the problem—the mountain—is increasingly cast into the sea. The bondage is broken, the fear has gone and the victory is there. Praise God!

Key thought: Pray until you have a conviction of faith that all is well.

Our Loving Father, we confess that we're so often in bondage so that we are affirming the problem. Father, we would repent, and we would so pray in depth that we would draw upon the victory of Christ and the power of the Holy Spirit so that the problem is cast into the sea by the power of God. Father, we would be those who follow Jesus who prayed all night in anticipation of a need the next day, and to find, as he did, victory because of prayer. In Jesus' name we pray. Amen.

What is a Faith Affirmation? – 1

'Then he opened their minds so they could understand the Scriptures.'
—Luke 24:45

Scripture reading: Ephesians 3:1–13

Sometimes, when people ask me about healing, I tell them: 'Healing is not something you get out of a drawer; it's not waving a magic wand. Healing is understanding the dynamic of how God works and putting it into practice'. If we are to have this understanding we have to know three things:

First, we must know what is the 'great and precious promise' of God that is relevant to our need (see 2 Peter 1:4). God has drawn close to us and made a covenant with us that we call the New Testament, and we search the Scriptures to see what are the promises he has covenanted to give us. One of those promises is that the Prayer of Faith will raise up the sick man or, as the New International Version of the Bible helpfully puts it: 'the prayer offered in faith will make the sick person well' (James 5:15). I like plain English, and that's good, plain English.

Secondly, we pray the Prayer of Faith that the promise might be made effective in our lives. And, as I say—and I don't mind saying it every day of the week—we understand the Prayer of Faith in conversion. It is the only area of Christian experience where we do understand the Prayer of Faith! And so I say to people: 'Are you a Christian? If you know how faith is exercised in conversion, then you know how faith is exercised for any of the promises of God, because it is still faith!'. In conversion we know there is a promise of God and we accept it so that we make a decision—we accept God's blessing. We accept it so that it is what we accept. Or, to use words from the Bible, we believe we have received it so that we do not doubt in our heart (see Mark 11:23, 24).

Key thought: Healing is not a magic wand; it is finding out what God wants to give us and following his guidelines.

Father, we ask that you will open our minds so that we will understand from your Word the promise relevant to our present need.

What is a Faith Affirmation? – 2

'By faith Abraham, even though he was past age—and Sarah herself was barren—was enabled to become a father because he considered him faithful who had made the promise.'
                                              —Hebrews 11:11

Scripture reading: Daniel 9:17–23

Having learned which of God's promises is relevant to our situation, and having accepted it, the third thing we need to do is to affirm it by faith.

Two people from the country came to see me because of a need they had. When I said they should know the relevant promise of God for their situation and should pray the Prayer of Faith, they said: 'We've been doing that but we're not quite sure we see any change for the better'. So I told them that this is where we must understand what it is to thank God by faith. Faith is thanking God before you have the blessing by sight, and it doesn't mean saying: 'but it's not working'. Faith affirms something before we have it, to the point where we do not doubt, and we continue to affirm it irrespective of the time which is involved.

Now you can see what a 'faith affirmation' is—knowing the promise of God, accepting it for yourself, and affirming it by faith. That is what I do when I pray about needs that are either my own or those of others. I bring to mind the promise of God. I accept it, so it is *what* I accept, and from that time on I discipline my mind and spirit to thank God by faith.

Key thought: If you are going to make a faith affirmation, you must affirm the answer, and not the problem.

Father, we understand how the Prayer of Faith works in conversion. We now affirm your blessing in the other areas of need we have brought to you. We affirm that we have the answer you have provided. In Jesus' name.

What is a Faith Affirmation? – 3

'and to know this love that surpasses knowledge—that you may be filled to the measure of all the fulness of God.'   —Ephesians 3:19

Scripture reading: 2 Corinthians 10:1–5

Dr Ainslie Meares is a well known and respected Melbourne psychiatrist who specialises in secular meditation. I know nothing about secular meditation and I don't particularly want to. The only meditation I'm interested in is that which is in the name of the Father, the Son, and the Holy Spirit. However, I have read some of Dr Meares' case histories and I was very interested in a certain point which he made.

There was a woman who was in an advanced stage of cancer who drew upon the meditation prescribed by Dr Meares. She put on weight and the cancer began to recede. Then Dr Meares went away for three-and-a-half weeks and she was left to her own devices. When he came back he found that her condition had deteriorated. He asked her what she had been doing differently from what he had told her to do; it was this—she was believing that she was being healed of cancer! She was believing that she was being healed of *cancer*; she had put a label on herself! And she was going downhill. Under the doctor's instruction she came back to a more simple and totally positive affirmation in meditation that did not include the concept that she was being healed of cancer. And again she began to progress so that healing was increasingly being drawn upon.

I fully understand Dr Meares' position, because people come to me and ask, 'Can I be healed of rheumatoid arthritis?' or of some other thing, and I say: 'No! As long as you've got that label on yourself you'll never be healed'.

Key thought: Take off the label of sickness.

Father, we would affirm your blessing and not the problem, and we do this now. In Jesus' name. Amen.

What is a Faith Affirmation? – 4

'and to put on the new self, created to be like God in true righteousness and holiness.'
—Ephesians 4:24

Scripture reading: Ephesians 4:17–32

What are we to do positively? What is a faith affirmation? It is a faith affirmation about the answer and not about the problem. This is why I hate asking people about their need because they affirm the problem. We have to avoid focusing on the problem and all the negativity that surrounds it. I don't mean that we ignore the problem. I get so annoyed when people say, 'Oh, you mean we ignore the problem'. We don't ignore the problem. We react to the problem by affirming the answer.

When I make a faith affirmation, I think of the area where blessing is needed (I will go as far as this to bring the problem into focus). I affirm that I am a new creation in Christ. I affirm that all things are made new. I affirm that I'm filled with all the fullness of God. I affirm: 'Praise God! Thank you, Father. Thank you, Jesus. Thank you, Holy Spirit.'

Now, I'm not sure that I've brought this into focus so sharply, so starkly, so uncompromisingly, before. I've believed it before, and Dr Meares' work reinforces that belief. His patient deteriorated when she affirmed she was being healed of *cancer*, and it was not until she returned to a simple, positive affirmation that she began to recover. So let us get our faith affirmation right, so that it's a faith affirmation about the answer.

Key thought: We don't ignore the problem. We *react* to the problem by affirming the answer.

Loving Father, we affirm that we are a new creation in Christ and that all things are made new. We are filled with all the fullness of God and have received the blessing we have asked of you. Thank you, Father; thank you, Jesus; thank you, Holy Spirit. Amen.

Meditation In Action – 1

'Then Caleb silenced the people before Moses and said, "We should go up and take possession of the land, for we can certainly do it."'

—Numbers 13:30

Scripture reading: Numbers 13:1, 17–33; 32:10–12.

A faith affirmation is knowing the promise of God; it is accepting the promise of God; and it is affirming the promise of God by faith. Now, Christian meditation is just that. It is having that understanding, it is making that affirmation, it is resting in that reality. It is affirming it, it is resting in it, it is growing in it, it is living in it, it is having it, in depth—in depth.

You've got to have theory but theory has to be put into practice, and often there's a great strain in putting it into practice to begin with because it is quite a jump from talking about a thing, and doing it. I look upon the Healing Service as a school—a School of Prayer—and, ultimately, we are concerned with helping people 'do it'.

I always begin prayer by saying: 'In the Name of the Father, and of the Son, and of the Holy Spirit.' My intention is to put myself in the presence of the Triune God, and to believe for his blessing, and his blessing alone. Not least, I am believing that I am protected by the armour of God and, above all, by the shield of faith.

Key thought: Christian meditation is resting in the reality of our faith affirmation.

Thank you Father. We accept your perfect blessing for us. We affirm it by faith. We thank you for it. We praise your name. We affirm its reality. We continue in depth more and more. Thank you, Lord. It is our faith affirmation. We draw on it more and more; we have it more and more.

Meditation In Action – 2: Steps in Christian Meditation

In the Name of the Father, and of the Son, and of the Holy Spirit. Amen.

Prayer: Father, we would be still and know that you are God. We believe for your perfect blessing and protection over us, so that we are only being ministered to by the Father and the Son and the Holy Spirit. It is our Prayer of Faith. Through Jesus Christ our Lord. Amen.

First of all, be relaxed physically. Consciously quieten your body; feel that your body is being relaxed; consciously relax the muscles.

Relax your mind, let the cares of the day roll away; and now relax your spirit. Open it to God Most High—Father, Son and Holy Spirit.

Confess any sin for which you need forgiveness and cleansing.

Prayer: Father, we confess those things whereof our conscience accuses us; the things we are carrying that are a burden; the things we may have done that have disfigured our relationship with you today. We confess our sin; we admit our sin. We are willing to leave our sin behind, and we do that now. We believe for your forgiveness and cleansing through Jesus Christ and the Holy Spirit. Amen.

Now go on to draw on the blessing God has for you. Because we are one with God, he provides newness: 'if anyone is in Christ, he is a new creation; the old has gone, the new has come!' (2 Corinthians 5:17). This newness includes healing. In other words, we are drawing upon all the fullness of God (see Ephesians 3:19)—God's perfect blessing; God's perfect provision; God's perfect healing—all things made new.

Our meditation brings us to the point where we are consciously resting in God's perfect blessing, perfect provision and perfect healing. That is what we are appropriating. That is what we are experiencing now. Praise the Lord. Rest in it now. You have it now.

Safety Rules for the Healing Ministry – 1

'"Amen! Praise and glory and wisdom and thanks and honour and power and strength be to our God for ever and ever. Amen!"' —Revelation 7:12

Scripture Reading: 2 Kings 20:1–7

A book which I read recently mentioned a number of people in the United States who had drawn on divine healing—but it had been a disaster. The only thing that followed this ministry was hurt and disillusionment. I felt very concerned and read the book carefully to see what characterised their ministry. I found, as far as my examination could go, that they had, as a sign of their faith, left off all medical treatment.

In my book, *Your Healing Is Within You*, I have set out clearly what I believe our relationship with the medical profession needs to be:

- Continue to draw upon the medical treatment as prescribed by the doctor and do it with a good conscience;

- Tell the doctor that you are attending a service of divine healing and keep him informed as to the results;

- Do not let the medical prognosis limit your faith expectation. Look past the treatment and prognosis to God and believe that with him all things are possible. Let that become the measure and reality of your faith.

Let me say plainly, to avoid misunderstanding, if you are drawing on the medical resource and you wish to draw upon divine healing as well, you are not showing faith by discontinuing the medical treatment. On the contrary, and I say this advisedly, you are being very foolish indeed, and I could accept no responsibility for what you do.

Key Thought: To draw upon divine healing does not mean you have to stop your medical treatment as a sign of faith.

Thank you, Father, for your provision of the medical resource. Our prayer is praise for the blessing of wisdom you have bestowed upon the doctors we consult, as we draw upon this resource in faith. Amen.

Safety Rules for the Healing Ministry – 2

'They devoted themselves to the apostles' teaching and to the fellowship, to the breaking of bread and to prayer.'
—Acts 2:42

Scripture Reading: Acts 2:40–47

Now, the second of the reasons which led these people into trouble was that they were drawing on the healing ministry on their own. It is not only important, but vital, to draw upon the healing ministry in a corporate or congregational way.

In a congregational setting you are drawing on the faith of other people as well as your own. If you have faith to come and draw upon the faith of others, ultimately it is the responsibility of the church to exercise the faith required. No-one should be told, or be given the impression, that his personal faith was not good enough.

Also, when you draw upon the healing ministry in association with other people you are drawing on the fellowship which others provide. It is so difficult, when we are on our own, to keep going with faith that does not doubt. We need the support and encouragement of other people. The New Testament knows nothing of the Christian who goes it alone!

Another reason why we need to draw upon this, and indeed any ministry, in a corporate way is because we need the knowledge and the insights of others. If you go it alone, you are, in effect, doing what is right in your own eyes. In the Old Testament, this was considered to be idolatry. With the healing ministry there is so much to learn, and we all need the insights, knowledge and wisdom which come from the Body of Christ. 'In the multitude of counsellors there is safety' (Proverbs 11:14 KJV).

Key Thought: We are not meant to 'go it alone'.

Our loving Father, we pray for your blessing on us as we reflect on these things. We pray that we might have wisdom in exercising this ministry. Through Christ our Lord. Amen.

You Can Be a Channel of Healing – 1

'"Whoever believes in me, as the Scripture has said, streams of living water will flow from within him."'   —John 7:38

Scripture reading: John 7:37–44

In the Healing Service we are constantly concerned to help people exercise the healing ministry of the church in a way that is scripturally sound and pastorally effective.

If we are going to be a channel for healing, the first requirement is always to know what God has provided and promised to give. The second requirement is that we must appropriate the promised provision in the way in which God has revealed; that is, to exercise repentance, faith and obedience.

What I want to emphasise now is that the promise of God is made effective when the Holy Spirit is flowing into us and through us as rivers of living water. 'For the Scriptures declare that rivers of living water shall flow from the inmost being of anyone who believes in me' (John 7:38 TLB). It is the rivers of living water—this is the way Jesus spoke of the Holy Spirit—which make effective the promises of God in the life of the believer, as the result of faith. This means that any prayer ministry that is effective has to be concerned with the person and ministries of the Holy Spirit. The Spirit flows into us for our own blessing, and the Spirit flows out of us for the blessing of others—in each case making real the promises of God.

Key thought: The Holy Spirit makes the promises of God effective in the life of the believer.

Father, we come to you in repentance and faith, seeking your forgiveness for anything we have done which has been abhorrent to you. We submit ourselves to trust and obey you in word, thought and deed. We believe for the living water of your Spirit to flow through us as we seek your blessing for others. In the name of Jesus Christ, our Lord. Amen.

You Can Be a Channel of Healing – 2

'He who believes in Me [who cleaves to and trusts in and relies on Me] as the Scripture has said, From his innermost being shall flow [continuously] springs and rivers of living water.' —John 7:38 (The Amplified Bible)

Scripture reading: Matthew 8:5–13

You can be a channel of healing for others when faith is linked with the promise of God. What happens is that the Holy Spirit flows through you to others to bring about healing. That is what you need to know and that is what you need to apply. An illustration of this is in the laying on of hands during the Healing Service. Those who lay on hands are being channels of healing for those who have had faith to come and ask for prayer. Let those who lay on hands have it clearly in mind that they are believing the promise of God for healing, and that they are being channels for the rivers of living water.

If this is going to happen, there is at least one more thing we need to have in our minds and act upon, and this is: *it is happening now*. The Bible says it was at the very moment when the centurion believed that his servant was healed. You see, where there is a promise and you are exercising faith, the Spirit is automatically flowing and it is an ongoing action which you can rely on, if you are getting your part right.

We might need to persevere in prayer. I am fond of saying that if our Lord had to pray all night at certain crucial times in his ministry, we may need to pray believing prayer all day at crucial times in our ministry.

Key thought: It is the Holy Spirit flowing through us which brings healing to others.

Dear Father, we repent of our sin; make us clean channels for your healing power. For your glory alone. Amen.

You Can Be a Channel of Healing – 3

'Then Peter said, "Silver or gold I do not have, but what I have I give you.
In the name of Jesus Christ of Nazareth, walk."' —Acts 3:6

Scripture reading: Acts 5:12–16

When I was in America as one of the speakers at the Order of St Luke Conference in Salem, Oregon,[1] I wanted the people attending one of my lectures to see that healing is something we can all do, and do now. So I invited anyone to come forward who had pain at that time. A woman came forward and said that she had a severe headache. I asked her to sit near the platform, and asked people to come forward and lay hands on her. I stood back and let those who came to lay on hands act out what I had been saying. They rested their hands on her head and they put into words what I had been sharing. Before the prayer had concluded, the woman cried out in surprise and joy, saying: 'The pain has gone!'. The people were so captivated by what had happened in front of them that they burst into spontaneous applause, in praise of God.

If you will remember what I have said and put it into practice, you can be a channel of healing for others. When you get it right you will find what I have said is true. You will have the joy and thrill of seeing it work for you. So start to get it right now and persevere.

Key thought: You can be a channel of healing for others when faith is linked with the promise of God.

Our loving Father, we thank you for your promise of healing which we affirm by faith. We believe that the rivers of living water are flowing through us now and bringing healing to others in Jesus' name. Amen.

---

[1] In June 1980 Canon Glennon spoke at meetings of the Anglican Renewal Centre in Victoria, British Columbia, and at the conference of the Order of St. Luke held at Willamette University, Salem, Oregon.

Make Sure Your Channel Isn't Blocked – 1

'Heal the sick, raise the dead, cleanse those who have leprosy, drive out demons. Freely you have received, freely give.'   —Matthew 10:8

Scripture reading: Mark 11: 22–26

When a promise of God is drawn on by faith, the Holy Spirit flows out as 'rivers of living water' making the promise a reality. It is most important to understand that this is how prayer works and to act on it. It will be as we get this fact more settled in our minds, and as we become more practised in believing it, that we will find we are drawing upon more and more of God's blessing. That is how we draw on healing. I have also made the point, and I would make it again, that this might well need to be applied in a continuous way. Faith is added to faith and healing is added to healing. 'Here a little, there a little' the Bible says, or 'First the blade, then the ear ... '.

However, if we act on what has been said and there isn't the blessing we need, we should ask the question: 'Is our channel blocked?' The Bible says that the Spirit can be grieved and quenched—those rivers of living water stopped. How? By sin. By acting contrary to God's will and continuing in unrepented sin.

One of the main ways in which our channel can be blocked is by an attitude of unforgiveness. This is one of the most important things that any sensitive Christian must know about if he is to be a channel, not only of healing but of any, and all, of the promises of God.

Key thought: We can't be a blessing to other people if there is sin in our lives.

Our Father, show us the sin in our lives preventing us from ministering healing and blessing to others. Give us grace to repent, and cleanse us through the blood of Jesus. For his sake and for your glory. Amen.

Make Sure Your Channel Isn't Blocked – 2

'Who can discern his errors? Forgive my hidden faults.' —Psalm 19:12

Scripture reading: John 4:1–14

In Mark chapter 11, when our Lord describes faith in prayer, he immediately goes on and says something else: 'And when you stand praying, if you hold anything against anyone, forgive him ...'. He goes further and adds: 'so that your Father in heaven may forgive you your sins' (Mark 11:25).

If we have unforgiveness in our hearts towards other people, it follows that this is going to affect the effectiveness of our prayer, because our Lord said—not only here but in other places—that this would so affect our relationship with God that he would not forgive us. If we have not forgiven others, and God has not forgiven us, how can we expect the rivers of living water to flow out?

To put it positively, this means that we are to have oneness in our minds and hearts with the person for whom we are praying. But, more than that, we are to have oneness in our minds and hearts about everyone, whether we are praying for them or not. It seems to be impossible! Yet, this is what God requires of us.

Humanly speaking, I think anyone would be entitled to say: 'This is a requirement I just cannot live up to'. At best, it is inevitable that we will have some feeling about some people. At worst, we can have a longstanding grudge against someone else. And, so often, the devil of these things is that we may be the innocent victim of other people's unkindness.

Key thought: An attitude of unforgiveness will block the flow of the Holy Spirit through us.

Come, Holy Spirit. Make us aware of any attitudes we are harbouring which grieve you and drive you away. Make us clean and worthy channels for your love and healing power. In Jesus' name. Amen.

Make Sure Your Channel Isn't Blocked – 3

'Forgive us our sins, for we also forgive everyone who sins against us.'

—Luke 11:4

Scripture reading: Luke 19:1–10

The reason why we find it difficult to forgive others is because we only go halfway. We might forgive one person, or some people, but not all. Or, we forgive but do not forget, and we find the problem can easily recur.

What success I have had in this matter has been dearly won because I have not found it easy to act it out. I have found that it is only when we forgive everyone, and from our hearts, that it is possible to do it at all.

Recently I ministered to a member of our staff who had had a bad headache for a fortnight. As I made myself a channel for the living waters, the pain in his head was taken away. He told me he had difficulties in his relationships with certain people. Part of the ministry time was to enable him to forgive those people, and this he did. He told me that the next morning he thought of the people concerned and reacted negatively. When he did, the pain came back. Then, remembering the need to forgive everyone, he again forgave from his heart. He told me that when he got it right, without saying or affirming anything else, the pain left him again.

There is nothing more needful than that we forgive—completely forgive from our hearts—all those whom we need to forgive. Only then can God forgive us, and only then can the Holy Spirit make real the promises of God.

Key thought: We forgive because we have to—yet we choose to.

Our loving Father, we confess that so often we have blocked the channel of your blessing. We would repent of any sin that hinders the flow of the Spirit. We would in particular forgive all others, as we ourselves need to be forgiven. In Jesus' name. Amen.

The Greatest Problem of All Is Loneliness – 1

'And Mary said: "My soul praises the Lord and my spirit rejoices in God my Saviour ..."'
—Luke 1:46

Scripture reading: Genesis 2:18–23

I have heard medical practitioners and social workers say that the biggest community problem of all is loneliness. One of my colleagues in the Healing Ministry told me that when ministering to someone in the service a week or two ago he asked what it was the person wanted prayer for, and was told 'loneliness'.

Loneliness affects all kinds of people—those who have no family, and those who have; those who are married, and those who are single; Christians and non-Christians; rich and poor. It is no respecter of persons.

What can we do to counter this problem? In order to deal with it we have to admit it is there. To repress it, to pretend it doesn't exist, only makes it worse. If you repress something, you don't get rid of it. You might disguise it in some way which deceives you and others but that means it is still there.

If loneliness is a problem, you should look it squarely in the face and admit that you are lonely. There might well be the need to tell some trusted person what is really on your mind and heart—or at least talk to God and have, what we call in social work, a catharsis or a release of feeling. I don't say that this is necessary for everybody. I do say that it can be necessary for many. It may be accompanied by tears and can be a very traumatic experience, but it has to be worked through if it is to be got rid of.

Key thought: The problem must be faced.

Father, there is nothing hidden from you. We invite your Holy Spirit to search us and enable us to release our hurts as we cast them upon Jesus. Amen.

The Greatest Problem of All Is Loneliness – 2

'A friend loves at all times, and a brother is born for adversity.'

—Proverbs 17:17

Scripture reading: Psalm 25

Christian people sometimes get the idea that it is wrong to admit they have a problem. Absolute nonsense! Christians have as many problems as other people, and it is not being Christian—it is being downright un-Christian—to attempt to ignore them.

Having admitted our need, we are to adopt a positive attitude to the problem, believing that God is dealing with it. This means we are looking forward to the future with hope and faith; we believe God is in the process of meeting our need.

Once you begin to affirm that God is changing your circumstances, and to affirm that you are no longer lonely, you will be amazed at how things start to change for the better. Indeed, you will increasingly find the Bible true when it says: 'Perseverance must finish its work so that you may be mature and complete, not lacking anything' (James 1:4).

So, if you are lonely, whether it be known to others or only to you and God, face it, have a release of feeling if that is relevant and important (it's more important than people realise or admit) and then start to believe that God is changing things. As you begin to have faith for that, you will find you are moving forward and God is in the process of making you complete, lacking in nothing.

Key thought: We are to adopt a positive attitude to the problem of loneliness, believing that God is dealing with it.

Our loving Father, we admit to being lonely in some part of our life, at one time or another, to a greater or lesser extent. We now start to believe that you are changing things, and that old things pass away and all things become new. Amen.

The Problem of 'Making Up Your Mind' – 1

'for waging war you need guidance, and for victory many advisers.'
—Proverbs 24:6

Scripture reading: 2 Chronicles 10

Many people have a problem in making up their minds. It can be to do with our work, our home, our church, ourselves or other people.

It might help if, first of all, I say that a main cause of the problem is emotional insecurity arising from our early life experience. Of course, we may have covered up our insecurity. We may have forgotten that we are insecure. But, nevertheless, that is an important reason why people in adult life find it difficult to reach a decision and to act on it.

There are two things in God's Word which will help us to resolve this difficulty and come to decisions that are balanced and effective. The first of these is from that wonderful book in the Old Testament, the book of Proverbs. It says: 'in the multitude of counsellors there is safety' (Proverbs 11:14 KJV). So, we can be helped in our decision-making by the advice of other people.

Now, there is a right and a wrong way of using help and advice from other people. Spurgeon, the great preacher of the nineteenth century, said, 'It is just as important to know what something is not, as to know what it is'. There is advice we get from other people which can be unhelpful. Frequently we ask for advice, not in order to listen to it, but rather because it reflects our own insecurity and uncertainty, and the end result is that it adds to our confusion.

So, if you want help from other people, make sure that you are not just going to them because you are confused and are not really going to listen to them at all. If you do go to other people in that way, you will find your problems only increase.

Key thought: Other people can help you arrive at a balanced decision.

Thank you, Father, for your blessing as we seek wise counsel.

The Problem of 'Making Up Your Mind' – 2

'The kisses of an enemy may be profuse, but faithful are the wounds of a friend.'
—Proverbs 27:6

Scripture reading: Proverbs 1:1–9

We can profit from the ideas, experience and advice of others. An illustration of this is my book, *Your Healing Is Within You* which was favourably reviewed by reputable journals, overseas as well as in Australia. If the book can stand the test of examination it is because, over all the years of my involvement in the healing ministry, I have listened to other people. After conducting missions and giving my teaching (of which a large part is in my book) I would have varying reactions from people. I would listen to what they said, so that increasingly what I was saying reflected the guidance of others, as well as my own understanding. Sometimes I didn't appreciate being given this information. I'd feel a little hurt that people were disagreeing with me or being critical, but I'm able to say that, as far as my book is concerned, I have sought to profit from advice given to me and this has lent the book what strength and balance it has. What people have said is reflected in its pages.

I value, more than words can say, the opportunity I have each day of receiving guidance from other people. Let us always be open to the insights of other people. If you listen to others you can be helped to make up your mind because you have the advantage of their experience.

Key thought: In making decisions we can be helped by the advice and experience of others.

Thank you, Father, for the advice of trusted Christian brothers and sisters as we seek to profit from their wise counsel in times of perplexity. Amen.

The Problem of 'Making Up Your Mind' – 3

'Whether you turn to the right or to the left, your ears will hear a voice behind you, saying, "This is the way; walk in it."'   —Isaiah 30:21

Scripture reading: Psalm 32

Asking others for advice is important, but there is something more important still. On one occasion, our Lord Jesus Christ had to make up his mind as to who would be the members of his team. What did he do? The Bible says that he prayed all night. Now, if our Lord had to pray all night to reach his decision, will we need to do less? In other words, we, too, will need to employ prevailing prayer.

Prevailing prayer means that, whenever the matter comes to mind, you discipline your mind and spirit to affirm the blessing by faith: 'Thank you Father, you are giving me your guidance. Thank you Father, you are enabling me to make up my mind. Thank you Father, you are helping me to come to a decision'. And, if you continue to affirm the blessing in this way, you will find—increasingly, if not all at once—the guidance of God coming through more and more, and feel the Holy Spirit saying, 'This is the way, walk ye in it.'

You are not to continue to affirm the problem—'Oh, dear me, I don't know what to do'. If you do say that, it becomes your 'faith'. You've got 'faith' for indecision. And because you've got 'faith' for indecision, that is what will continue, in an ever-growing way.

Key thought: We need to prevail in prayer and, by faith, believe that we receive God's guidance.

Our loving Father, we thank you that we can turn to others and to you. We do this now, and believe you are leading us to the decision we need to make in the circumstances of our own personal lives. Thank you Father, through Christ our Lord. Amen.

The Problem of 'Sticking At It' –1

'"For I [David] have kept the ways of the LORD …All his laws are before me; I have not turned away from his decrees."' —2 Samuel 22:22,23

Scripture reading: Matthew 13:1–23

Once we have made a decision, and assuming that we have had God's guidance in making it, we must stick to it and make it work.

This was brought home to me when I was confirmed by Bishop Venn Pilcher who spoke on the text, 'He who stands firm to the end will be saved' (Matthew 24:13). I am glad that, at that tender stage in my Christian walk, I learned that it is not enough to make a decision; we must keep to it in an ongoing way.

Jesus said we will 'stick with it' in varying degrees. He gave us the magnificent story of sowing seeds. He said that with some people their decision would not last; it would be as though they hadn't made a decision at all. With others, it would be like seed sown in shallow ground—it grows up quickly, but because it has no depth it doesn't last. We all know the people who make a decision for Christ and who are full of enthusiasm for a day or two, a week or two, a month or two—and then you never see them again.

Then there are those who make a decision with every good intention, but have so many other things going on in their lives—including things that will undermine the decision they have made—that they fall away.

Jesus also said that there are those who make a decision and persevere; they stick at it and they win through.

Key thought: Once we have God's guidance in a decision we have made, we must stick at it and make it work.

Father, give us grace to be among those who receive your word and persevere as Christians. Amen.

The Problem of 'Sticking At It' – 2

'Let us then approach the throne of grace with confidence, so that we may receive mercy and find grace to help us in our time of need.'
—Hebrews 4:16

Scripture reading: Matthew 24:3–14

At an earlier time in my life I really felt I couldn't continue with the decisions I had made. In that position of extreme difficulty, not being able to find a way through, I had an experience of God which changed my life. For the first time in my life I was spoken to by the Holy Spirit.

I have only heard the voice of God about four or five times, and always at times of extreme need or difficulty. On this occasion, God said to me, 'Is there anything you can learn from all your problems?'. That was the one thing I had not thought of. I could blame other people— which I did, not a little. I understood my problems, but that didn't help. I could be filled with fear and depression, but I had never thought there was something I could learn. So I could but listen, and he went on, 'You are to learn to depend on me more'. That changed my life! From then on I disciplined myself to react to my difficulties so that I depended on God more. And I continued in prayer each day until I got it right.

The problem of 'sticking at it' is a problem we all have. Come to your decision and then, if there are mountains to overcome, let the difficulties help you depend on God more.

Key thought: We need to learn to depend on God more.

Our loving Father, we are those people who have problems of sticking at it and we would so depend upon you that we draw upon more of your help and power, so that our goals are reached, to the glory of God. Amen.

Are You at the Crossroads?: Problems can lead to breakdown – 1

'this happened that we might not rely on ourselves but on God, who raises the dead.'
—2 Corinthians 1:9

Scripture reading: Romans 8:18–27

If the truth be told, many people are at the crossroads. It might be because of things that have accumulated over a long period of time or because of a crisis situation or financial troubles.

Whatever the circumstances, I want to say that you are not alone. Many people who have solved their problems were in that situation at an earlier time. Help is available, but you must know what to do, and then you must do it.

First of all, I need to say that, if you react to the difficulties in terms of the problem, you are following a certain law. Things will continue to get worse until you cannot bear it any longer—which means you will come to breakdown point. I know, because in the earlier part of my life that is how I reacted, and that is what happened to me!

It is understandable that people do react to their difficulties in this way. After all, they are only affirming what they see. They are only affirming what they have. It might even seem to be irresponsible *not* to react in terms of the difficulty—and sometimes I have been told as much by well-meaning people when I have spoken on this theme. But the fact remains that, if you affirm your difficulties they will continue, and you will finally reach 'rubout' point.

I am not saying that we should ignore our difficulties. It alarms me when someone says: 'I'm trying to forget them'. I don't mean that at all. What I mean is that we are to react to our problems in a different way— you react to them by affirming the blessing that God wants you to have.

Key thought: We need to learn a different way of reacting to our problems.

Dear Father, we affirm the blessing you have for us in every situation of difficulty and need; we do that now. In Jesus' name. Amen.

Are You at the Crossroads?: Problems can lead to breakdown – 2

'My eyes stay open through the watches of the night, that I may meditate on your promises' —Psalm 119:148

Scripture reading: Isaiah 43:16–21

It is hard for people to draw on healing when they have been reacting to their problems in terms of the difficulty.

If you have been reacting to your problem in those terms for a long period of time, so that your mind is filled with that kind of thought and affirmation, it isn't going to be easy for you to switch over and affirm something positive. In a word, it is going to be very difficult for you to start affirming healing.

Sometimes, when people come to me for counselling—and shall we say they have learned to react in a different, positive and healing way—they may say to me, 'but I'm no different'. I then use the simile of a ship: their ship has been going full speed astern for so long that it is going to take time for it to slow down and eventually stop. Then, it will begin to move forward, slowly at first, until it gathers speed and is finally moving ahead in a positive, creative and healing way.

So, keep these things in mind and understand the consequences of continuing to affirm the problem. Not least, remember there are a lot of things to *unlearn* before you can *re-learn* things in a way that is going to make for healing and wholeness.

Key thought: Stop affirming your problems.

Our Loving Father, we believe you are speaking to us, myself included. We confess that so often we are going full speed astern as we react in terms of our difficulties and the things that we see. So bless us that we will see the end result which is unhappy and destructive, and that we will learn to react in a positive and believing way for good. Through Christ our Lord. Amen.

Are You at the Crossroads?: Problems can lead to healing – 1

"'I am your brother Joseph, the one you sold into Egypt! And now, do not be distressed and do not be angry with yourselves for selling me here, because it was to save lives that God sent me ahead of you.'"

—Genesis 45:4,5

Scripture reading: 1 Samuel 1:1–20

How can we react to those problems that have brought us to the crossroads of life so that we have, not breakdown, but healing? That is the question. We not only need to know the answer ourselves but, if we are to help others who are at the crossroads, we must be able to explain it to them as well.

I want to say three things. The first is this: *the purpose of the problem is to bring us to faith.* This is what Paul found and what he recorded in 2 Corinthians 1:8,9. Paul's experience of problems not only brought him to the crossroads but, he said, to the end of his tether. Death stared him in the face. He was brought to breakdown point. So he put on his 'theological thinking cap'. He knew that everything, without exception, works together for good to those who love God, and asked himself what was 'the good' towards which his problems were working. Then, inspired by God, he came up with the answer. The problems were to bring him to faith.

That is what God is wanting us to know. That is how we are to react. The problems that have brought you to the crossroads are to bring you to faith. If you have that understanding, it makes sense of problems, and it makes sense—and I say this reverently—it makes sense of God.

Key thought: The problems that bring us to the crossroads are to bring us to faith.

Our loving Father, we thank you for those permitted difficulties that have brought us to the crossroads because they work together for good. Through Christ our Lord. Amen.

Are You at the Crossroads?: Problems can lead to healing – 2

'God is not a man, that he should lie, nor a son of man, that he should change his mind.'   —Numbers 23:19

Scripture reading: Numbers 23:13–23

My second point is this: our problems are to bring us to faith, but *faith in what?* Faith in God, yes, but more than that—faith in what God has promised to give.

The whole idea of the New Testament is summed up in 2 Peter 1:4 'he has given us his very great and precious promises'. God has drawn close to us in Christ. He has committed himself to us and made promises. If we, with all our frailty, know what it is to make and keep a promise, how much more will God, who is without frailty, keep the promises he has made?

I feel sorry for people who say, 'I don't know what God's will is'. Search the Scriptures and see the great and precious promises of God in the New Testament, because they reveal God's will. Now, I am going to be frank and say that there are many Christian people, including theologians, who apparently do not believe this. They are not sure whether God wants to keep his promises. My own understanding, and I will stand or fall on this point—the whole Healing Ministry in the Cathedral stands or falls on this point—is that God has made us a promise of healing: 'the prayer offered in faith will make the sick person well' (James 5:15).

Healing is not only a promise but a broad theme in the New Testament to which there are no exceptions. My position is that this promise, and this theme, reveals the will of God.

Key thought: God has committed himself to us in his promises.

Thank you, Father, that you have revealed your will to us through the great and precious promises which you have given to us.

Are You at the Crossroads?: Problems can lead to healing – 3

'partakers of his promise in Christ by the gospel'– Ephesians 3:6 KJV

Scripture reading: John 3:1–15

If we can't rely on any and every promise of God which is clearly set out in the New Testament, we are of all men most miserable. We haven't even got the assurance of salvation. Our whole relationship with God is wholly dependent on the promises of God. If it is God's will to keep one promise, it is God's will to keep *every* promise.

My third point is this: Jesus has instructed us to believe that we have received what we ask for in prayer (see Mark 11:24). In the area of conversion we say we 'accept' Christ, or we 'make a decision' and we affirm it by faith. If you will act out faith for healing in the same way as you act out faith for conversion, you will find it will work.

May I add this—I spend time every day in what I call 'prayer-thinking', that is, getting it right for myself and for my prayer activity for the day. I have such an unruly mind. I'm so easily caught up with the problems, so I sit down and take time to be with God until I am not reacting in terms of the problems, but coming to faith in the promises of God, and believing for them.

I am giving you principles about the Healing Ministry that are fundamental. God guide us all.

Key thought: If it is God's will to keep one promise, it is his will to keep every promise.

Thank you, Father, that our permitted difficulties bring us to faith in the promises of God of which we are partakers. Thank you that we know how to exercise faith for conversion; help us that we will get it right for healing and all the promises of God. Through Christ our Lord. Amen.

Are You at the Crossroads?: Problems can lead to conversion – 1

'"But the Counsellor, the Holy Spirit, whom the Father will send in my name, will teach you all things and will remind you of everything I have said to you."'   —John 14:26

Scripture reading: Titus 3:1–8

As well as God giving practical help with our real-life situations, he is concerned to provide us with those blessings that last beyond this life into eternity. The point is, we all need to be forgiven our shortcomings. Jesus provides forgiveness through what he has done for us on the cross and, when we accept this work as having been done for us personally, we are reconciled to the Father, both now and for eternity. We speak of Jesus as the one who saves us; he is therefore our Saviour. He forgives and, as a result, we are forgiven. *That is ultimately the most important blessing God has for those who are at the crossroads of life.*

What brings people to God when they are at the crossroads of life? The plain fact is that people who are in need, who no longer feel self-sufficient and who have had the pins knocked from under them, are now ready to turn to God.

People don't have to come to a Healing Service to find God in their difficult circumstances. That can happen anywhere at all. But, because we are orientated to helping people with the help God gives, we have a greater concentration of people who are at the end of their tether and who are more likely to find God than at other times.

Another reason why people find Christ in the Healing Service is that, when we pray for people, the Holy Spirit is being drawn upon to meet their needs and, because the Holy Spirit is the Spirit of Christ, he shows Christ to the person concerned.

Key thought: The most important blessing is to be forgiven.

Thank you, Father, that you forgive us because of what Christ has done for us.

Are You at the Crossroads?: Problems can lead to conversion – 2

"'Who is he, sir?" the man asked. "Tell me so that I may believe in him."'
                                                                    —John 9:36

Scripture reading: Joshua 24:14–24

If a church wants people to put their faith in Christ, it cannot do anything more conducive to that end than to have a balanced and effective healing ministry.

Here is one family's testimony: The woman had a serious physical problem that required surgery. She was effectively ministered to by a member of our congregation who also ministered to her husband. She was a Christian, though not deeply committed at the time; her husband had wandered from his earlier faith position. As a result of the ministry, which helped her physically, she came back to Christ; her husband, and at least one of her children, was converted as well. I have all this information in a letter that the husband and wife jointly wrote to me.

This testimony could be repeated many, many times. If a ministry is enabling people to come to Christ, that ministry is effective in the ultimate and most important sense of the word.

Key thought: Are you at the crossroads? Remember, problems can lead to conversion. Accept Christ as your Saviour and Lord now. God bless you!

Our loving Father, we thank you for those circumstances that bring us to you. We come to you now, even to Jesus our Lord. In his name we pray. Amen.

My Prayer of Commitment: *I take God the Father to be my Lord. I take God the Son to be my Saviour. I take the Holy Spirit to be my Sanctifier. I take the Word of God to be the rule of my life. I take the people of God to be my people.*

And I now commit myself – mind, body and spirit to my Lord and Saviour Jesus Christ. In the name of the Father and of the Son and of the Holy Spirit. Amen.

Getting Well Again: Learn your lesson – 1

'Later Jesus found him at the temple and said to him, "See, you are well again. Stop sinning or something worse may happen to you."'

—John 5:14

Scripture reading: John 5:1–15

I have earlier referred to the time when I was very sick with emotional problems. I suppose that is why I have some understanding of people who have emotional difficulties, because usually there is not much they have experienced that I have not experienced myself. When I had finally reached breakdown point the Holy Spirit spoke to me, saying that what I needed to learn was to depend on God more. The idea that I could learn from what had happened to me had not crossed my mind, so this was the important question that God needed to raise with me.

I am calling the three addresses which begin tonight, 'Getting well again', and the emphasis this evening is 'Learn your lesson'.

The Bible says 'everything that does not come from faith is sin' (Romans 14:23). 'Sin' means anything that is less than faith. This means that we can interpret the word 'sin' in a general way to mean that we are to learn our lesson and come to faith. If we are getting well again, we are to learn our lesson lest a worse thing happens to us.

Are you getting well again? What is the lesson you need to learn? This will vary from person to person. Let me refer to one kind of lesson for the moment—stress.

What part has stress played in your sickness? How much is that the lesson you must learn, if you are to remedy the underlying causative factors and so draw on wholeness and enduring healing?

Key thought: What is the lesson God wants us to learn?

Loving Father, thank you that when we are weak your strength enables us to depend upon you more. Help us now as we cast all our burdens upon Jesus. Amen.

Getting Well Again: Learn your lesson – 2

'"Then neither do I condemn you," Jesus declared. "Go now and leave your life of sin."'
— John 8:11

Scripture reading: John 8:1–11

I was once in hospital for an ophthalmic problem and, when the medical specialist came to examine me, he caught a glimpse of my neck. I shall never forget his astonishment and concern as he exclaimed, '... do you know what you've got? You've got multiple skin cancer!'. I looked back on my life to what might have been an underlying causative factor, and I didn't have far to look. Eighteen months beforehand, I had had a serious argument with somebody. Whenever I thought of this person, I would boil with resentment. I felt convicted that it was this continued burden of resentment and unforgiveness that was the underlying causative factor of my multiple skin cancer.

I wrote to the person concerned and said something like this: 'I am sorry for my part in our disagreement'. I suppose I was taking a bit of a risk. Anyway, he got in touch with me and, calling me by my Christian name, said that he could see I was sincere. He wanted to tell me that he was sorry for his part in our disagreement.

I solemnly record that, from the time I forgave him and he forgave me, the multiple skin cancer completely disappeared of its own accord and without any medical treatment. It has never recurred. I am not suggesting that we do not need medical treatment, but I didn't need it in those particular circumstances.

Key thought: Sickness is often caused by underlying factors which need to be understood and remedied.

Our loving Father, thank you for the lessons we learn. Bless those of us who are getting well again that we will learn our lesson, and make things right—in the way they need to be made right, both now and in an ongoing way. For Jesus' sake. Amen.

Getting Well Again: Set your goals – 1

'I press on towards the goal to win the prize for which God has called me heavenwards in Christ Jesus.' —Philippians 3:14

Scripture reading: 2 Corinthians 4:7–18

At every point in our lives we ought to have goals that we set and press towards. I want to suggest three goals relevant to those who are getting well again and who are drawing on the healing ministry of the church.

The first is: *react to your sickness in a positive way and don't ignore what remains of your sickness.* If you ignore your problems you will find they will only continue and get worse. On the other hand, don't fill your mind with what remains of your sickness so that it becomes an overwhelming and almost obsessional preoccupation.

Often, a person who is drawing on both the medical resource and the Prayer of Faith is very conscious of a wonderful improvement. However, there is a tendency, as time goes by, to move from being thankful for what progress has been made, to becoming preoccupied with what remains of the sickness. Your goal should be to react to what degree of sickness remains by affirming healing in a continuing way.

Let me give an illustration from my own experience. I once used to go swimming regularly and, on one occasion, I pulled a leg muscle. I felt no pain at all in my everyday activities but, whenever I went swimming and did a certain stroke, I experienced pain in my leg and had to stop. Eventually, I put into practice what I am talking about here. I didn't ignore the problem, neither did I become preoccupied with it. I reacted to it in a positive way; when I felt the pain I would affirm healing. One thing became something else. The negative was turned into the positive. Then I drew on healing and the pain disappeared.

Key thought: Don't ignore what remains of your sickness but don't become preoccupied with it in an exclusive way.

Help us, Father, to keep pressing on towards the goal—to take hold of all you have promised to give us. Through Jesus our Lord. Amen.

Getting Well Again: Set your goals – 2

'Praise the LORD, O my soul, and forget not all his benefits. He forgives all my sins and heals all my diseases'   —Psalm 103:2,3

Scripture reading: Exodus 17:8–15

The second goal to set is this: react to what degree of sickness remains by *affirming healing in a continuing way*. This might require sacrificial prayer. You have got to sacrifice time and effort, and be disciplined so that you are affirming this blessing in a continuing way— '"I will not let you go unless you bless me." '(Genesis 32:26).

The third point I want to make is: as we react to our sickness in the way that has been described, we come to the point where *we get this right every day*.

You can't rely on the faith capital of yesterday. I find that the more I begin the day by reacting to what remains of my sickness by affirming healing by faith, the sooner I come to that level of faith whereby I am doing this in an effective way. We might have something of a struggle to get it right. We may find that we oscillate between affirming our sickness and affirming the answer. We need to come to the point where we truly get faith right, so it is that which is ticking over in our minds, hearts and prayers all the time. The sooner you start doing it during the day, the easier it is to come to this victory position and hold to it.

It is not something you are to do only when you are having a formal time of prayer. It is what happens moment by moment. It is called 'fractional prayer'.

Key thought: Affirm healing in a continuing way.

Father, we believe that when we pray you hear us, and we continue to be watchful in the same with thanksgiving as you fulfil your perfect healing for us now. In Jesus name. Amen.

Getting Well Again: Set your goals – 3

'Not one of all the LORD's good promises to the house of Israel failed; every one was fulfilled.'   —Joshua 21:45

Scripture reading: Joshua 23:1–8

Harry, not his real name, is a clergyman of the Church of England. He had a severe back injury and was told by his medical advisers that he needed surgery to immobilise his back in the area which was injured. He accepted healing in a Healing Service, in the same way as one accepts Christ as Saviour, and others affirmed faith with him.

There was a remarkable improvement but he seemed to get stuck just at that point. Harry realised that he needed to react to what remained of the sickness and come to faith that God would complete the healing. He made it a point of getting this right every day; he would continue in prayer every morning until he had come to that point of faith.

Harry told me he did this faithfully, day by day and time by time, for three weeks, and during the whole of that time the pain did not let up. However, as he continued to affirm healing for what needed to be healed, the time came when the pain disappeared and the healing was there in perfection. When I was in Melbourne recently I met him in the church where I was ministering and asked, 'Harry, how is your back?'. He replied, 'Jim, it has remained perfectly healed for the last fifteen years'.

Key thought: We need to win the battle of faith every day and not rely on yesterday's faith.

Our loving Father, we thank you that we can react to what remains of our sickness in this positive way and come to faith now, and continue to affirm our blessing. We do this for ourselves and for one another. Through Christ our Lord. Amen.

Getting Well Again: Walk with God –1

'"All that belongs to the Father is mine. That is why I said the Spirit will take from what is mine and make it known to you."'   —John 16:15

Scripture reading: 1 Peter 1:1–12

I remember someone coming to me who had drawn on God's blessing through the Healing Service for a knee that had been damaged in a car accident. He said, 'Would you please not talk about the healing of my knee because what has happened to me spiritually is much more important'.

My experience is that, irrespective of whether or not people draw upon physical and/or emotional healing, they all draw on a blessing of Jesus mediated through the Holy Spirit.

This blessing of Jesus will take varying forms. There is nothing rigid or stereotyped about it. It will be the blessing of Jesus that is relevant to each person; it is, if you like, 'tailor made'.

With many, it will mean that they come into the experience of conversion. With others, who are already converted, it might well mean that they draw upon the fullness of the Holy Spirit.

Others will experience growth in their understanding of prayer or find their Bible reading much enlivened as it takes on new meaning and reality. For some there will be a release of Christian love and compassion in their relationship with others or a growth in fellowship, ministry and Christian service. Not least, it can mean that people enter into fulltime Christian work as a result of the blessing of Jesus they have drawn on through coming to the Healing Service.

Key thought: The Holy Spirit, the 'Spirit of Christ' who quickens our mortal bodies takes of Christ and shows him to us.

Father, we thank you that as we draw upon your promises for healing, you give us the blessing of being brought into a closer relationship with you. Amen.

Getting Well Again: Walk with God – 2

'For I received from the Lord what I also passed on to you'
— 1 Corinthians 11:23

Scripture reading: 2 Corinthians 1:1–7

I have a preoccupation with the Healing Ministry. It is not just that I am interested in people being healed. I *am* interested in that; I have a healthy preoccupation with it. However, I am more concerned with them drawing on the deep eternal blessing of Father, Son and Holy Spirit, which is what the Healing Ministry brings about.

If we have drawn on blessing from God we have a price to pay; the price is that we are to share that blessing with others. What we are given, we are to give away. The comfort we have drawn on from God is the comfort that we are to share with other people in their need. If you are drawing water out of a well and you continue to draw the water, the well will remain full. If you stop drawing water, the supply of water will dry up and the well will, ultimately, be useless.

One of the most important things which those who are drawing on the Healing Ministry must understand is that they should comfort others with the comfort they themselves receive from God. Or, to put it in another way, they have a ministry which they then share with other people. It is a solemn obligation. It is the way we say 'thank you' to God, and it is necessary for our own ongoing spiritual blessing from God.

Key thought: Getting well again? Praise God, then continue to walk with God more and more.

Our loving Father, we thank you for the blessing of the Holy Spirit who shows us Jesus. We return thanks for the abundant blessings we have drawn upon in seeking healing and would share them with others, more and more. Amen.

Faith In Action – 1

'God did not give us a spirit of timidity, but a spirit of power, of love and of self-discipline.'
—2 Timothy 1:7

Scripture reading: Philippians 3:12–21; 4:4–7

Faith in action begins in the mind—in our thoughts. Our ongoing thoughts are extremely important. We have to discipline our minds, and this isn't easy. I have found that to achieve 'faith thoughts' I take a simple repetitive phrase which expresses my faith in action, and I say it in my mind. For example, 'Thank you Lord, you are healing me' or 'Thank you Lord, you are healing (someone else)'. In repeating this simple affirmative phrase over and over again, my thoughts are being disciplined and get used to acting out the faith I have expressed at an earlier time in my prayer. You can develop this further and use what a theological lecturer called 'sanctified imagination'.

Agnes Sanford favoured the idea of forming a 'faith picture' in our mind. She would ask the person she was helping: 'What do you like doing when you are well?'. Let us suppose the answer was, 'I like gardening'. Agnes would then say to the person: 'In your thoughts, form a picture of yourself doing the garden; see yourself in your garden doing the work you are accustomed to doing, and train your mind to think in terms of that faith picture'. This advice is profoundly good and right and helpful.

So, discipline your thoughts. A repetitive phrase can help tremendously—especially if you are distracted by pain or anxiety. Keep on affirming these repetitive phrases to express your faith; then you can form a faith picture of God's healing being there, so that you see yourself doing what you are able to do when you are well.

Key thought: Faith in action begins in the mind.

Thank you, Father, for the peace of God which guards our hearts and our minds in Christ Jesus.

Faith In Action – 2

'It is Jesus' name and the faith that comes through him that has given this complete healing to him, as you can all see.'   —Acts 3:16

Scripture reading: Acts 3:11–16

Faith in action begins in the mind and expresses itself in what we do— in our activity. For instance, if you need to forgive someone, it isn't enough to pray the Prayer of Faith about it. It has to be expressed in what you do.

A young lady who was having problems in relating to her fellow students came to see me. Although she forgave them when she prayed, there was no change whatsoever in the actual relationships. When you pray the Prayer of Faith and nothing happens, it means that in some way you haven't prayed it right. So I asked her what she had done to show her forgiveness and oneness with the other students. She said that she had not done anything—only prayed. 'Well,' I said to her, 'what about going out on a limb and speaking to the students, assuring them that you want your relationship to be good and perfect and right?'.

She was a courageous young woman, a fine Christian, and that is what she did. She found it to be such an enjoyable experience that she didn't stop until she had spoken to all the students, expressing her desire for oneness and fellowship with them. When she next came to see me her face was radiant. She had become a doer of the word and *that* brought the healing.

Key thought: We need to act out our faith.

Loving Father, we invite your Holy Spirit to minister to us so that our actions and faith —what we believe—are of one accord. Holy Spirit, go before us and give us courage and tact to be 'doers' of the Word, through Jesus Christ our Lord and Saviour. Amen.

Faith In Action – 3

'So he [Naaman] went down and dipped himself in the Jordan seven times, as the man of God had told him'　　　　　　　　—2 Kings 5:14

Scripture reading: 2 Kings 5:1–14

I want to give two examples to illustrate how to be a 'doer of the word'. The first was given from this pulpit by Norman Vincent Peale. A man was told by his doctor that he was heading for serious physical trouble. Then the doctor said, 'I believe, under God, that this prognosis can be altered so that you do not end up in trouble but will end up in healing'. He told his patient to go outside, admire the beauty of God's creation and, as he breathed in, to affirm that he was breathing in God's perfect creative blessing.

When the man went back to the doctor, he was told that the process of worsening sickness had been arrested and that his health had greatly improved.

The second example relates to a couple with serious physical and emotional problems. I tended to give them a more scriptural or theological explanation as to how they were to exercise faith. And, as far as that went, I believe it was right, but they didn't get better. Finally, they went to another clergyman in the Anglican Church who told them to affirm, 'God is healing me now through Jesus Christ' (and to refer to the area where healing was needed), then to breathe in as an outward sign that this was what was inwardly happening at that moment. They did this twelve or twenty times, twice a day.

These people *were healed by God* because they were given a simple, practical way of putting their faith into action.

Key thought: The Prayer of Faith must be expressed in what you do.

Loving Father, we thank you for your miraculous healing power. Help us to put our faith into action as we affirm that you are healing us now, through Jesus Christ our Lord. Amen.

The 'Crunch' Line In Prayer – 1

'A righteous man may have many troubles, but the Lord delivers him from them all'   —Psalm 34:19

Scripture reading: Acts 12:1–11

I imagine that all adult people have, at some stage in their lives, had the experience of their problems being so great that they felt they couldn't bear the strain any longer.

There may be times of sickness, of anxiety, resentment or family problems; it may even be persecution. You name it—difficulties can rise up and we can be overwhelmed. Not least, there is the reality of bereavement that comes, sooner or later, into everyone's life.

Our self-sufficiency is the greatest hindrance there is to our drawing on the power and blessing of God. I should have said, our *fallen* self-sufficiency. Self-sufficiency, or self-protection, is one of the primal instincts; we cannot set it aside just because we want to. Our fallen self-nature always has to strive to preserve itself. If God is to enable us to come to the point where we are trusting in him alone, he has to bring us to the end of our fallen self-sufficiency. He does this by permitting a difficulty such that it brings us to the end of our tether.

I well recall a member of the congregation saying, when summing up her experience, 'When I thought I was "going down the drain" I found myself, instead, floating on the calm sea of God'. When you have been taken past the point of self-sufficiency, you find that God is there and you are trusting in him alone.

Key thought: Our permitted difficulties are to bring us to the point where we are not trusting in ourselves, but in God.

We thank you, Father, that our permitted difficulties bring us to trust, not in ourselves but in you who can raise the dead. We put our trust in you now. In Jesus' name. Amen.

The 'Crunch' Line In Prayer – 2

'"My son, do not make light of the Lord's discipline, and do not lose heart when he rebukes you, because the Lord disciplines those he loves"'

—Hebrews 12:5,6

Scripture reading: 2 Corinthians 12:1–10

I want to refer briefly to three things that you can expect to happen when you are enabled to trust, not in yourself, but in God.

- You may well experience some degree of revelation. The times in my life when I have been spoken to by the Holy Spirit, so that I could say, 'Thus says the Lord', have all been in times of extreme stress. If it is not an actual 'word from the Lord', it might be some scriptural truth that God makes real to you in a special way.

- You will find a new sense of freedom in serving God.

- Finally, and not least, there will be a release of the Holy Spirit in power to do the work of God.

May I say again—because I cannot share with you anything that will be more productive of God's blessing—react to the difficulties that God has permitted by letting them move you closer to him. As you get that right, and you continue to get it right, you will experience God's Word, God's freedom and God's power. If you always pray like this, you will always draw on the power of God for your own life, and in reaching out to others.

Key thought: Let your permitted difficulties help you move closer to God, and God will provide for all your need.

Our loving Father, we embrace this 'crunch line' in prayer. We hear the word of the apostle: 'when I am weak, then I am strong', and we would come and depend on you more now, and continue to depend on you more and so have your blessing in abundance. Amen.

Insecurity: How insecure are you? –1

'Now Moses was a very humble man, more humble than anyone else on the face of the earth.'   —Numbers 12:3

Scripture reading: 1 Peter 2:13–25

We are all, to some degree, insecure. The only person who has ever lived who was whole in spirit, mind and body was the Son of God. You can be secure in some areas of your life, and in other areas you can be very insecure. Insecurity is anything to do with fear, apprehension, worry, anxiety, an inferiority complex, or difficulty in relationships. It just means being unsure of yourself.

What are some of the ways in which insecurity can show itself? One way is for a person to become bombastic or overly assertive. Very often this covers up one's insecurity.

A friend, for whom I have a sincere regard, was a very imperious person before she changed jobs. Her new supervisor reminded her of her mother, a domineering person who had kept my friend under her thumb, making her very insecure. This new supervisor reminded her so forcefully of her mother that all her commanding manner evaporated. Her insecurity reasserted itself. Finally, she left that position because it was intolerable, and it was interesting to see how quickly she sprang back into being that same kind of imperious person again—to an even greater extent than before. Do you see how insecurity can turn us into people who compensate for our feelings of inadequacy?

Insecurity can also make us critical of others. By seeing the faults in others we can avoid facing the reality of problems within ourselves.

Key thought: We all have areas of insecurity in our lives.

Loving Father, our prayer is praise that you have provided for us to be whole, and secure, in body, mind, and spirit. We confess that we have areas of insecurity in our lives and thank you that you have healed us. We hold to our healing with ever grateful hearts. Through Jesus Christ our Lord. Amen.

Insecurity: How insecure are you? – 2

'" I am the LORD who heals you."'   —Exodus 15:26

Scripture reading: Psalm 91

Another example of insecurity manifests itself in the person who is always right. He, or she, may well have a quiet personality. The quiet person never offends, never says a thing out of place. To move into more demanding situations would make life intolerable for them. It would awaken their deep insecurity.

Then there are the people, God bless them, whose insecurity is shown in a negative self-image. They know that they are inadequate for the demands of life and they have an inferiority complex which makes them unhappy, miserable, lonely and afraid.

The insecure person tries to cover up or compensate for his insecurity by erecting what we call defence mechanisms—for example, by criticising others. These defence mechanisms keep out hurt and harm, but they also keep out love and other things that the growing person needs and wants!

I have said insecurity is fear, and that fear is the opposite of faith. Fear cancels out faith, or reduces its effectiveness. The more insecure you are, the more you are unable to exercise faith. I don't say you can't exercise faith, but you have a more difficult task than the person who is relatively secure.

We need to bring these things into the open if we are to find an answer. The reason for my speaking as I have is because it may help you to face your insecurity and to go on to draw on God's blessing in order to be healed, so that old things pass away.

Key thought: We need to face up to our insecurities and be healed.

Father, we want to enter in to all the blessing you have for us. We confess the sins which have hindered us, and thank you for the cleansing you give us now through Jesus' blood. Amen.

Insecurity: How did it begin?

' be made new in the attitude of your minds'   —Ephesians 4:23

Scripture reading: Acts 20:7–12

I remember a mother bringing her daughter to see me. The child was having a lot of trouble in school. She was thought to be a sneak, mainly because she was unable to look other people—including her fellow schoolmates—in the face.

My first question was, 'How long has she been like this?'. The mother replied that it had been right from the time when the child could be conscious of relating to other people. So I asked, 'What were your circumstances like when you were carrying the baby', and she replied that it was during the war. Her husband was in the armed forces and she was apprehensive about his safety. It was their first child and she was frightened. At night she would lock all the doors and windows, and having done it once she would go round again to make sure everything was locked. Right from the time of birth, the child seemed to be afraid and insecure and, ultimately, unable to relate to people and look them in the face. I have no doubt that the mother's anxiety was communicated to the child before birth.

Insecurity can begin before the person is born; it can also happen through a particular experience after birth and can be something people initially learn to live with but which later becomes a problem they can no longer handle.

Key thought: Everyone is affected by insecurity to some degree, and by a variety of causes.

Father, we realise that we have all been affected by problems of insecurity, and not infrequently because of circumstances over which we had no control. Lord, we know that we are still affected and we ask that you will come to us now and enable us to face up to these things so that we can go ahead and draw on healing. Through Christ our Lord.

Insecurity: How to have healing – 1

'But Abram said, " …I remain childless"' —Genesis 15:2

Scripture reading: Genesis 15:1–6

How can we draw on healing from God for our insecurity? The first requirement is that we be willing to face our problem and do something about it. Now, this is not as easy as it sounds. Instead of looking at themselves, insecure people get used to looking at others and finding fault with them. So you see, it is not the easiest thing for an insecure person to face up to his, or her, problem. Indeed, facing the fact of our own insecurity can, to begin with, make us more insecure because we are realising what we are really like. It might be that we can only do this gradually and increasingly. But let it be clear that, if we are to have any healing from God, we must have some awareness of our difficulty, some willingness to face it and draw on God's help—whatever the future may hold.

The second thing which must be understood is that God provides perfect help. Look at that beautiful verse in Timothy which says: 'God did not give us a spirit of timidity but a spirit of power, of love and of self-discipline' (2 Timothy 1:7). Now, that's next door to saying that God has not given us insecurity. We need to realise that, as far as God is concerned, we don't have to be insecure. The Bible says it is the love of God which casts out the insecurity, or timidity, or fear. God's provision, because of Christ and by the Holy Spirit, is that we be 'perfect and complete, lacking in nothing' (James 1:4 RSV).

So, have in your mind a clear understanding of the perfection of blessing that God provides.

Key thought: As far as God is concerned, we don't have to be insecure.

Father, we thank you for your love which casts out all our insecurity. We accept this blessing now. Through Jesus our Lord. Amen.

Insecurity: How to have healing – 2

'"For nothing is impossible with God."' – Luke 1:37

Scripture reading: Genesis 21:1–7

It is most important that we know what God has provided for us. So often, the Christian churchman does not know that God provides his perfect blessing. All we hear so very often is, 'My grace is sufficient for you' (2 Corinthians 12:9), as though God just bolsters us up—keeps us going. Well, he does that, but he does much more than that, and the 'much more' is that 'old things are passed away ... all things are become new!' (2 Corinthians 5:17 KJV).

ALL things become new! Have in your mind a clear understanding of the perfection of blessing that God provides, and that it is his will that love will cast out all timidity and all your insecurity.

The third requirement for drawing on healing for our insecurity is that we go on to accept this love, this healing, this newness—so that God is making all things new, and old things are passing away. I say— and I say again and again—we accept *all* of God's blessings in the same way as we accept Christ for salvation, because, when we accept Christ for salvation, whether we realise it or not, we are praying the Prayer of Faith about a promise of God. And faith is always the same, whether it is for salvation, or for being filled with the Spirit, for healing, or for any of the other promises and provisions of God.

If you know how to exercise faith in one area you know how to exercise faith in another. You accept God's blessing for the healing of your insecurity in the same way as you accept Christ for salvation.

Key thought: God keeps his promises.

Dear Father, we thank you that your provision for us is not fear and insecurity but power, love and a sound and disciplined mind. We accept this now. Through Jesus Christ. Amen.

Insecurity: How to have healing – 3

'*where the Spirit of the Lord is, there is freedom.*' —2 Corinthians 3:17

Scripture reading: 2 Corinthians 3:7–18

As insecurity comes from past experiences, it might be that we need to accept God's healing of our memories. However, if we accept healing for ourselves as we are now, it will mean that the past will be healed too.

When I visited Pretoria, South Africa, I called on Elsie Salmon, a great woman in the healing ministry. I asked, 'Mrs Salmon, do you always have to know what it is in the past that needs to be healed?'. She replied: 'Not necessarily. God knows what the need is. All you have to do is to believe'. This gave me a lot of reassurance, and I share that reassurance with you.

The kind of healing we are talking about is often healing that needs to go very deep. It is a big prayer job, and what takes time is the healing of the defences that we build around ourselves, so that the love of God can come in and go all the way through.

Accept healing and continue to affirm it, even though you may not see much change at first. I'm not suggesting that it always has to be over a period of years, but I think that it is right and wise to say that, not infrequently, this long-range approach is necessary.

Key thought: If you accept healing for yourself as you are now, it will lead to the healing of those past experiences that make you insecure.

O Father, we praise your name that you provide your perfect blessing for us, and that it is your will that we be perfected in love. We would affirm that you are changing us. We accept this by faith, we accept it now, and we thank you that you are bringing it about in our lives at the present time. Through Christ our Lord. Amen.

Do You Want to be Made Whole?: Accept Christ as Saviour – 1

'"He [the Holy Spirit] will bring glory to me by taking from what is mine and making it known to you."'   —John 16:14

Scripture reading: John 16:5–16

When people came to Christ for healing, he did not say, 'You have to be forgiven by God before you can be healed'. The only requirement he ever laid upon those who came to him for healing was faith that he would heal. There were no strings attached to his ministry. He healed because of his compassion; he healed because it was the will of God; he met people at the point of their felt need.

It is the same with the healing ministry of the Christian Church today. If you seek healing—that is enough. *God will meet the need you and others have, and there are no strings attached.*

When a person is healed by God, it is the Holy Spirit—that person of the Trinity who is in the world today—who does the work. The Bible says he quickens, makes alive or heals our mortal bodies (see Romans 8:11).

In 1 Peter 1:11 the Holy Spirit is described as 'the Spirit of Christ'. The Bible also says that the Spirit takes of Christ and shows him to us. This means that, when you come to God for healing and God gives healing, *the Holy Spirit takes of Christ and shows him to you*—that is, the Spirit is forming Christ within you, always and automatically.

Key thought: The only requirement Jesus laid on the sick was that they have faith to believe that he could heal.

Thank you, Father, that our Lord Jesus had love and compassion for the sick and met them at the point of their felt need. We come to you now, believing that you will meet our need today. In Jesus' name. Amen.

Do You Want to be Made Whole?: Accept Christ as Saviour – 2

'And if the Spirit of him who raised Jesus from the dead is living in you, he who raised Christ from the dead will also give life to your mortal bodies through his Spirit, who lives in you.'   —Romans 8:11

Scripture reading: Acts 2:14–21

It is through Christ, and through Christ alone, that we are made to be one with the Father. By ourselves we are not good enough, but Christ has come and, if we put our faith in him and in what he has done for us on the cross, our shortcomings are forgiven. For this reason we speak of Christ as our 'Saviour'. So, when you come for healing, the Spirit who is doing the healing is forming Christ in you—Christ, who is our salvation, who provides forgiveness and reconciles us to the Father.

For this ministry to be fully effective, it requires us to come to the point where we accept for ourselves the work that the Holy Spirit is doing. God takes the initiative, but we have to respond because God has given us the right of choice. It is possible for the Spirit to be ministering to someone, yet he, or she, chooses not to respond. That is the person's right. But I would prefer to put it positively and say that the individual concerned must come to the point where he accepts Christ for himself as the One who saves him, as the One who forgives him, as the One who makes him right with God—both now and always.

Key thought: It is through Christ alone that we are reconciled to God, our Father.

Loving Father, our prayer is praise that, when we were far off, you met us through your Son. We accept Jesus as our Lord and Saviour; we accept your healing which leads to wholeness. Thank you Father, thank you Jesus, thank you Holy Spirit. Amen.

Do You Want to be Made Whole?: Accept Christ as Saviour – 3

'Here I am! I stand at the door and knock. If anyone hears my voice and opens the door, I will come in and eat with him, and he with me.'

—Revelation 3:20

Scripture reading: John 3:16–21

It needs to be constantly emphasised in the Church that we each have the responsibility of accepting Christ as our Saviour. We can help one another to do that. We can believe for one another but, in the final analysis, there is no alternative but for the individual to respond and accept Christ for himself.

I thank God that, as a young man, I was in a church where this was constantly and rightly emphasised. There came a day when a mission was conducted by the late Canon H.M. Arrowsmith, and he put it to us just like I am trying to put it to you tonight and invited us to make our response. Not knowing much of what I was doing, except that I wanted to respond, I indicated that I accepted Christ as my Saviour. There was much water to flow under the bridge, but that was when I began. No-one could do it for me. I had to do it myself.

And so with you. You come for healing. God will meet you where you are. The Spirit will show you Christ. You need to respond by accepting Christ in your heart, by opening your life to him and believing that he will come in.

Key thought: The Holy Spirit shows Christ to us; we need to respond.

Let us all take a moment to hear Christ knocking at the door of our lives; then let us respond, accepting him as Saviour and opening our lives to him, so that he comes in as our Lord. You can do it very simply by just saying: 'Jesus, I accept you as my Saviour. I open my life to you, and I believe you are coming in now. Thank you. Amen.'

Do You Want to be Made Whole?: Be filled with the Spirit – 1

'Do not get drunk on wine … be filled with the Spirit' —Ephesians 5:18

Scripture reading: Acts 9:10–18

It is one thing to be healed and another thing to be made whole. You can be healed by God but that doesn't necessarily mean that you have been made whole.

I have said that the most important aspect of being made whole is to accept the Lord Jesus Christ as your personal Saviour. I now want to bring into focus another aspect of being made whole—it is the fullness of the Holy Spirit.

On the road to Damascus, Saul, known also as Paul (see Acts 13:9), called Jesus 'Lord', and the Bible says that no man can call Jesus 'Lord' except by the ministry of the Holy Spirit (see 1 Corinthians 12:3). It is agreed in Christian thought that Paul's experience on the road to Damascus was the occasion of his conversion. He accepted Christ so that he called him 'Lord'. He was 'born of the Spirit' (see John 3:5).

The Bible goes on to say that, three days later, Ananias, a lowly disciple whom we would not otherwise have known about, was told by God to go to Paul to bring healing and the fullness of the Holy Spirit. Ananias said to Paul: '"Jesus … has sent me so that you may see again and be filled with the Holy Spirit."' (Acts 9:17). The important point is that there was a separation of three days between Paul's conversion and his being filled with the Spirit. Once you have an interval of three days between these two events, you can have any interval at all.

Key thought: To be healed and whole, we need to be filled with the Holy Spirit of God.

Thank you, dear Father, that your Holy Spirit brings us to faith in Christ, and that you want us to be filled with your Spirit and made whole. Amen.

Do You Want to be Made Whole?: Be filled with the Spirit – 2

' … they prayed for them that they might receive the Holy Spirit,'
—Acts 8:15

Scripture reading: Acts 8:9–17

I am going to tell you, in brief, about my own experience. It happened when Agnes Sanford came to Sydney at Easter 1961. I had begun the Healing Ministry in 1960 and found that I needed more of the Holy Spirit if the ministry was going to continue and be effective.

Often, this is the way people go forward from being born of the Spirit to being filled with the Spirit. They have a practical need which cannot be met in any other way.

I told Mrs Sanford of my need and she said, 'Do you know that if you have not yet been filled with the Spirit, you *can* be?'. I said to her: 'Well, I have always had the impression that, when you are converted, that is what is meant by being filled with the Spirit, but I have a need and, if there is more to draw on, I would be glad if you would pray for me'.

Agnes Sanford prayed for me on three occasions, in considerable depth and with remarkable discernment, and I was filled with the Spirit. It was an overwhelming experience. I felt that I was being immersed in the Holy Spirit. The experience was important at the time, but its importance was nothing by comparison to the value of the ongoing experience. For, if my experience of conversion had made me alive unto God, I found that my experience of being filled with the Spirit gave me power for service.

Key thought: We need to be filled with the Spirit to have power for service.

Father we invite your Holy Spirit to fill us now. Thank you. In Jesus' name. Amen.

Do You Want to be Made Whole?: Be filled with the Spirit – 3

'Again Jesus said, "Peace be with you! As the Father has sent me, I am sending you." And with that he breathed on them and said, "Receive the Holy Spirit."'
—John 20:21, 22

Scripture reading: Acts 2:1–13

So often, people are trying to serve God out of the experience of the Holy Spirit which is only intended for conversion. This is why we so often try to extend the Kingdom of God with man-made resources. We are trying to *organise* the Kingdom of God. But the only way you can extend the Kingdom is through a ministry of the Holy Spirit.

Let me say two things which will help you to be filled with the Spirit:

1. Be very clear—you must be 'born again'; you must have accepted Christ as your Saviour.

2. Accept the fullness of the Spirit so that this is the decision you have made, and is what you affirm in your heart and mind from now on.

Now, the great difficulty in all these things is that sometimes nothing happens, and the natural reaction is to say: 'But nothing has happened', and, as long as you say this, nothing *will* happen. Faith means praising God before you have the blessing by sight. So, when you have accepted the fullness of the Spirit, thank God by faith. This means you should praise God before you have the reality of the blessing.

Those are the two things. Get them right and then there is no limit to what God can do when you are drawing on his promises. It is simple, it is definite, and it is effective.

Key thought: Accept the fullness of the Spirit, so that it is what you accept and what you affirm.

Our loving Father, we thank you for your gracious provision that we can be filled with the Spirit, and we would believe for that now. Through Christ our Lord. Amen.

Do You Want to be Made Whole?: Prosper and be in health – 1

'But seek ye first the kingdom of God, and his righteousness; and all these things shall be added unto you.' —Matthew 6:33 (KJV)

Scripture reading: 3 John 1–8

I have said that wholeness is more than healing, and that the most important aspect of wholeness is our conversion—our acceptance of Christ as our Saviour. Wholeness also includes being filled with the Spirit which, like conversion, we draw upon by faith. What I now want to emphasise is that wholeness includes material provision and health. One of the promises of God, and part of wholeness, is for the provision of our material needs. Jesus said that, if we make God and his Kingdom our priority, what we need of clothing and food will be ours as well. God's concern for us is such that even the very hairs on our heads are all numbered (see Matthew 10:30).

As with everything else to do with the Bible, and indeed with everything that has to do with life, it is important for us to maintain balance in this matter of material provision. God will provide for our needs but not make us rich for the sake of being rich. Balance will also mean that we must be equally concerned about God being enabled to meet the needs of others.

So let us, for ourselves and for others, accept God's gracious provision of meeting our material needs. Let us so accept this provision from God that it is the decision we have made, and is what we are affirming by faith, and in a continuing way.

Key thought: It is right to believe that God is meeting our material needs.

Dear Father, we accept your gracious provision of meeting our material needs. We accept it for ourselves, and for others, so that it is the decision we have made, and is what we affirm by faith in a continuing way. Through Jesus Christ our Lord. Amen.

Do You Want to be Made Whole?: Prosper and be in health – 2

'Beloved, I wish above all things that thou mayest prosper and be in health, even as thy soul prospereth.'   —3 John 2 (KJV)

Scripture reading: Deuteronomy 7:6–15

Health is God's provision for us. We are used to thinking of God providing healing, and that is right and good. But he also provides *health*. This is the fence at the top, rather than the ambulance at the bottom. We need to accept health as part of God's wholeness for us as followers of Christ; we need to accept health for others, so that it is what we accept and what we believe.

I believe I can say that I think of myself as having health. Because of what I accept and affirm, I very seldom have to go to a doctor or take medication. As I say quite regularly in the Healing Service, the healing ministry of the Church seeks to work in full association with the medical profession. However, with 3 John 2 in mind, surely it is logical to affirm *continuing health* as the regular experience, the usual experience, the nearly-invariable experience we ought to have as the children of God.

Remember—you have what you accept. Do you agree that there is much to think through as far as this is concerned? My own position is that, if we thought through these things so that we believed God was meeting our material needs and providing health for us, it would give us a different approach to life.

How practical God is! How practical Christianity is! How practical the Healing Ministry is!

Key thought: We need to accept health as part of God's provision.

Our loving Father, we thank you for the wholeness that you provide, and we draw on it now, in all its ramifications, for our benefit, for your glory, and the increase of your Kingdom. Amen.

How to Have Perfect Faith –1

' Jacob replied, "I will not let you go unless you bless me."'
—Genesis 32:26

Scripture reading: Genesis 32:24–28

In chapter eleven of Mark's Gospel, verses 20 to 26, our Lord Jesus gives his prescription for prayer—the Prayer of Faith. The faith which God requires in order to have prayer answered is faith which *believes* that prayer is being answered, and it has to reach the point where we do not doubt in our hearts. In other words, it is perfect faith. If our Lord Jesus Christ said our faith needs to be perfect, it means that he is not setting before us something which is impossible, for that would be ridiculous. It is plainly possible, otherwise he would not have prescribed it as necessary.

How, then, can we have perfect faith that God is answering our prayer? I want to say three things and I trust they will be helpful.

If we are going to have perfect faith, the first requirement is that we have to have God's blessing. Jacob said to the man with whom he was wrestling, 'I will not let you go unless you bless me'. Some people feel this is being presumptuous but the man from God didn't say that Jacob was presumptuous—he commended Jacob and blessed him mightily.

An up-to-date illustration of this principle involves the Healing Ministry here at the Cathedral. Some people might wonder why it has prospered. It is because, when it began, we went so far 'out on a limb' that it just had to succeed if our position was to be justified!

Key thought: We must, like Jacob, hold on to God until he blesses us.

Thank you, Father, for Jacob's example of persistence in prayer. Our need is such that, like him, we will not let you go unless you bless us. In Jesus' name. Amen.

How to Have Perfect Faith – 2

'And God placed all things under his feet and appointed him to be head over everything for the church, which is his body, the fulness of him who fills everything in every way.' — Ephesians 1:22, 23

Scripture reading: Ephesians 1:15–23

The second requirement for having perfect faith is that you fill yourself and whatever is the situation—perhaps to do with another person—with the perfection of God's resource, his perfect blessing. I won't name particular problem areas, but our whole difficulty is that we tend to try to rise up through the problem. Instead, we must seek to bring the answer—God's perfect blessing—down to us.

We bring God's Kingdom down to us by our acceptance of it. We draw upon it so that it fills our whole being and our whole need. We so draw upon that fullness that it 'turns fear out of doors' (1 John 4:18 The Amplified Bible); it turns anxiety out of doors; it releases us from bondage to the problem. It is as we do the positive thing that the negative thing is cast out. Paul reminds us that God did not give us anxiety or fear (see 2 Timothy 1:7). He gives us himself. He gives us his Kingdom, his healing, and it is to fill us in spirit, body, mind and circumstance. The consequence of this is that God has cast out the fear and anxiety, the sickness, the infirmity and the problem.

You draw down God's Kingdom until it is there. You affirm that you have that perfect blessing because of your perfect acceptance of it. You keep affirming it until you have the witness in your heart that it is so. Keep on keeping on.

Key thought: We bring God's Kingdom—his perfect blessing—down to us by our acceptance of it.

Loving Father, we thank you that you have not given us a spirit of fear but a spirit of love and soundness of mind. We come to you in confidence, and accept the blessings of your Kingdom for our need.

How to Have Perfect Faith – 3

'When I said, "My foot is slipping," your love, O LORD, supported me.'
—Psalm 94:18

Scripture reading: Romans 7:1–6

The third requirement for having perfect faith is to be prepared to win the battle of faith day by day. I wouldn't have the impertinence to speak to people who have serious health problems, where sometimes their very lives might be at stake, if I wasn't being totally honest. There is a battle of faith to be fought in drawing upon the fullness of God's blessing until you have accepted it perfectly, and you will have to renew that perfect faith every day. Some days, you might find it comparatively easy; at other times it is difficult.

Don't be concerned if faith doesn't come easily. When you have given up, try again! It is when we are at the end of our tether—our self-resources—it is then that we are enabled to trust, not in ourselves, but in God (see 2 Corinthians 1:9).

If you want to have perfect faith, the faith that does not doubt, let God put you in the position where you must have that blessing. Then, bring it down by your acceptance of it. Continue to accept it until it is there, and until you know that you believe perfectly for it. This is a wonderful experience. You know that you believe perfectly, with no doubt at all and that God is doing it now. That is perfect faith. Remember that you may have to win the battle day by day. Don't be surprised by this, but, if you do your part, God will do his.

Key thought: Each day we appropriate the fullness of God's Kingdom blessing until the point is reached where we have it perfectly.

Thank you, Father, for the strength you give to encourage our faith day by day. In Jesus' name. Amen.

Can We Be 'On Top' Every Day? – 1

'This poor man called, and the LORD heard him; he saved him out of all his troubles.'
—Psalm 34:6

Scripture reading: Psalm 34:1–10

There are two ways to give a sermon. One is to begin from the Word of God, seeking to explain it, and then relating it to the needs people have. The other way, which I personally follow in these sermons at the Healing Service, is to show an understanding of the pressures, the strains, the sicknesses that come to us all, and then show that there is an answer in God's Word. When we realise that help from God is available, and we draw on that help in our real-life situations, it is good news—which is what the word 'gospel' means.

So, I begin by asking the question, 'Can we be "on top" every day?' I am sure you know what I mean. Can we have the ball at our feet every day? Can we have an experience of confidence, praise and blessing every day? Can we be on top of our circumstances, rather than our circumstances being on top of us?

You will notice that I didn't say, 'Can we be "on top" all the time?' If I had put the question like that, I would have had to admit that I, myself, am not on top all the time.

When I pose this question I do not mean to imply that we are not going to have problems. What I am saying is that we are to react to our problems so that we come to the point where we are on top of them every day.

Key thought: The way in which we react to our problems determines whether we shall be 'on top' of them.

Thank you, Father, that in your Word we find the answer to all our needs. We accept your provision now. Through Jesus Christ. Amen.

Can We Be 'On Top' Every Day? – 2

'In you our fathers put their trust; they trusted and you delivered them. They cried to you and were saved; in you they trusted and were not disappointed.' —Psalm 22:4, 5

Scripture reading: Psalm 22:22–31

It cannot be over-emphasised that our difficulties (you think of yours and I will think of mine) are permitted by God. They are not sent by God. They may well come from the devil himself; they may be caused by our personal and corporate disobedience. But we must have in our minds the understanding that the Bible gives, which is that problems are permitted by God and they are used by God, and work together for our good.

We need to have a theology or an understanding of the difficulties that come our way which will enable us to react to them in such a way that 'we should not trust in ourselves, but in God' (2 Corinthians 1:9 KJV). It means that we will come to faith in the promises and the provision of God. We do this by an act of the will. Faith is a decision of the will. We do it with our minds, both at the time and in an ongoing way.

When we have this understanding and we discipline ourselves to react in this way, we will find that we are drawing upon a release of the Holy Spirit which is blessing from God appropriate to our needs. Perhaps another way of putting it is to say that when we are weak God is strong and he helps us. The mountains are moved and we are 'on top' in the best sense of the word.

Key thought: Our difficulties, which are permitted by God, work for our good.

Father, we give you praise that, through our problems we learn to depend upon you more and that nothing can separate us from your love. Amen.

Can We Be 'On Top' Every Day? – 3

'give thanks in all circumstances, for this is God's will for you in Christ Jesus.'
— 1 Thessalonians 5:18

Scripture reading: Acts 4:23–31

Christians who are persecuted or under pressure are strong and effective. The reason is that, whether they realise it or not, they are reacting to their difficulties so that they are depending on God more and there is a subsequent release of the Holy Spirit. That is why they are strong! That is why they have blessings in their lives! That is why they are on top of their permitted circumstances.

In the long run, though perhaps not in the short term, people experiencing persecution, and who have this understanding, even thank God for their difficulties. All things have worked together for good. They are depending on God and not on themselves, and they have a blessing of God that they didn't have before and wouldn't otherwise have had.

This is the secret of the Healing Service. We set out to minister to troubled people and, both individually and corporately, we react to the problems by drawing closer to God. It is no virtue on our part. It is no virtue on my part. We have no alternative but to depend on God more, but, when we do, the blessing of God is released in a way which meets people's needs.

If we are going to come to the point where we are on top every day in this balanced scriptural sense, we have to choose to react like this in a meaningful and continuing way.

Key thought: In all things, God works for the good of those who love him (see Romans 8:28).

Father, help us to depend on you more for the answer to our needs. Thank you for the gift of your Holy Spirit in our lives which brings us joy and peace in our hearts, with your blessing and provision. Through Jesus Christ, our Lord. Amen.

Can We Be 'On Top' Every Day? – 4

'I will walk about in freedom, for I have sought out your precepts.'
—Psalm 119:45

Scripture reading: Psalm 119:41–56

I am never tired of saying that if our Lord had to pray all night, we will have to pray all day. I know what it is like—and so do many of you—to pray every moment of the day, without so much as putting in a comma. This is what is meant by *'Pray without ceasing'* (1 Thessalonians 5:17 KJV).

It is something you are doing all the time because you choose to; it is a continuing act of the will. I am not saying it is easy. I am not giving some short-term answer that will deliver the goods. I am saying that you may well have to react like this so that you are doing it in an ongoing way.

Well, you are going to be affirming something all the time, so make sure that what you are affirming is always positive and creative, enabling the blessing of God to be released. The Mary Sisters say you have to 'fight the battle of faith every day' if you are going to come out on top. I like that; it is realistic and it is what we must do.

'Can we be "on top" every day?' Yes, certainly. We can arrive every day at the point where we are affirming God's blessings to the extent that we do not doubt in our hearts. We do it by an act of the will, and we continue to do it until we are 'on top' of our circumstances for that day.

Key thought: We fight the battle of faith every day.

Our loving Father, we thank you that we can so react to our problems that we depend on you more and come to faith, and have your blessing. We would do that now and every day, and be 'on top'. In Jesus' name. Amen.

The Theological Basis of the Healing Ministry – 1

'"When you enter a town and are welcomed, eat what is set before you. Heal the sick who are there and tell them, 'The kingdom of God is near you.'"'

—Luke 10:8,9

Scripture reading: John 14:5–14

One of the things we all need to have in mind, especially those involved in ministering to people, is that we 'give thanks in all circumstances, for this is God's will for you in Christ Jesus' (1 Thessalonians 5:18). If we give thanks in all circumstances, we will find that this will stir up faith within us so that at all times we are able to be used in ministry and pray the Prayer of Faith effectively; and one reason why we can give thanks in all circumstances is because of what is available to us as far as healing is concerned,

There are a number of things which can be said in relation to the theological basis for the Healing Ministry, one of which is recorded in the Epistle of James: 'the prayer of faith shall save the sick, and the Lord shall raise him up' (James 5:15 KJV).

The particular basis for the Healing Ministry to which I now want to refer relates to three texts from Luke's Gospel. The first is Luke 10:9 — our Lord Jesus' commission to the general group of disciples to go out and preach the gospel, 'Heal the sick who are there and tell them, "The Kingdom of God has come near to you"'. What Jesus means is this: when a person is healed, he has drawn on part of a greater reality called the Kingdom of God. In other words, the Kingdom of God is God's perfect blessing, and healing is part of it.

Key thought: Jesus showed us that healing is part and parcel of the gospel message.

We praise you, Father, and thank you for your provision of salvation and healing.

The Theological Basis of the Healing Ministry – 2

'*"the kingdom of heaven is like a merchant looking for fine pearls. When he found one of great value, he went away and sold everything he had and bought it."*' —Matthew 13:45,46

Scripture reading: John 17:20–26

My second text referring to the theological basis for the Healing Ministry is Luke 17:21 where Jesus said: 'the kingdom of God is within you'. This is the other side of what he reveals about the Kingdom of God. It both belongs to the end of the age, and it has already been established—it is within you.

The art of interpreting the Bible is to see all that is said about a subject and relate one part to another. Jesus said the Kingdom of God has two sides to it. One side is that it belongs to the end of the age when Jesus will come again in power and glory and wind up this present world order—when the kingdoms of this world will become the Kingdom of our Lord and of his Christ (see Revelation 11:15). This is something to which all Christians look forward, and it is something of a heavenly and spiritual nature.

Our Lord Jesus Christ also said—and he made many, many references to this effect—the Kingdom of God has already been established and is for the 'here and now'.

If we realise that the Kingdom of God has been established, and is that greater reality of which healing is part, we can see how available healing is. It is available in response to faith because it is part of the Kingdom of God. As someone once said to me: 'it doesn't even have to be asked for; why ask for something you've got?'.

Key thought: The blessings of the Kingdom of God are ours now.

Father, thank you that we are reconciled to you through Jesus Christ, your Son, and that you have restored the Kingdom to us.

The Theological Basis of the Healing Ministry – 3

'"... the kingdom of God ... is like a mustard seed, which a man took and planted in his garden. It grew, became a tree, and the birds of the air perched in its branches."'
—Luke 13:18,19

Scripture reading: Mark 8:22–26

Let me go on and introduce my third text, Luke 13:19, where Jesus compares the Kingdom of God to a grain of mustard seed which grew into a tree big enough for birds to perch in its branches.

Our Lord Jesus Christ gives us more information about how the Kingdom shows itself. He said it is like seed scattered on the ground which, without the farmer understanding how, produces 'first the stalk, then the ear, then the full kernel in the ear' (Mark 4:28).

When you plant a seed you don't see anything to begin with, but it is there. If you could see it, it would be breaking its case and sending down its tap root; then the shoot would begin to come up and the merest slip of green would show through the soil.

In summary:
• The Kingdom of God is God's perfect blessing and healing is part of it;
• Healing is available in response to faith because it is part of the Kingdom of God;
• The Kingdom of God, which includes healing, is like a seed which grows.

This is part of the explanation for divine healing. Not only does it give great authority and assurance, but if the principles which I am sharing with you are understood and put into practice, you will find that they give you great guidelines as to how the ministry of healing is to be exercised. There is much to think about. For some, it might be that these are new insights and worthy of the most serious consideration.

Key thought: The Kingdom of God is within us, like a tiny seed; and its property is to grow.

Thank you, Father, that healing is part of your Kingdom provision.

The Theological Basis of the Healing Ministry – 4

'Hearing this, Jesus said to Jairus, "Don't be afraid; just believe, and she will be healed."'   —Luke 8:50

Scripture reading: Luke 13:10–17

I have spoken before about my friends with the child who had a curvature of the spine. It was a very bad curvature and the medical prognosis was not good.

My friends began to read the Bible with a new interest and saw that healing was part of the greater reality called 'the Kingdom of God'; they saw that the Kingdom of God doesn't even have to be asked for—'it is within you'; and they saw that the characteristic of the Kingdom is like that of a plant whose nature is to grow. All I can say is that they believed these things, and that they believed them on behalf of their child.

They said: 'By faith, we see in our child the Kingdom of God; it includes healing; we don't even have to ask for it; it is within, and its nature is to grow from being small to being big'.

They continued in this way for more than three years. There was never anything spectacular. It was all hard going, but at the end of more than three years their child was completely straight!

So often what we accept is the problem. My friends had the vision and faith to accept the answer and believe it was growing, so that old things passed away and all things became new.

Key thought: We have what we accept.

Our loving Father, we thank you for these real, moving and wondrous things which are more than perhaps we have ever dreamed of before, but they have only been waiting to be understood and acted out. So we would believe these things in our circumstances here and now. We do this so that your Kingdom will be extended, not only in this way, but in all good ways. So our prayer is praise; and, indeed, we give thanks in every circumstance. Through Jesus Christ our Lord.

Faith Is Your Frame of Mind – 1

'the mind controlled by the Spirit is life and peace'   —Romans 8:6

Scripture reading: Hebrews 4:12–16

Faith is a frame of mind. In chapter eleven of Mark's Gospel there are recorded the well-known words of Jesus where he describes the Prayer of Faith. He says: "whosoever shall say unto this mountain, Be thou removed, and be thou cast into the sea; and shall not doubt in his heart, but shall believe that those things which he saith shall come to pass; he shall have whatsoever he saith" (Mark 11:23 KJV). Faith means that we believe we receive these things so that we do not doubt in our hearts. We are sure. You might say this is hard. But that isn't the point. The point is that this is what we have to do if we are to have God's blessing. It must be our frame of mind.

The difficulty is that, while we are seeking to exercise the faith which does not doubt, with our eyes we see the problem—the mountain; it is so hard to divorce ourselves from what we see, what we have—for example, the headache—so that we believe to the point at which we do not doubt that we receive something else. Yes, it is hard.

Let us face the difficulty. Faith means we are thanking God so that we are sure, *before we see the answer to our prayer.* It is not impossible, and once we realise what we have to do and we set about doing it, it can become astonishingly easy.

Key thought: It is hard to believe so that we are sure, but it is not impossible.

Thank you, Father, for the faith to believe before we see the answer to our prayer.

Faith Is Your Frame of Mind – 2

'"Did I not tell you that if you believed, you would see the glory of God?"'   —John 11:40

Scripture reading: Mark 8:14–21

We do have a frame of mind whether we realise it or not, and whether we like it or not. If not in terms of faith and the answer of God, we have a frame of mind about what we see, that is, the mountain or the problem. If we do not accept the answer by faith so that it is our frame of mind, we are accepting the difficulty. Do you see? The Bible says: 'What I feared has come upon me; what I dreaded has happened to me.' (Job 3:25).

Have you ever wondered why your prayers are not answered? Nine times out of ten it is because, despite your prayer procedures— meaningful and sincere as they are—your frame of mind majors on the problem. You have what you accept, for good or for ill.

It is not easy to switch over from what you see or what you have or what you are, to what you have faith for so that you do not doubt. But let us realise that, when our frame of mind is anchored to a problem so that it is what we talk about, then that is what we are bringing about or, if the problem already exists, it is what we are perpetuating.

Key thought: Faith means that we are thanking God before we see the answer.

Father in Heaven, we are broken before you when we realise that the way we think is for good or for ill. Lord, help us to understand the consequences of our frame of mind, and enable us, by your grace, to accept your Kingdom blessing. In Jesus' name. Amen.

Faith Is Your Frame of Mind – 3

'The only thing that counts is faith expressing itself through love.'
—Galatians 5:6

Scripture reading: Galatians 3:1–14

Whenever I have thought of people in terms of their presenting problems—for example, their need for conversion or for healing—I have had terrible experiences of seeing problem situations continuing and getting worse. But, when I have come to the point (usually because I'm at the end of my tether) where the Holy Spirit is able to minister to me in prayer so that, by faith, I switch over from a negative frame of mind to one which is positive, those people can be changed. The change can begin to happen, literally, overnight.

When I say my prayers I try to be still before God so the Holy Spirit can show me those areas, either to do with myself, with other people or the world, where my frame of mind is negative. When I feel God has shown me this, I then accept by faith the Kingdom reality for myself, for those people or for that situation. I seek to accept it as I accept Christ as Saviour. I accept the blessing, whether it be for conversion or for healing, or for the 'whatever you ask for' (Matthew 21:22) so that this becomes my frame of mind. It will not be what I see. It will be what I have faith for, and faith is 'being sure of what we hope for and certain of what we do not see' (Hebrews 11:1). I then live by faith in that particular area of prayer. Then, if not all at once, progressively, the mountain is moved.

Key thought: The Holy Spirit is able to help us change from a negative frame of mind to one which is faith-filled and positive.

Loving Father, so bless us that by your grace we will live by faith—thought by thought, moment by moment, night and day—always. O Father, teach us to live by faith, through Christ our Lord. Amen.

Repentance for the Christian – 1

'Godly sorrow brings repentance that leads to salvation and leaves no regret, but worldly sorrow brings death.'   —2 Corinthians 7:10

Scripture reading: 2 Corinthians 7:8–16

Meaningful repentance comes from a conviction of sin and of having fallen short as far as God and our relationship with our brothers and sisters is concerned (see Romans 3:23). There is no repentance that does not issue in deep contrition, a deep inward hurt we feel because of the burden of our failure. We might well be moved to tears because of that conviction. Would to God that it was a more frequent experience for us all!

I am sure that repentance is something about which we should talk more, although it is not a popular subject. If you ask what, in my opinion, is the main single reason why there is not a spirit of revival in the Church, I would say it is because we lack the godly sorrow that leads to repentance; we lack the conviction of the Holy Spirit that enables us to turn from that which grieves God so that we might go on to a more complete experience of God.

The purpose of repentance is not only to bring about a godly sorrow: it is to enable us to draw upon more of the experience of being perfected in love, which is what God has provided for us if we repent, and if we believe, and if we obey.

Key thought: Meaningful repentance must issue in godly sorrow and contrition.

O Father, we come to you, knowing that it is your work and your Church that are languishing in the world because those who are called by your name do not repent, but rather are proud and self-satisfied, having rationalised things away. We turn from our sin and thank you for your blessing. Through Jesus Christ. Amen.

Repentance for the Christian – 2

'Therefore confess your sins to each other and pray for each other so that you may be healed. The prayer of a righteous man is powerful and effective.'
—James 5:16

Scripture reading: Matthew 3:1–12

In the book, *Realities*, the Mary Sisters tell how, with their own hands, they built their chapel in Germany. They had a little cart which ran on rails which they used for carrying building materials to the site. The cart kept jumping the rails. The Sisters did their best to find out the cause—they even had an engineer look at it—but it still kept jumping the rails. So, at last (and sometimes we do the essential thing last), they gathered in their prayer tent, near the work site, and began to pray.

God gave them a different focus when they looked away from the presenting problem and prayed. One of the Sisters confessed that she had a grudge against one of the others and that she had not forgiven her. She confessed this to God and asked the other Sister for forgiveness. This led to one Sister after another being convicted by the Holy Spirit that there was something wrong in their own lives—resulting in a time of heartfelt and meaningful repentance, reconciliation and renewal. And, they solemnly record that the cart never jumped the rails again!

I believe the lesson of this story is so deeply theological that we should write it on our hearts and act it out in our lives. God provides his times of refreshment, his perfection of love, his material provision, his Kingdom. There is no reason why we can't have things just as he intends us to have them. The only thing which prevents it happening is our unrepented sin.

Key thought: We should ask God to reveal those things of which we need to repent.

Show us, Holy Spirit, those things which we need to set right in order that we might draw on all the blessing our Father has for us.

Victory Over Satan – 1

'Then Jesus came to them and said, "All authority in heaven and on earth has been given to me."'   –Matthew 28:18

Scripture reading: Acts 28:1–10

When the general group of disciples (not the Apostles) had returned from their first preaching-healing tour Jesus said to them: "I saw Satan fall like lightning from heaven. I have given you authority to trample on snakes and scorpions and to overcome all the power of the enemy; nothing will harm you. However, do not rejoice that the spirits submit to you, but rejoice that your names are written in heaven" (Luke 10:18–20).

Now, let us rejoice about the last part of what Jesus said as being of primary importance, but don't let us ignore the first part. Satan is the author of all problems, including sickness and infirmity, and Jesus said that when the disciples went out preaching the Kingdom and healing the sick he saw Satan fall like lightning from heaven! In other words, the reality of the Kingdom meant that Satan was overcome.

Jesus went into certain details about what this means. The words which are particularly relevant to us are these: 'I have given you authority over all the power of the enemy; and nothing shall hurt you'. If we accept the Kingdom reality, it follows that we have power over other things which would be potent to harm us except for the Kingdom of God.

The real crunch of what I want to say is that, in my view, we do not accept the reality of the Kingdom in such a factual way that we believe that this is what it means. What I can't get people away from is their acceptance of sickness and infirmity, in the sense that it is a giant over which they hope to have the victory—but don't.

Key thought: Jesus gives us authority over all the power of the enemy.

We do rejoice, Lord Jesus, that our names are written in heaven.

Victory Over Satan – 2

'"The kingdom of heaven is like a mustard seed … it is the smallest of all your seeds, yet when it grows, it is the largest of garden plants and becomes a tree"'
—Matthew 13:31, 32

Scripture reading: 1 Kings 18:16–21

People don't realise that, as we draw upon the Kingdom, our Lord gives us power over all things, and nothing will hurt us. Until people do understand, and it becomes the kind of way they live their lives, they will never draw upon the healing ministry—as well as other areas of Kingdom blessing—in the way that they need to.

Of course, what Satan wants us to do is to have a foot in both camps. He loves people to say they believe in the healing ministry, provided they are still in bondage to the potency of the things that they wrestle against.

The Kingdom of God, the greater reality of which healing is a part, is within you. This means that we have authority over all the power of the enemy and, Jesus said, nothing can harm us. Do you believe it?

Key thought: We need to accept the reality of the Kingdom of God.

O Father, we say we love the Word of God, but yet we do not believe it. We say we have faith in these things, but we don't act them out. Father, we would say tonight that what we've really got is the spirit of fear, whereas what you have given us is power and love and a sound mind, and the reality of victory over Satan in all his forms. O Father, bless this to our understanding by the ministry of the Holy Spirit. Lord, hear our prayer, and let our cry come unto you. Amen.

We Can Have Faith for *One* Thing

When We Have Faith for *All* Things – 1

'So I will always remind you of these things, even though you know them and are firmly established in the truth you now have.' —2 Peter 1:12

Scripture reading: 1 Thessalonians 5:12–28

Part of the reality of God's Kingdom is with us now, and the reality of the Kingdom blessing we have now is that Jesus said we have *power* over all the enemy and nothing shall by any means hurt us. This is an extraordinary reality which we are hardly conscious of, yet it must be at the heart and centre of the Healing Ministry. Healing means that we are drawing on the Kingdom of God; it means that we have power over all the work of Satan, of which sickness and infirmity are a part. Would that those words were written on our hearts and that not a day passed but that we sought to make them operative in our real-life situations.

I make no apology for repeating myself. I have to repeat myself to *myself* every day! I find that even something that is clear in my mind and heart concerning God's blessing and which I have made effective in my own, or someone else's life, can be quickly lost—the reality of that belief being taken away by the evil one, so that it has to be recaptured, realised again and applied again. I don't think anyone will mind the repetition of things that are of central importance. So I say again that the reality of God's Kingdom in our real-life situations must be accepted; also the reality that we have power over Satan so that nothing shall by any means hurt us. That is what we must accept.

Key thought: Satan is a defeated foe.

Lord Jesus Christ, you have won the victory over the enemy and have given us the authority to overcome all Satan's power. We accept your provision with thanks and praise.

We Can Have Faith for *One* Thing

When We Have Faith for *All* Things – 2

'When Jesus saw him lying there and learned that he had been in this condition for a long time, he asked him, "Do you want to get well?"'

—John 5:6

Scripture reading: Romans 10:1–13

You have what you accept and, so often, what we accept is the problem. We can all do that with marvellous efficiency! But we must accept the answer—accept the Kingdom, accept the victory over Satan, so it is *that* which we accept—it is *that* which is to fill our minds; that is what we are to affirm. It is the way we are to react to the problem—the problem in front of us at the time, or any recurrence of the problem. The 'real you' is the Kingdom blessing and the victory over Satan; that is what you affirm by faith. It might not be what you see—and, of course, that is the difficulty; we are to affirm it by faith.

It will be when we are weak that we are strong; when circumstances have brought us to the point where there isn't anything of ourselves left to trust in that we shall be able to believe these things. We do these things and we get them right when we *have* to, yet we choose to.

I make no apology for repeating this because I have to say, very lovingly, that there isn't anyone I know who really gets it right. And there are many times when I don't get it right myself!

Key thought: The 'real you' is the Kingdom blessing and the victory over Satan; that is what you affirm by faith.

Heavenly Father, we want to get these things right. We affirm that your Kingdom is the reality and that, through Jesus Christ our Lord, we have victory over all the power of the enemy.

We Can Have Faith for *One* Thing
When We Have Faith for *All* Things – 3

'Test everything. Hold on to the good.'   — 1 Thessalonians 5:21

Scripture reading: Psalm 119:89–105

I have often pondered over a verse from the eleventh chapter of Mark where Jesus says: ' whatever you ask for in prayer, believe that you have received it, and it will be yours' (v. 24) and 'when you stand praying, if you hold anything against anyone, forgive him' (v. 25). I used to think this to be so difficult, so impossible, and so unrealistic as far as I was concerned, that I never really faced up to it. I would see the need to forgive the particular troublesome person for whom I was praying, or other individuals who were causing me difficulty at that time. However, I have been convicted recently, when in situations where I have had to go further in God's blessings, that when we pray the Prayer of Faith about anything we desire, we are to forgive from our hearts *anyone* and *everyone*—no exceptions.

When I began to face up to this, the Lord showed me other things, and I saw this verse in the Bible: 'give thanks in all circumstances, for this is God's will for you in Christ Jesus' (1 Thessalonians 5:18). This means that, in every conceivable situation—again there are no exceptions—we are to give thanks because it is the will of God. So, again I see that God has told us to be wholehearted in forgiving everyone, and he has said that everything should evoke thanksgiving.

Key thought: We can't pick and choose who we will forgive.

Help us, loving Father, to be obedient to your word and wholehearted in doing what you command.

We Can Have Faith for *One* Thing
When We Have Faith for *All* Things – 4

'"But my righteous one will live by faith."'   —Hebrews 10:38

Scripture reading: Romans 1:8–17

As I considered Jesus' words in Mark 11:24 and following, I realised afresh that we are to live by faith: faith is not what you see, but what you hope for, and what you believe you receive so that you are sure you have the Kingdom blessing (see Hebrews 11:1). Remember that to live by faith means our faith goes on moment by moment and breath by breath. It is a continuous experience that allows no kind of interruption. That is what God says we are to do, and it means we are not living by what we see, or have, or are.

In 1 Timothy 2:1 Paul says: 'I urge, then, first of all, that requests, prayers, intercession and thanksgiving be made for everyone'. Intercession is the kind of praying that Jesus does in heaven—the kind of praying that the Spirit does, with 'groans that words cannot express' (Romans 8:26). It means that we are to believe for all men, that is, everyone who is in need of prayer in the whole world.

Friends, I believe that the reason we find it impossible to accept the Kingdom blessing and the victory over Satan at *one* point, is because we do not do it at *every* point. If only we believed in faith for every area at every time and in every way, then we would find we could do it for the particular matter which is of such pressing concern to us. I share this part of my own pilgrimage with you, trusting that it will enable us all to go further forward.

Key thought: Forgiveness, thanksgiving, faith and intercession should be for every situation, all the time.

Loving Father, increase our understanding of these things and give us grace to accept your Kingdom blessing always, and in all things. Amen.

The Healing Congregation – 1

'How good and pleasant it is when brothers live together in unity!'
—Psalm 133:1

Scripture reading: Ephesians 4:1–6

The Healing Ministry in the Cathedral is hosting a residential seminar [May 1983]. People have come from New Zealand and all States of the Commonwealth, except Queensland. On the two occasions when I have attended I spoke about the promises of God and about drawing on the promises by repentance and faith. I told participants that I would also like to speak about the role of the 'healing congregation' in drawing upon healing from God. This topic is immensely important to us at the Healing Ministry. It is equally important to those who will read our sermon notes because it is vital that we all understand something of the role of the congregation in drawing upon blessing from God.

I want to make it clear that I am not only referring to the congregation here, although most of what we say and do comes out of the Healing Service in the Cathedral on a Wednesday night. Therefore, I will pose a question and give my answer. The question is: What are the characteristics that enable us to say that any group at all—any Christian group—is a 'healing congregation'?

The first characteristic of a healing congregation is unity. Paul tells us to: 'Make every effort to keep the unity of the Spirit through the bond of peace' (Ephesians 4:3). There is to be a unity that is of the Holy Spirit, something that is experienced not only with the mind but with the heart. It is vital. It has to be prayed about and worked at. It means that we have to keep 'short accounts' with God and with one another.

Key thought: We are all one in Christ Jesus.

Thank you, Father, that we are in Christ Jesus who gave himself for us on the cross, and because we are in him, we are joined to one another. Amen.

The Healing Congregation – 2

'Jesus wept'   —John 11:35

Scripture reading: Mark 1:40–45

The Bible says that the Holy Spirit can not only be stirred up and flow out as rivers of living water, but can also be grieved and quenched. There is no more potent cause of grieving the Spirit than when there is disunity in a congregation. I always have this point at the forefront of my mind on any and every occasion, because it is absolutely vital, if we are going to have the person and ministries of the Holy Spirit operative and effective, that we maintain 'the unity of the Spirit through the bond of peace'.

The second characteristic of a healing congregation must be compassion for those in need. One of the marks of our Lord Jesus Christ in his own healing ministry was that he had compassion on those who were sick. It is very easy to become case-hardened. You get so used to troubled people— 'Oh, here's another one', so to speak. I am very easily moved to tears by the problems that people have and, if the day comes when I am not, I will hand over this ministry to someone who does have the compassion of God for people in need. That compassion is shown in the welcome at the door; it is shown in the greeting time and in the laying on of hands; it is shown in the letters we write and in any other activity to do with our ministry. It mightn't solve the problem but it enables the problem to be solved in other ways. Compassion is love. It is extended in the name of Christ to all, and each, who are in need, and it is an essential requirement in a healing congregation.

Key thought: We must be compassionate, like Jesus.

Help us, Father, to live in peace with one another, and to show your compassion to those in need. Through Christ our Lord. Amen.

The Healing Congregation – 3

'"I served the Lord with great humility and with tears … I have not hesitated to preach anything that would be helpful to you but have taught you publicly and from house to house … "'   —Acts 20:19, 20

Scripture reading: Philippians 2:1–11

The third characteristic of a healing congregation is this: there must be 'an informed ministry'. By that I mean that there is a knowledge of the provisions of God; there is a capacity to draw on them by repentance, faith and obedience, and those who minister act in a way that will be effective because of this.

It is not enough to say: 'Oh well, we will have a prayer'. We *will* have a prayer, but the prayer must be the vehicle of an informed ministry. We must know the promises that are available. We must draw on them with a faith that pleases God. This informed ministry will come from instruction; it will come from experience; and it will come from correction. No-one should mind being corrected if it is serving a positive purpose. We seek to provide—any congregation must seek to provide—an informed and effective faith ministry. By 'we' I don't just mean those 'out front'. We believe in, and we practise, the ministry of all believers. I can't hide behind the fact that I am supposed to be 'informed' in my ministry, because the ministry here is exercised by the rank and file of the congregation. I have to be concerned about that too—we all have to be concerned about that too. It is the business of us all to minister in an informed, scriptural and effective way.

Key thought: We can't leave it to the minister, the person 'up front' in a healing congregation to know all the answers. It is everyone's responsibility.

Dear Father, we want to be able to minister your healing grace to those in need. Help us to become fully equipped to be your means of blessing. In Jesus' name. Amen.

The Healing Congregation – 4

'How, then, can they call on the one they have not believed in? And how can they believe in the one of whom they have not heard? And how can they hear without someone preaching to them?'   —Romans 10:14

Scripture reading: Acts 4:1–14

Unity, compassion, and an informed ministry are three important characteristics of a healing congregation. A fourth characteristic is ultimately the most important: it is that we present the Lord Jesus Christ as, not only Healer but also as Saviour and Lord. He is the one who makes us right with the Father, both now and in eternity. He is the head of the Church and he must be the head of this congregation. It must be Jesus who walks the aisles; it must be Jesus who lays on hands; it must be Jesus who is introduced to people. If people are not being converted to Jesus, or being enabled to go further in their walk with Jesus, our ministry is not being effective.

I must give an illustration of this. One of our members brought a man with whom he worked—a man who was not a believer—to the Healing Service. The man's wife came with him. They had a newborn baby who had, humanly speaking, a condition that could not be altered for good; it was terminal. They came that night, brokenhearted, with their baby, and they were so touched by the concern of those members of the congregation who related to them, that they accepted Christ as Saviour in the service the first night they came. Their baby subsequently died but they continued on in their faith and have since become members of one of our parishes. It was their conversion to Christ that stood them in good stead in their tragic circumstances, and it was something they drew on through the Healing Congregation.

Key thought: Healing introduces people to Christ.

Our loving Father, we thank you for these insights. Help us to build them into our lives, for your glory and our blessing. Through Christ our Lord. Amen.

What Do You Want Out of Life?: I want to be accepted – 1

'To the praise of the glory of his grace, wherein he hath made us accepted in the beloved.'   —Ephesians 1:6 (KJV)

Scripture reading: Psalm 92

We are all looking for something out of life. One of the things we all have in common is that we want to be accepted by other people. I suppose one could substitute the word 'love' and say we all want to be loved by other people, and I would be very happy to put it like that. But I think the word 'accept' has a wider application.

Many people feel rejected; they feel on the outer. They will even affirm that other people don't like them. They may keep up a pretence, an outward form of conviviality, but inwardly they feel alone, rejected and unhappy.

This problem comes from insecurity stemming from a person's experiences while growing up. The feelings of insecurity may be covered up but deep down they are there, whether the person knows it or not. To put it more positively, there are areas in everyone's life where we would like to have a deeper and more satisfying experience of being accepted by other people.

When Dr Robert Schuller was in Australia conducting schools for church leadership he spoke about loving ourselves. This gripped people's attention because we are so used to thinking of ourselves as having no good thing dwelling within us (see Romans 7:18 KJV). Even our righteousness is as 'filthy rags', the Bible says.

However, in chapter one of Ephesians Paul reminds us that we are ' … accepted in the beloved' (v.6). The Living Bible, which is a free translation of the original text, puts it like this: 'We belong to his dearly loved Son'.

Key thought: Everyone wants to be accepted by other people.

Thank you, Father, that through Jesus we are righteous and accepted by you as your dear children. Praise God. Praise God. Praise God.

What Do You Want Out of Life?: I want to be accepted – 2

'But Barnabas took him and brought him to the apostles.' —Acts 9:27

Scripture reading: Acts 9:20–31

The wonderful thing about the Christian religion is that, because of Christ and his work on the cross, we have the assurance that we are acceptable to God the Father, both now and for eternity. We need to realise this; we need to emphasise it and keep it in mind, moment by moment. We are people who are accepted by God because we belong to his dearly loved Son.

It is a whole new ball game. We are not only forgiven, but we are accepted by God and, because we are accepted by him, we are accepted by one another. Because we belong to Christ we belong to one another. We are brothers and sisters in Christ.

This understanding transforms the problem about being accepted. There is no reason why we should continue to have a low self-esteem and feel rejected. The Christian should have a high self-esteem because he has a new self that comes from being accepted by God through Christ. The Christian also has a new relationship with everyone else who has been accepted by God—they with him and he with them.

However, if we affirm that other people don't accept us, we will inevitably find that this is what really happens because we are affirming the problem; we have not realised our full position in Christ and are not believing for it by faith.

Key thought: 'I want to be accepted'. You are accepted in Christ and you are accepted by all who are joined to Christ. Affirm it by faith and grow into the reality of it.

Father, I now stop being sorry for myself and begin to praise you because you accept me; and I start to believe that I am entering into the same kind of positive relationship with every Christian I know. Thank you, Father. Amen.

What Do You Want Out of Life?: I want to succeed at work – 1

'"Do not let this Book of the Law depart from your mouth; meditate on it day and night, so that you may be careful to do everything written in it. Then you will be prosperous and successful."' —Joshua 1:8

Scripture reading : Joshua 1:1–9

One of the things any self-respecting person wants is, I believe, to succeed at work. Let me say straight away that I am interpreting 'work' in the widest possible sense, that is, as our vocation. It will not only be a nine-to-five job; it will be what we do in our waking hours more generally. This means that what a wife and mother does is work; certainly she would think of it like that! So, whether you are an accountant, a cleaner, a carer, a typist, a plumber or a 'washer-upper' — whatever you do — that is what I am talking about. I believe we should enjoy our work, and I believe it is right to succeed at it.

The first thing I want to say is that *we should choose the work for which we are suited.* If you are working in an occupation for which you are not suited — change your job. We all have some capacity which we need to recognise and develop by training in order to undertake work in that field.

Whatever abilities we possess were given to us by God — through our parents, yes, but given to us as individuals. Paul says: 'What do you have that you did not receive?' (1 Corinthians 4:7). When we recognise this, it immediately gives our work a special quality and motivation. Our work is no longer just a job but, rather, it could be called a ministry.

Key thought: Part of what we call ministry is doing the job for which God has fitted us.

Gracious Father, thank you that you have created us as individuals, each with special abilities. We open our lives to your Holy Spirit now so that these gifts can be used for your glory. Amen.

What Do You Want Out of Life?: I want to succeed at work – 2

'Be still before the LORD and wait patiently for him; do not fret when men succeed in their ways, when they carry out their wicked schemes.'
—Psalm 37:7

Scripture reading: Proverbs 16:1–20

Secondly, *our God-given work should succeed.* God told Joshua that if his people would walk in his way they would be prosperous and successful. The New Testament or Christian equivalent would be to say that, if we believe the Christian faith and live the Christian life in a way that is truly meaningful, God will bless our work and we will have good success.

Having said all that, how are you getting on in your job? Are you in the job for which God has equipped you? That is the first question, and I include in that the need to develop your potential so that it increases your capability. Assuming that to be the case—are you successful in your job? Some people are, and some are not.

If you are not having success in your work, examine your relationship to God. If you are someone who calls himself a Christian but who is still not having success in your work, then God is telling you there is something wrong; you need to find out what it is and put it right. You might be so used to yourself—your strengths and your weaknesses—that you cannot be objective; you might need a skilled Christian counsellor to whom you can speak in confidence who will help you work through these insights. When things are truly right between you and God, then things will work out; Joshua 1:8 makes that plain and definite.

Key thought: We will prosper in our work if we keep our relationship right with God.

Dear Father, we thank you that your will is to prosper the work of our hands. Grant that we might glorify your name in our daily work. Amen.

What Do You Want Out of Life?: I want to succeed at work – 3

' "This stone that I have set up as a pillar will be God's house, and of all that you give me I will give you a tenth." '   —Genesis 28:22

Scripture reading: Luke 18:9–14

If we are so walking with Christ that God is giving us success in our work, what should be our response? I suggest that in such circumstances we are under an obligation to give generously from our finances to the work of God.

In the Old Testament the rule was to give a tenth of one's income to the work of God. Now, we are not under the law; we are under grace. We don't follow a rigid rule; it is the grace of God that controls our responses. However, many Christians do return a tenth of their finances to the work of God.

One person, a foundation member of the Healing Ministry, said: 'I cannot afford not to tithe'. Many would say they cannot afford *to* tithe but tithing was part of this person's Christian walk. So, I share this with you and I address it to myself. If God should lay this upon us, then he will enable us.

You want to succeed at work? Then assess the abilities God has given you and get into that kind of work. If you walk with true Christian meaningfulness you will find that he will make your work successful. And, as a sign of your thanksgiving for God's blessing, one of the things that you could do is to tithe your income so that a tenth is given to the work of God.

Key thought: Giving part of our income to God is a way of thanking him for his blessings.

Loving Father, we all want to succeed at work and we believe that you will lay these insights from your Word upon our hearts, that we might have your blessing in our daily life. Through Christ our Lord. Amen.

What Do You Want Out of Life?: I want to be forgiven – 1

'"Forgive us our debts, as we also have forgiven our debtors."'

—Matthew 6:12

Scripture reading: Isaiah 53

There is one thing we all want out of life at one time or another. We want to be forgiven—forgiven by God, forgiven by others and, not least, forgiven by ourselves.

The forgiveness of God is a central theme in Christianity. Assuming that we do what is required of us, we have repeated assurances in Scripture that we are forgiven by God.

By and large, people think that, because they obey the Golden Rule or because they would not do a bad turn if they could do a good one, this will make them right with God. That is not the Christian position.

The Christian position is that we all fall short of what God requires, and that we need to be forgiven. What Christ has so wonderfully done on the cross is to provide for God's forgiveness if we will admit our need and draw on that forgiveness by faith. We can be sure we are forgiven by God, simply because we have accepted his forgiveness in the same way in which we would accept any gift.

We must look at things in a balanced way and go on and say that, if we draw on forgiveness from God, it carries with it an obligation to forgive others. Indeed, our Lord said that if we do not forgive others in the way we have been forgiven, we will not be forgiven by God (see Matthew 6:15).

Key thought: We all want to be forgiven by God.

Dear Father, we are full of praise and gratitude that you have forgiven us our sins and shortcomings. We remember what Jesus has done for us on the cross and accept your forgiveness with deep thanksgiving. Amen.

What Do You Want Out of Life?: I want to be forgiven – 2

'"if you are offering your gift at the altar and there remember that your brother has something against you, leave your gift there in front of the altar. First go and be reconciled to your brother; then come and offer your gift."'   —Matthew 5:23, 24

Scripture reading: Colossians 3

Let us accept forgiveness from God and have an assurance that this is what we have drawn on. Let us also remember the words of our Lord that, just as we have been forgiven, so we must forgive others. That is the evidence of sincerity that God is looking for.

There is a second aspect to forgiveness—we want to be forgiven by others. This is part of the forgiveness story. If someone has something against us—which means we have offended that person—then we must realise this and act on it. It is important to know that the responsibility lies with us. Jesus said that, if someone has something against me, it is my duty to go to that person and seek reconciliation.

This might not be easy to do. It is never easy to go to others and ask to be forgiven—to admit that one has done something that is wrong and caused offence. It is so easy to justify one's position and say, 'I only did what was reasonable'. Nevertheless, we have an obligation to seek the forgiveness of others where we know it is appropriate. We may have to make restitution to bring about a heart-reconciliation on both sides. That is part of being forgiven.

Key thought: We must be prepared to forgive those who have sinned against us.

Our loving Father, we praise you that we are forgiven because of Christ and his shed blood. Give us wisdom to know when we need to ask the forgiveness of others. Enable us to be sensitive as we seek reconciliation. For Jesus' sake. Amen.

What Do You Want Out of Life?: I want to be forgiven – 3

'"So if the Son sets you free, you will be free indeed."' —John 8:36

Scripture reading: John 8:31–40

The third aspect of forgiveness—our need to forgive ourselves—is very important. If something goes wrong, we might find this very difficult because we tend to think the worst about ourselves.

I once knew a lady who had done something wrong. She had appropriated God's forgiveness by faith and she had been forgiven by others who were involved, but her insecurity on one hand and her guilt on the other were such that she could not forgive herself. As a result, she slowly worried herself into a nervous breakdown and ended up going to a psychiatrist.

She was fortunate in choosing a Christian psychiatrist who told her, 'Your real need is to forgive yourself', and she said, 'I have tried, but I can't'. He said: 'Let us kneel down; you confess your fault to God and then I am going to add my faith to yours—that you are forgiven all the way through, including forgiving yourself'.

The lady prayed her part and then the psychiatrist said a prayer something like this: 'Lord, thank you that you promise to forgive all the way through, and I now add my faith to my sister's faith that she is forgiven and that she forgives herself, because of Christ and by the Holy Spirit. I believe this with her and for her.'

The lady told me that, from then on, all the feeling of self-guilt rolled away.

Key thought: If we can't forgive ourselves, we need to go to some trusted and informed person who will add his or her faith to ours, so that we experience forgiveness all the way through.

Our loving Father, we believe that you have forgiven us our sins and failures and that Jesus has set us free. By your grace we now forgive ourselves. Through Jesus Christ our Lord. Amen.

What Do You Want Out of Life?: I want a new start – 1

'"Forget the former things; do not dwell on the past. See, I am doing a new thing!"' —Isaiah 43:18,19

Scripture reading: 1 Corinthians 15:3–11

A man who had been an alcoholic once told me, 'No-one can be given a new start unless they want a new start'. He had been an alcoholic and had been healed of that problem, and other problems too, through Alcoholics Anonymous.

When I was in America I visited the great work of Teen Challenge in New York. Don Wilkerson, the brother of David, invited me to go with him to interview a man who was a drug addict. I always remember Don Wilkerson saying to the man, 'Do you want a new start?'. There was a sense in which the man did want to break away from his destructive habits but they had him too strongly in their grasp, and he finally said, 'No'. We had to leave him because he didn't want to be helped at that time. I have never ceased to pray for this man and to believe that God enabled him, at a later time, to come to the point of wanting a new start.

To want a new start means we have to come to the point where we know our lives are in a mess. We are at the end of our tether and no longer have answers that meet our need. It is not easy to make that admission but, if God is going to help us work things out, we need to be in the position where there is only God to depend on.

Key thought: We have to want a new start in life before we can have it.

Father, some of us need a new start in life. We want it, deep down, and admit our great need. Help us as we depend on you; enable us to draw on all your provision. Through Jesus, our Lord. Amen.

What Do You Want Out of Life?: I want a new start – 2

'You have made known to me the paths of life; you will fill me with joy in your presence.'
— Acts 2:28

Scripture reading: Acts 9:1–6

Why is it that we have to be in a mess before we can have a new start? I personally believe one of the reasons is because the Bible says, 'no flesh should glory in his presence' (1 Corinthians 1:29 KJV). No-one is going to say to God on the Day of Judgement that he, or she, has contributed by one jot or tittle to what God has done.

At one time or another in our lives we all come to the point where we know we haven't got the answer and we have to leave it to God. We have found that, when this happens, phoenix-like, a new life arises from the ashes and we have new opportunities.

When we do come to this point we find that, in a most wonderful way, God does the work: God gives us a new vision; God gives us new power; God gives us a new start. It is no longer what *we* are doing. That is why it is easy. It is what God is doing. For this reason Paul says, ' ... when I am weak, then I am strong' (2 Corinthians 12:10). He means that when we have no ability to carry on, God's strength is released in us and through us. He gives us help in the way we need. It is a whole new ball game which God provides.

Key thought: When we are at our wit's end, God is there to help.

Dear Father, we praise and thank you for your provision for us, but feel we have come to the end of our tether. Come, Holy Spirit, and teach us to learn to depend on God more. In Jesus' name, we pray. Amen.

What Do You Want Out of Life?: I want a new start – 3

'But God was with him and rescued him from all his troubles.'
—Acts 7:9,10

Scripture reading: Acts 7:1–10

When we come to the end of our self-dependency and depend only on God, it doesn't mean we won't have any more difficulties. Anyone who is walking closer with God would say that things can become even more difficult. Not only is the Spirit of God stirred up but there is a sense in which Satan is stirred up as well—the Bible says he 'prowls around like a roaring lion looking for someone to devour' (1 Peter 5:8). Notwithstanding, when God comes in with his new start there is a new effectiveness in ministry; a new increase of the Kingdom; a new joy and peace in believing; a new reality of the Holy Spirit and a new love for our Lord Jesus Christ. We draw upon healing and wholeness for ourselves, and for other people.

These blessings become so much of a reality that we ultimately thank God for our difficulties, including those very circumstances which brought us to the point where we were in a mess and had no answers. Not that the problems were good in themselves. The Bible doesn't say that; they may have come from the devil but *they work together for good* (see Romans 8:28).

Thank God, a new start is part of the Christian resource; a new start at certain crucial times in our lives; a new start every day—time by time and circumstance by circumstance. This is what God is saying to us.

Key thought: God turns our difficulties around so that they work out for our good.

Thank you, loving Father, for the blessing of a new start. We accept it and believe for it. Through Christ and by the Holy Spirit. Amen.

The Occult and Deliverance – 1

"'Do not turn to mediums or seek out spiritists, for you will be defiled by them. I am the LORD your God.'"   —Leviticus 19:31

Scripture reading: Acts 13:4–12

Recently, a couple was referred to me because of strange happenings in their home. Furniture was moving; crockery was being thrown from one part of a room to another; there were eerie and unexplained noises and the feeling that someone was there. The couple was frightened by these happenings and they had no idea what to do. I asked if they had had any contact with the occult, and they said that, four years earlier, the man had used what is called a ouija board. Since that time things had been going wrong.

I have had a low-key involvement in this kind of ministry for nearly twenty years and have no hesitation in saying that, as far as my knowledge and experience goes, this kind of thing is increasing. The explanation is that, consequent upon the flight from true religion where we worship the active presence of Father, Son and Holy Spirit, a vacuum has been created whereby wrong spirit-forces are being released through activities which, in effect, are calling them up. Those activities, and the manifestations which come from them, are called the occult. The Bible warns that Satan may come disguised as 'an angel of light' (2 Corinthians 11:14) and deceive even the elect of God (see Matthew 24:24).

When people involve themselves in occult activity—in ouija boards, water-divining, horoscopes, séances, spiritism, fortune-telling and the like—something happens that is beyond any human explanation. Things don't always go wrong but, when they do, my experience is that it can be traced back to this kind of activity.

Key thought: God forbids any involvement with the occult.

We praise you, Father, that Satan is a defeated foe and that through the blood of Jesus we are delivered from all his power. Amen.

The Occult and Deliverance – 2

'Jesus said to him, "Away from me, Satan! For it is written: 'Worship the LORD your God, and serve him only.'"'   —Matthew 4:10

Scripture reading: Acts 19:11–20

I want to strongly advise against amateur deliverance ministries. I assure you that it is easier to make things worse than it is to make them better. Once the devil has got his grip it takes all the experience and all the resource you can lay your hands on to make yourself free or to obtain deliverance for another person. Only go to someone who can be trusted, who is experienced, and who will draw upon the faith and wisdom of the Church.

Having said that, I want to emphasise that not all unusual problems are caused by this kind of thing. People have sometimes been referred to me because they were supposed to be demon-possessed, but I would find that the problem they had was nothing to do with what I am talking about. It just needed someone to understand emotional behaviour and the things that can go wrong. Again, you need to go to someone who is able to help in an informed way.

If you have had contact with occult activity, I urge you, in the name of Christ, to repent. Turn from it! Have nothing to do with it! Leave it behind! Put your whole trust in Christ as Saviour and worship him as Lord in your life. Depend only on the ministry of the Holy Spirit, in fellowship with the Church.

Key thought: Repent of any involvement with the occult. Put your whole trust in Christ as Saviour.

Father, we turn from any occult activity we have shared in and totally repudiate those things. We believe you are loosing us from any inroads that Satan has made. We depend only on Christ and affirm the protection of the armour of God and, above all, the shield of faith wherewith we quench the fiery darts of the wicked one. Amen.

Divine Healing: Why some people are not healed – 1

'O LORD my God, I called to you for help and you healed me.'
—Psalm 30:2

Scripture reading: 2 Timothy 2:14–21

Why are some people not healed? There is a lot that could be said about this. One of the reasons is that people have been fed the idea that, because Paul asked for healing three times and God said to him, 'My grace is sufficient for you' (2 Corinthians 12:9) it might not be God's will for them to be healed.

However, Paul had responsibilities in the early Church that were more than we can fully understand. He was the Apostle to the Gentiles. To equip him for this unique ministry, the Bible says he was given 'visions and revelations from the Lord'; that he 'was caught up to Paradise' and 'heard inexpressible things, things that man is not permitted to tell' (2 Corinthians 12:1,4). Paul said it was to prevent him from becoming proud because of this unique experience, that he was given a 'thorn in my flesh' (v. 7).

It is bad Bible exegesis to make a general deduction from a unique premise but, unfortunately, this is what we so often do. We should realise that Paul's sickness, if it was a sickness, was because of a unique set of circumstances which do not apply to us.[1]

I suggest that, when we correctly understand Paul's 'thorn' and then read the gospels to get a general teaching about healing which God reveals to us in Christ, we see that, without any exceptions whatsoever, God wills us to be healed. Jesus healed all who came to him. If only people would be sure that God wanted them to be healed, they would be halfway to experiencing the healing.

Key thought: Jesus healed all who came to him.

We praise you, Heavenly Father, that it is your will to heal us, and we accept your blessing now. Through Christ our Lord. Amen.

---

[1] For a fuller version of Canon Glennon's teaching on 'Paul's thorn', see chapter 10 of his book, *Your Healing Is Within You.*

Divine Healing: Why some people are not healed – 2

' all of them were healed.'　　　　　　　　　　　—Acts 5:16

Scripture reading: Matthew 4:18–25

Another reason why some are not healed is because there isn't faith in the Church. Let me explain this.

I want to make it completely clear that it is unscriptural to tell a person who is sick, and who is not healed, that it is because of lack of faith, nor is it scriptural to say to the family of such a person—a husband, a wife or a parent—that it is because they don't believe in the right way

When an epileptic boy was not healed by the disciples, his father brought him to Jesus and said, 'Your followers prayed for him but he wasn't healed. I'm bringing him to you' (see Matthew 17:15,16). Then Jesus healed the boy. It is important to notice that Jesus didn't say to the person who was sick, 'You haven't got enough faith'; nor did he say to the father, 'You haven't got enough faith'; Jesus said to the other people who had prayed for the boy, 'YOU haven't got enough faith'.

So often, unfortunately, there isn't faith in the Church for healing. It is something which congregations would know little about. I am not wanting to make a critical or negative point, only to say we need to realise this is a potent reason why some people are not healed; we haven't a believing Church as far as divine healing is concerned.

It is the prayer of the Church, the Christians, that is the vehicle of faith for the person to be healed. If the person is not healed, God says it is because of lack of faith on the part of those who pray for the person— that is, the Church or the congregation.

Key thought: The Church has the responsibility to exercise faith for the healing of the sick.

Thank you, Father, that you have provided the body of believers, the Church, to exercise faith for our healing. Amen.

Divine Healing: Why some people are not healed – 3

'After he had dismissed them, he went up into the hills by himself to pray.'
—Matthew 14:23

Scripture reading: Matthew 14:22–36

Even though we may be convinced it is God's will to heal, and even though the Prayer of Faith might be prayed by the Church, it could still happen that the person is not healed. Why? Jesus said, 'this kind goeth not out but by prayer and fasting' (Matthew 17:21 KJV). In effect, what he is saying is that this particular problem was a bigger 'mountain' to be moved; the sickness was more advanced; the boy had had this problem all his life and a greater reality of believing prayer was necessary.

Here is a story to make my point. A friend of mine, an Anglican clergyman in another diocese, was asked if his church congregation would join in prayer for someone who was sick. My friend, because he believes in the healing ministry, summoned the church together that they might pray for the sick person. They held a very meaningful service of divine healing. At the end of the service the person wasn't healed. The Anglicans felt they had 'fulfilled all righteousness'—they had prayed the Prayer of Faith—and they went home. Now, there was at the service a group of people who belonged to the Pentecostal Church; they stayed on and prayed for the sick person all night. The next day some other Pentecostal people came along and took over, as it were, and they prayed all day. Still the person wasn't healed and then they came back and again prayed all night. Then the person was healed.

Key thought: Persistence in prayer is necessary.

We praise and thank you, Father, that you enable us by your grace and the power of the Holy Spirit to go deeper into prayer for our own needs, and for the needs of others. Amen.

Practical Help for Your Daily Prayer:

The Prayer of Faith in slow motion – 1

'For no matter how many promises God has made, they are "Yes" in Christ. And so through him the "Amen" is spoken by us to the glory of God.' —2 Corinthians 1:20

Scripture reading: Mark 5:24b–34

Tonight I want to speak about 'The Prayer of Faith in slow motion'. Jesus said, '"According to your faith will it be done to you"' (Matthew 9:29). It is good to be able to understand in a succinct form what we mean by the Prayer of Faith.

The first thing I want to say is that we have to know about the promises of God because all the promises of God reveal the will of God in the here-and-now Kingdom. That is a sentence worth remembering, for it contains a great deal of insight, help and truth. The Bible says that God has made 'very great and precious promises' through which we 'may participate in the divine nature' (2 Peter 1:4); it also says that the promises have their 'Yes' and 'Amen' in Christ (2 Corinthians 1:20).

We search the Scriptures so that we might know what are the broad themes of scriptural promise. It hardly needs me to say that healing is one of the broad themes of scriptural promise; it runs right throughout the New Testament, and one promise that is immensely relevant to us is in James 5:15: 'The prayer offered in faith will make the sick person well'. That is a promise as clear and as definite and as easily understood as any promise in Scripture. This is step one, which is relevant not only to prayer for healing, but prayer for anything—we are to know what God has promised to give, for the promises of God reveal the will of God in the here-and-now Kingdom.

Key thought: The promises of God reveal the will of God.

We thank and praise you, Father, that healing is your perfect will for us in Jesus Christ our Lord. Amen.

Practical Help for Your Daily Prayer:

The Prayer of Faith in slow motion – 2

'I do not hide your righteousness in my heart; I speak of your faithfulness and salvation.'
—Psalm 40:10

Scripture reading: Psalm 40

The second thing I want to say concerns the exercise of faith itself. Someone came to me the other day and he said something like this, 'I have prayed the Prayer of Faith for healing, but I'm not healed yet'. In a nice way I said to him, 'Well, if you continue to pray like that, you are not going to be healed in a hundred years'. Of course, I went on to explain where he was inadequate in his understanding and practice of faith. I told him about my conversion as a late teenager when I believed that Christ had come into my life and how, after some weeks, I went to the rector and said, 'Rector, I'm praying to be saved, but nothing has happened,' and he said to me, 'Jim, you will never be converted like that—not in a hundred years'.

When we believe on Christ for salvation we are taught to say, and rightly so, 'I am saved'. When the rector taught me to say 'I am saved', I then said, 'But I'm no different'. He then said that I was to affirm: 'I am saved, *by faith*'. That made all the difference. I stopped saying, 'I am praying to be saved, but I am not saved yet'. On the contrary, I believed I had received these things—in this case salvation—and I affirmed it by faith.

Key thought: The Prayer of Faith means that you believe a promise of God and affirm that you have it.

Our loving Father, we thank you for your promises, and that we are to be partakers of them. We thank you for faith, whereby we believe that we have received these things. In Jesus' name. Amen.

Practical Help for Your Daily Prayer:

The Prayer of Faith in slow motion – 3

'Continue in prayer, and watch in the same with thanksgiving'
—Colossians 4:2 (KJV)

Scripture reading: Psalm 95

The third aspect of the Prayer of Faith has to do with thanksgiving. There is only one instruction in the New Testament about how we are to continue in prayer. It is found in Colossians 4:2, 'Devote yourselves to prayer, being watchful and thankful'. To begin with, we are thanking God before we have the blessing by sight. The Bible, in Hebrews 11:6, says that without this kind of faith it is impossible to please him. However, we are also looking for answers to prayer; first the blade, then the ear, then the full corn (see Mark 4:28 KJV), but whether it be that we are thanking God by faith, or whether it be we are thanking God for the blade—let alone the ear and the full corn—the way we continue in prayer is by thanksgiving.

When you have the laying on of hands for healing for the first time, it means that you accept healing. If you ask for the laying on of hands on a subsequent occasion, it means that you are thanking God by faith to begin with, then, increasingly, by sight—first the blade, then the ear. That is what your ongoing prayer is all about; it is about thanksgiving.

These, then, are the principles of the Prayer of Faith—the promises of God; the Prayer of Faith itself, and watching in the same with thanksgiving. Promises, faith, thanksgiving.

Key thought: We are to continue in prayer, thanking God by faith for the answer.

Our loving Father, we thank you that we can have a succinct and clear statement of what we understand by the Prayer of Faith. And we thank you that we are to praise your name with thanksgiving, both by faith and by sight, and we do that now. In Jesus' name. Amen.

Practical Help for Your Daily Prayer:

How to avoid 'striving' in prayer – 1

'Then Jesus told him [Thomas], "Because you have seen me, you have believed; blessed are those who have not seen and yet have believed."'

—John 20:29

Scripture reading: Psalm 55:16–23

Even when we have the principles of prayer right, we might find ourselves *striving* to have faith, and that is counterproductive.

When, on the last Wednesday of September 1960, we began the Healing Ministry in the Cathedral, what happened by way of answered prayer and people being healed was straight out of the New Testament. We believed, and we left it to God, and the blessing was there. But within six months the wonderful blessings with which we had begun were tapering off. Why? As I look back on it, I realise that what we were doing was developing a kind of self-effort to make the problems go away. Our fallen human nature, the very reality for which we needed blessing and prayed for blessing, caused us to begin to try to generate faith. But no flesh will glory in his sight. All we can do is to 'let go and let God'. How, then, can we pray the Prayer of Faith so that our fallen human nature, which cannot help but want to strive, does not get in the way?

I want to emphasise that the first requirement, if we are going to pray the Prayer of Faith and not strive, is to know that God has taken the problem away. I would refer, in particular, to 1 Peter 2:24: 'He himself [Jesus] bore our sins in his body on the tree, so that we might die to sins and live for righteousness; by his wounds you have been healed'.

Key thought: We must not try to *make* things happen.

Forgive us, Father, when we try to make things happen by our own efforts. Help us, in simple faith, to believe you and give you the glory. In Jesus' name. Amen.

Practical Help for Your Daily Prayer:

How to avoid 'striving' in prayer – 2

'"The kingdom of heaven is like treasure hidden in a field. When a man found it, he hid it again, and then in his joy went and sold all he had and bought that field."'   —Matthew 13:44

Scripture reading: John 1:29–34

When God made things in the beginning, he saw that they were good. That is what God is like—he creates what is good; his will is good; his provision is good. But man stepped outside the limitations that God had placed around him, and so we have coming into reality what the Bible calls 'the sin of the world'.

The sin of the world is the root cause of all our disharmony and disease—let it take what form it may. Jesus came in the fullness of time to take away the sin of the world. When, on the cross, he cried out, 'My God, my God, why have you forsaken me?' it meant he was paying the price of the sin of the world, which is separation from God. And, when at the end he said, 'It is finished!', he meant that the sacrifice for sin had been made; nothing more could, or need, be added to it—it was finished.

In the Healing Ministry we affirm that the problem has been taken away because Jesus took the sin of the world upon himself, and because the Bible says that we have been healed 'by his wounds'. If you are going to pray the Prayer of Faith without striving, then know of a surety that Jesus has taken away the problem. He took it away 2,000 years ago and we are appropriating that now.

Key thought: Jesus has taken away the sin of the world.

Our loving Father, we thank you that Jesus came to take away the sin of the world and that he has taken upon himself our sickness and our infirmity. Praise God! Amen.

Practical Help for Your Daily Prayer:

How to avoid 'striving' in prayer – 3

'"Heal the sick who are there and tell them, 'The kingdom of God is near you.'"'
                                                                    —Luke 10:9.

Scripture reading: Luke 9:1–6

We need to know that Jesus has taken away the sin of the world and that the sin of the world is the root cause of our sickness and infirmity. We also need to know that, because we have been reconciled to the Father if we trust in Christ, the Kingdom has been restored to us. Healing is one of the signs of the Kingdom and is available to us now. The Kingdom is not far away; we do not have to ask for it; the Kingdom order has been restored to us and is within us now.

We affirm this by faith. We believe it before we have it. The Bible says that 'faith is being sure of what we hope for and certain of what we do not see' (Hebrews 11:1). You have to believe it before you have it because the Bible also says that without faith—without believing what God has done before we have it in reality—we cannot please him (see Hebrews 11:6).

We know the problem has been taken away; we know the Kingdom order has been re-established; we accept this for ourselves and we affirm it by faith. That is why we do not have to strive. We are just resting in what God has done in Christ. That is what enables our prayer to be answered so that faith becomes reality—if not straightaway, then first the blade, then the ear.

Key thought: Faith means that we rest in the finished work of Christ and leave it all to God.

Dear Father, we want to be those who please you by believing your Word and affirming it by faith. Help us to live by faith and not by sight. Help us not to strive in prayer but to rest in what you have done in Christ. Amen.

Practical Help for Your Daily Prayer:

How to avoid 'striving' in prayer – 4

'"when the Son of Man comes, will he find faith on the earth?"'

—Luke 18:8

Scripture reading: Psalm 61

Let me tell you a story. A woman with cancer in both breasts—one breast as hard as stone, swollen so that at any moment the skin might rupture—her tummy swollen with cancer fluid, her eyes sunken—accepts that Jesus has taken it away (by his wounds we have been healed) and that God has restored his Kingdom order, of which healing is a sign. She accepts it and rests in it. Perhaps it is important to say she rests in it hour after hour. It becomes the way she lives and moves and has her being—not striving but resting. The breasts soften; the stomach returns to its normal shape; her face fills out; strength returns. A miracle!

But then—so often it is when you have blessing that self rises up—without realising what she is doing, she begins to try to make it go away. There is a complete relapse. The cancer comes back again as it was to begin with. But at least she realises where she has gone wrong—instead of just resting in the finished work of Christ she had begun striving. She learned her lesson and returned to the 'rest of faith', affirming: 'God has done it all. I accept it and I rest in it'. The cancer regresses again! Doesn't that grip you? It does me. He has done it all. The Kingdom order has been restored. We affirm it by faith and we *rest in faith*. That is how you avoid striving and that is how you have the blessing of God.

Key thought: God has done it all. We accept it, and we rest in it.

Our loving Father, we take this to ourselves in a new way—heartened and chastened, instructed, built up—that we might rest in faith. Amen.

Learn to Pray: Repentance, Faith, Obedience – 1

[John] 'went into all the country around the Jordan, preaching a baptism of repentance for the forgiveness of sins.' —Luke 3:3

Scripture reading: Luke 3:7–18

Jesus, in his death, took our sickness and our infirmity upon himself (Isaiah 53:4,5) and we are to believe that what otherwise is our problem has died with Christ. As a result we affirm in a single-minded way, the Kingdom healing, the Kingdom perfection.

If you are going to pray effectively, the first requirement is to know what God has provided. The second requirement, complementing the first, is to know what we have to do to appropriate his blessing.

You often hear people saying in a casual way that they are 'praying about' something. Well, I am not rubbishing that. I am sure anything that is called Christian prayer is valuable and used by God, but I wish I could pick up from them that they are praying in an informed way — that is, that they are doing the things that God says we have to do. God has done his part through Christ. We must do our part. Our part is to *repent*; to *believe* and to *obey*. Those are the three things we have to do, in an informed way, so that we pray effectively in drawing on what God has provided.

What do we mean by repentance in the context of prayer? I will refer to those things that are especially relevant to people who wish to draw upon healing. They have to repent of *fear* and *resentment*. If you have not done that, this is what is meant by repentance as far as you are concerned.

Key thought: Our part in accepting God's provision is to repent.

Dear Father, we have often been afraid instead of trusting you, and we have often harboured resentment against others. We repent and are sorry for all our sins. Forgive us and cleanse us through the blood of Christ, we pray. Amen.

Learn to Pray: Repentance, Faith, Obedience – 2

*'The life I live in the body, I live by faith in the Son of God, who loved me
and gave himself for me.'*   —Galatians 2:20

Scripture reading: Galatians 3:1–9

The late Father John Hope was a true pathfinder for the Christian
healing ministry in this country. He had a marvellous healing ministry
in Sydney for forty years before we had ever thought about it here at
the Cathedral. He said he had never known anyone to be healed who
was afraid he would *not* be healed. Fear is the great enemy of faith; it
negates faith. You have to repent of fear by replacing it with what God
provides—power, love and soundness of mind (see 2 Timothy 1:7). To
turn from fear to power and love and soundness of mind is repentance.
It is turning from what is wrong to what is right.

As far as resentment is concerned, you overcome resentment by
forgiving other people who have wronged you, and, as you know, this
is constantly emphasised in the context of our healing services.

Let us now consider faith. We exercise faith according to what Christ
has said in Mark chapter 11: '"I tell you the truth, if anyone says to this
mountain, 'Go, throw yourself into the sea,' and does not doubt in his
heart but believes that what he says will happen, it will be done for him.
Therefore I tell you, whatever you ask for in prayer, believe that you have
received it, and it will be yours".' (vv. 23,24).

If you are not quite sure how to do this, remember how you exercise
faith for conversion—where you believe you have received Christ so
you do not doubt—and then apply the same principle in the current
situation.

Key thought: If we believe, Jesus said, our requests will be granted.

*Help us, Holy Spirit of God, to follow Jesus' guidelines in the exercise of
faith.*

Learn to Pray: Repentance, Faith, Obedience – 3

'As obedient children, do not conform to the evil desires you had when you lived in ignorance ... for it is written: "Be holy, because I am holy."'

— 1 Peter 1:14,15

Scripture reading: Matthew 21:28–32

Finally there is obedience: William Temple, a great Archbishop of Canterbury, had a piece of doggerel that expressed what he wanted to say about obedience. He said: 'It's not enough to say "I'm sorry and repent" and then to go on afterwards just as I always went'. Repentance and faith need to have ongoing expression in obedience.

Part of obedience is to always react to the problem in terms of faith. You can always gauge what sort of faith you have by how you react when the matter about which you are praying comes to mind. If you react in terms of the problem with: 'Oh dear me!', then that is your faith. But, if you have disciplined your mind to react by praising God with a full heart, then that is your faith that moves the mountain, and that is part of what is meant by obedience.

When you have your prayer time, get your mind working in an effective way. Put on your 'thinking cap'. Step 1: What has God provided? Step 2: What have I to do to make it mine? You have to repent, you have to believe, and you have to obey; when you are doing that meaningfully and effectively, you are not only praying, but your praying is moving the mountain. Praise God!

Our loving Father, we thank you for this teaching. We thank you for what you have provided—the Kingdom blessing. Bless us that we will pray in a truly informed way; that we will repent and believe and obey. We do that now, through Christ our Lord, Amen.

Take Off Your Label of Sickness – 1

'to bestow on them … a garment of praise instead of a spirit of despair.'
—Isaiah 61:3

Scripture reading: Psalm 86:1–13

A friend of mine who is both a medical practitioner and a clergyman, said that, when he had been told by his doctor that the results of his medical examination revealed that he had cancer, he felt 'the death sentence had been pronounced'.

This is often the reaction people have when they are given bad news—and not only about cancer, but about any condition where no medical resource or human aid can be effectively given.

In such circumstances, a person who is involved in the healing ministry of the Church affirms healing by faith, but, with conditions that are so serious, where 'the death sentence has been pronounced' or 'the bone has been pointed', often the healing ministry does not work. And so the question we need to ask ourselves is: Why?

It is not enough, as far as I am concerned, to set the matter aside and say: 'Well, they drew upon a blessing of the Spirit'. They might well have drawn upon a blessing of the Spirit but if we are going to go further in our understanding of the healing ministry so that we make it more effective, we need to ask: Why? Well, I can give at least part of the answer in one sentence: It has not worked because they have taken the problem into themselves so that it is what they accept about themselves. They make it alive; they keep it alive, and so it does its destructive work.

Key thought: We must not accept the problem.

Father, we turn from that death sentence. We turn away that pointed bone. We invoke what Christ has done and we cast the burden on the cross and believe that it will remain there. We affirm the Kingdom perfection, and that alone, in praise and in Jesus' name. Amen.

Take Off Your Label of Sickness – 2

'Surely he took up our infirmities and carried our sorrows'—Isaiah 53:4

Scripture reading: Matthew 8:14–17

We must not take a problem into ourselves so that we accept it. This does not mean we are to ignore the problem. That would be the height of foolishness and irresponsibility. Face the problem square on and take what remedial action is available—but do not take it into yourself so that you make it alive, for as long as it is alive to you the destructiveness of it is alive as well.

We are to know, and believe, that Jesus took our sickness and infirmity upon himself (see Matthew 8:17, Isaiah 53:4). You do not take the problem into yourself because you affirm that it died with Christ. This is the Healing Ministry position.

You affirm this by faith. Again, this is where you have to know what the Bible says. There are no marks for being ignorant. Search the Scriptures so that you know what God has revealed, what God has said. What does God say about faith?— 'faith is the substance of things hoped for, the evidence of things not seen' (Hebrews 11:1 KJV); this means that the things which you see are the things you see—but that is not faith. Faith is not what you see. Faith is what you hope for, and what you believe you have received so that you do not doubt. And the Bible says again, the Christian lives by faith, not by sight (see 2 Corinthians 5:7). We affirm that the sickness and the infirmity has died with Christ and we believe it before we have it in reality—to the point where we do not doubt.

Key thought: Jesus has dealt with the problem on the cross. Leave it with him, and don't take it back!

Help us, Holy Spirit, to take the problem to Jesus and to leave it with him. Amen.

Take Off Your Label of Sickness – 3

'"Do not be afraid, Daniel. Since the first day that you set your mind to gain understanding and to humble yourself before your God, your words were heard"'   —Daniel 10:12

Scripture reading: 2 Corinthians 5:14–21

Put on your thinking cap when faced with difficulty; don't panic and lose your head; you might lose your life. Know what Christ has done; accept that reality in your inner spirit and affirm it by faith. You are getting rid of the negative reality so that old things have passed away, and in their place you have a positive reality. You are dead to the problem and alive to the answer. The Kingdom reality is God's perfect blessing; it is healing, it is wholeness; it is newness.

You discipline your mind to make this affirmation. I was doing this only yesterday and today. Instead of affirming a problem, say instead: 'I have the Kingdom reality only'. When you believe this for others, say the same thing: 'I take off the label of sickness; I affirm it has died with Christ, and on their behalf I say, by faith, that he/she has the Kingdom reality, the Kingdom healing only'.

If you would have a ministry of the Spirit so that you know these things, not only with your mind, but in your heart, then, like Daniel, set your heart to understand. You will need to have God make it real to you. Then the lethal aspect referred to earlier does not apply. And that is healing.

Key thought: Old things have passed away; all things have become new.

God, I believe you are making these things real to me, so I know the problem has died with Christ; so I know I have the kingdom reality; so I am affirming the answer only.

Let God Help You With Your Finances – 1

'Therefore I tell you, do not worry about your life, what you will eat; or about your body, what you will wear.' —Luke 12:22

Scripture reading: Luke 12:22–31

Jesus tells us we should not become worried and stressed about our need for food and clothing. As former Archbishop of Canterbury, William Temple, once said, Christianity, more than any other religion, is concerned with material things. This is something we need to know; we must understand what is meant, what is appropriate, and what is available. I can sum up my own understanding of this by saying: it concerns need, not greed.

I am not referring here to what is sometimes called 'prosperity Christianity' but to the financial needs and responsibilities we all have. Every family is concerned with the need to balance the budget. Parents are responsible for providing for their children. Those in business have to be concerned with profit and loss and, not least, those who are on a pension or a retirement income are very much concerned with finances. I am talking about meeting our material needs in a balanced, honest way.

We need to know that our heavenly Father is directly and absolutely committed to caring and providing for our every material need. Jesus illustrates this in a simple but graphic way when he says: 'even the very hairs of your head are all numbered' (Matthew 10:30). That is what God's concern for us is like.

The question is: how can we so relate to God that he will meet our material needs? The first thing you have to know is that we are to be dead to the problem—the shortage of money—which died with Christ on the cross, and alive to the Kingdom righteousness and perfection that God has restored to us (see 1 Peter 2:24).

Key thought: God's great love for us is beyond our understanding.

Father, we believe Jesus' assurance that you care for us and we believe for your provision in all things.

Let God Help You With Your Finances – 2

'Do not be anxious about anything'   —Philippians 4:6

Scripture reading: Philippians 4:4–20

Some five years ago I bought a unit intending to live there in my retirement. It so happened that I changed my mind about living there and I am now due to pay back the money I borrowed which enabled me to purchase the unit.

I had thought that, over the years, the unit would appreciate in value but, instead, I found it was worth $12,000 less than the purchase price. I was offered this amount and was advised to accept the offer and cut my losses. I was disappointed, but sought to put into practice the very things I am sharing with you now. I affirmed that the shortage died with Christ. I reacted to the situation by affirming the Kingdom provisions for my real-life situation.

I was at the end of my tether when someone came forward and offered to buy my unit for $10,000 more than I had been offered. The first person then matched this offer, whereupon the second person offered another $1,000—then the first person withdrew. In other words, I am getting only $1,000 less than what I paid for it and have been praising God because I believe it is part of the Kingdom provision to meet our material needs.

Don't take the problem into yourself; remember it died with Christ and you are to be alive to one thing only—the perfection of God. Get that right and everything else will be brought into line with what God has provided and with what you are believing for by faith and in praise.

Key thought: God meets our material needs.

Our loving Father, we thank you for the blessed provision that has come from the work of Christ and we would be alive to the Kingdom and its righteousness that you might meet our every material need for the glory and the increase of your Kingdom. For Jesus' sake. Amen.

Are You Spiritually Dry? – 1

' be clear minded and self-controlled so that you can pray.'— 1 Peter 4:7

Scripture reading: 2 Timothy 1:1–14

A potent reason why committed Christians can be spiritually dry is because they are overactive—overactive in doing the work of God!

I once knew a Christian doctor who said something to me that I have never forgotten. He said that, if he is too busy, he knows he is out of the will of God. I asked him how this could happen. He replied that it was like a dog chasing its tail. Which comes first? You are too busy, therefore your prayer time suffers—or is it that your prayer time suffers and then you are too busy? Whichever it is, he said, there is a connection.

That is my experience, too. I often find I am too busy, and what I want to say is—if you are too busy, it is because you do not spend enough time with God. Because you are too busy, and therefore to that degree out of the will of God, you will grieve—you will even quench—the Spirit. You will be spiritually dry.

So you have to go back to the reason—you need to pray more. If you pray enough, and the Spirit is being stirred up and poured out, you will not be over-busy. Do you see the positive corollary? If you are praying enough, and meaningfully enough, you will not be too busy. The Lord will so order your steps that the Spirit is stirred up and flows out, and you will not in any way run dry. Don't become too active, too busy, and, if you are, pray more; this will get things ticking over in the way they should.

Key thought: Lack of prayer can lead to spiritual dryness.

Thank you, Father, that we can come to you in prayer. Help us to make time to pray. Amen.

Are You Spiritually Dry? – 2

'Dear friends, if our hearts do not condemn us, we have confidence before God and receive from him anything we ask, because we obey his commands and do what pleases him.' —1 John 3:21,22

Scripture reading: 2 Samuel 12:1–13

Sin can be another cause of spiritual dryness. If you are doing something that is out of the will of God and different from what is God's will and provision for you, you will, of course, run dry spiritually. We must keep a clear conscience, both in our relationship with God and our relationships with everybody else.

Sex is one area where there can be sin—in adultery, in fornication. Adultery means that a married person is having sex with someone outside the marriage bond. Fornication means that you are not married, but are having sex with someone—obviously outside the marriage bond. But it isn't just about those who are having sex in a wrong way physically, because Jesus laid it on the line when he said you are sinning just as much if you entertain lust in your mind. So it applies to us all.

Sexual sin will make you and me run dry physically, but not only sexual sin. Anything at all that is sin will make you run dry spiritually. And, when you are in that position, you must come under the conviction of the Holy Spirit. You must confess the sin, repent and turn from it and be forgiven. If you can do this yourself—fine; if you are unable to do it you should seek some trusted Christian friend and do what the Bible says: '… confess your sins to each other and pray for each other so that you may be healed' (James 5:16).

Key thought: Sin of any kind will sap our spiritual vitality.

Search me, O God, and know my heart; test me and know my anxious thoughts. See if there is any offensive way in me, and lead me in the way everlasting (Psalm 139:23,24).

Are You Spiritually Dry? – 3

'"Give, and it will be given to you. A good measure, pressed down, shaken together and running over, will be poured into your lap."' —Luke 6:38

Scripture reading: 2 Samuel 12:14–25

A third reason for spiritual dryness is that we are just plain negative! Recently, I was talking about this with two Christian friends. After five minutes' conversation we became really alarmed as we reviewed our negative comments. If you want to be helped in this area, read Norman Vincent Peale's book: *The Power of Positive Thinking*. It helped me a lot in facing up to my negativity and in learning to be positive instead.

Let me say one thing by way of conclusion. If negativity is your problem, stop saying that you are spiritually dry and start affirming that God is refilling you with the Holy Spirit. Again, do not react in terms of the problem, but react in terms of the answer.

Are you dry, spiritually? What is your answer, deep down inside? What is mine? Friends, when I speak from the pulpit I am so often speaking about my own condition, and that is why people often say, 'You were speaking to me tonight', when I wasn't! I was speaking to myself! But because we are human beings we are so much the same— isn't that right? And so I am speaking about myself, and I am speaking about you.

Are you spiritually dry? Face up to what is causing you to be dry, and remedy it, by God's grace. Then start to affirm that God is enabling the Spirit to be stirred up in you and flow out so that you are full—God's blessing pressed down, shaken together and running over—that is how the Lord wants to give to you.

Key thought: Is your problem negativity?

Our loving Father, we believe for your blessing on us now, that insofar as we are dry spiritually, you will water our lives with your Spirit. In Jesus' name. Amen.

How I Prepare a Sermon – 1

'"[We] will give our attention to prayer and the ministry of the word."'
— Acts 6:4

Scripture reading: Acts 18:24–28

I have hesitated a good deal before deciding to speak about this subject, but I think that we would all agree that the sermon, whether given by myself or others, is an important part of our Healing Service. Therefore it might have some degree of importance and relevance for me to say, as far as my own sermons are concerned, how I go about preparing them. It is not just a personal statement, because I hope that you will feel that it has value for us all in our spiritual lives.

In principle, there are two ways to prepare a sermon. The usual way, which might be called the 'classical way', is that the preacher takes a verse or portion of the Scriptures and endeavours to explain this to his hearers, usually applying it to their own personal needs. He may well spend a great deal of time preparing his address which, I repeat, is designed to explain the Bible to those who listen. He will consult works of reference, such as commentaries and other books. That is the usual way of preparing and presenting a sermon.

There is another approach which I myself follow and find to be more helpful, as far as I am concerned. This works the other way round—the speaker begins with the real-life situation in which people are placed and then endeavours to show that the Bible has some message that is relevant to that particular situation. One approach begins with the Bible and works down to the need; the other begins with the need and shows that the Bible has a relevant answer. I am not comparing these methods; I am just explaining what I do.

Key thought: It can be valuable to start with a need and then show what the Bible's answer is.

Thank you, Father, that your Word provides the answers we need. Amen.

How I Prepare a Sermon – 2

'The earth is filled with your love, O LORD; teach me your decrees.'
—Psalm 119:64

Scripture reading: Psalm 119:65–72

I now want to go into some detail as to how I go about preparing a sermon and I trust that it will have some value and interest for you.

The real-life situations with which I am concerned are my own or those of people who come to see me, who write to me, or of whom I might hear. I nearly always find these real-life situations to be matters of urgency and, not infrequently (and I choose my words carefully), to be matters of life and death. They all need to be treated with the utmost concern. Although I listen to many problem situations, I think I can say that I am not 'case hardened' but that each one is important to me; I feel moved by the real problems, burdens and heartaches that people have.

These problem situations can be destructive. They can rub you out, and this is why, so often, people come to the Healing Service because their personal stress situations are a burden to them and are being destructive to them and to others.

I have learned that you can react to a stress situation, a sickness situation, in a constructive way so that you are enabled to move closer to God. This is the most important thing I have learned in my life next, of course, to dependence on Christ for salvation. So when I am listening to someone, when I am thinking about someone, I am endeavouring to depend upon God in an ever-increasing way. Do you follow me? I do that as meaningfully as I can, day by day and time by time.

Key thought: Stressful situations, whether our own or those of others, can be used as the means to depend on God more.

Help us, Holy Spirit, to learn to react to stress by learning to depend on God more.

How I Prepare a Sermon – 3

'"But when he, the Spirit of truth, comes, he will guide you into all truth."'   —John 16:13

Scripture reading: John 5:31–47

A preacher working according to the first method I described may well spend hours reading, studying and preparing his address. I don't spend time in that way but I can say that I spend an equal amount of time, if not more, in just translating those problems into my dependence on God. Of course, the preacher working according to the first method may well spend a great deal of time in prayer too—I am not making comparisons. But this—that is, the problem being translated into our dependence on God—is something that has to be followed day by day, circumstance by circumstance, and sometimes moment by moment, if it is to become a meaningful experience. It has to become a way of life.

I find that, as I do this, the Holy Spirit illuminates something of God to me as a result. The prime function of the Holy Spirit is to lead us into all truth and, when circumstances make us depend on God more, the Holy Spirit is stirred up within us and he leads us into some aspect of God's truth.

After I started to act in this way I was tremendously uplifted by the wonderful things which the Holy Spirit began to show me. You might be amused to hear that, after I had been acting like this for something like twelve or eighteen months, I realised that the wonderful things which the Holy Spirit was revealing to me were all in the Bible! It might be that I had read those words in time past; it might be that I had sought to explain them, but when the Holy Spirit makes truth to be truth, it is as though you had never heard it before!

Key thought: The Holy Spirit will lead us into all truth.

Open my eyes Lord to the richness of your blessings that meet my every need.

How I Prepare a Sermon – 4

'"you have hidden these things from the wise and learned, and revealed them to little children."'
　　　　　　　　　　　　　　　　　　　　—Matthew 11:25

Scripture reading: Psalm 119:105–112

I want to emphasise that, if you are relying on the Holy Spirit in this way, the things which are revealed to you must be what are in the Bible. It is no good hiving off on your own and making up your own 'revelation'. We are limited by the revelation of God's Word. Let there be no mistake about this point. The Holy Spirit illuminates the Word of God and none other.

I find that, when I use my circumstances to depend on God more, the Holy Spirit illuminates the truth which is contained in the Scriptures. It is quite remarkable how this issues in material for my Wednesday sermon, as well as for those people who come to me for counselling.

Sometimes people are generous enough to say that the sermon is relevant to their problem and simple to follow. If that it so, it is a work of God. It isn't difficult to understand that a sermon could be relevant to a person's needs, because that is how it began—from a real-life situation.

As far as simplicity is concerned—God is simple. Jesus is simple in his teaching. He spoke about people's real-life situations in thought-forms which his hearers would understand most clearly e.g. 'A farmer went out to sow his seed' (Matthew 13:3). He spoke of himself as being the Good Shepherd (John 10:11). One could give myriad examples of the simplicity of God's teaching as it is expressed by Jesus.

The faults are mine, but I believe that any relevance and simplicity in my sermons are blessings from God.

Key thought: The Holy Spirit's revelations to us will be in complete agreement with the Bible—the Word of God.

Thank you, Father, for your Word; a lamp to my feet and a light for my path.

How I Prepare a Sermon – 5

'May the words of my mouth and the meditation of my heart be pleasing in your sight, O LORD, my Rock and my Redeemer.'   —Psalm 19:14

Scripture reading: Psalm 19

When I give the address I think I ought to say that I am only half in the pulpit. The other half of me is in the pew, and I am listening with the utmost attention to what I am saying! Further, I need to say that I am in your shoes, as it were, seeking to listen with your ears and your heart and your need.

If I might say so, speaking generally and not personally, the weakness of many preachers is that they speak in a way which is edifying and stimulating to themselves, but they are not so concerned with what is edifying and stimulating to their listeners. Despite my own failures in the matter, I try to speak in a way that is of interest and value to those who listen, and is understood by them.

In principle, that is how I prepare, and that is how I give, a sermon. I begin with my need and the needs of other people. I translate those needs into the means of my personal dependence on God—and that is time-consuming. This issues in the Spirit making the truth to be truth, consistent with the revelation of the Bible. That, in turn, becomes my message to those to whom I relate in a counselling relationship, and issues in my sermon for a Wednesday night and at other times. And, in giving the sermon I am half speaking and half listening—with your ears, and mind, and need.

Key thought: When ministering to others it is helpful to be able to put ourselves in their shoes.

Help us, Father, to so depend on you in all our problem situations that you can safely use us to help others find your provision for their need. Through Jesus Christ. Amen.

God Is For Real: How to begin – 1

'God did this so that men would seek him and perhaps reach out for him and find him, though he is not far from each one of us.'   —Acts 17:27

Scripture reading: Acts 17:16–31

When I say: God is for real—how to begin, it means that I am starting right at the very, very beginning, so much so that I am not even going to talk about Jesus. There is something which is sometimes called 'pre-evangelism'—that which goes on before you come to thinking about Jesus. I am talking about pre-evangelism now.

It is as though you were at the very beginning point of a railway line. I think that there are people today, and I believe even in the Healing Service tonight, who are at that beginning point. They are looking for purpose in life, looking for meaning in life, looking for the answer to some problem or circumstance in their lives for which they know they haven't the answer and they hope to God that somebody else has!

When I talk about the very beginning of things, I am not only thinking of the person who fits into the category of what I've just said. I am also referring to people who might even be Christians in a kind of a way—certainly they might be church people; they may have spent many years going along that road, and it hasn't been without blessing. However, it might be that they have never been instructed as to how they can have God in their lives in a real way—not as a form but a reality.

Key thought: God gives meaning to life.

Dear Father, thank you for the meaning and purpose we have in life because we are your children and seek to get to know you. Amen.

God Is For Real: How to begin – 2

'But if … you seek the LORD your God, you will find him if you look for him with all your heart and with all your soul.'   —Deuteronomy 4:29

Scripture reading: Psalm 27

The Bible says: 'anyone who comes to him [God] must believe that he exists and that he rewards those who earnestly seek him' (Hebrews 11:6). Anyone who wants to come to God must believe that there is a God! That is the first and absolute beginning point. An atheist is someone who does not believe there is a God and, as long as he remains an atheist, he can never have God in his life. I do not say that such a person is doomed to endless failure as far as having God in his life is concerned, but I do say that he has to move from that position so that he believes there is a God before he can experience him.

At this point I am not going to talk about God in terms of Father, Son and Holy Spirit. I am not going to be theological or complicated. For the moment, you don't even have to call him God! You can think of him as being Someone out there who is bigger than, and different from, us. That's all you have to do at the very beginning. You may not be any more definite than that; it might be just a thought. I don't mind if he is called 'Mr Big'. This should be encouraging because some people, before they experience God, have difficulty in understanding and accepting what the Christian says about him. I think there are people who can be tremendously lifted up and encouraged and helped just to feel they are able to begin like this.

Key thought: People might come to a Healing Service just hoping that there is a God who can help them.

Thank you, Father, that those who earnestly seek you find you.

God Is For Real: How to begin – 3

'Jesus answered: " …Anyone who has seen me has seen the Father."'
—John 14:9

Scripture reading: Luke 15:11–27

The Bible tells us that God *rewards* those who earnestly seek him (see Hebrews 11:6)—he does things for us. The agnostic says, 'Oh, yes, there is a God but you cannot know him; he is far removed from this world and far removed from me'. So you can believe in God, and yet be an agnostic, meaning that you say you cannot know him and you cannot draw upon anything from him. I have to say again that, if you think like that, you cannot have a connection with God, you cannot come to know God and have his help and blessing and his presence in your life.

This is what Jesus says: if we know how to go to people and help them, despite the fact that we have so many hang-ups ourselves and can do things which are wrong, how much more will God who is good give good things to those who want them? (see Matthew 7:11). We have this assurance from the lips of Jesus Christ, that God, as a Father, wants to draw us to his side. So, if you can believe that God helps people and that he will help you, this is another of those 'beginning things' about which we need to be clear.

We are also told in Hebrews 11:6 that God rewards those who *earnestly* seek him. You've got to be on the level; God isn't mocked; you can't have it both ways with God. You have to sincerely hunger and thirst if you are to be filled. You have to be sincere if it is to work out. Let us face up to this, for you can very easily delude yourself and other people, but you can't delude God for a passing minute. He is God and he doesn't change for anyone.

Key thought: God wants to draw us to himself.

We praise you, O God, that, like the father in the parable Jesus told, you come running to meet us when we come to you.

God Is For Real: What God does for us – 1

'we have peace with God through our Lord Jesus Christ' —Romans 5:1

Scripture reading: Romans 5:1–11

Christianity, alone among all the religions in the world, provides the way back to God. All the other religions profess to be paths to God but say that *we* have to find the way! They are merely forms of self-improvement whereby you must follow certain standards—perhaps even sacrificially. Some affirm that, once you have tried your best in this life, you come back again as another person and begin from the point you had reached in your previous life. In the new life you make what further progress you can, then return in another life, and so, after many reincarnations, you reach the position where you are absorbed into the 'Infinite'. Christianity says this cannot be done. It affirms that *'man is destined to die once, and after that to face judgment'* (Hebrews 9:27).

Christianity teaches that Jesus takes away the barrier between us and God. This barrier is our wrongdoing, or sin, and, as we put our trust in Jesus, we are forgiven. *We are brought back to God because of Jesus Christ.* That is the most important thing to be understood about Christianity and is the point about which we need to be most clear—that it is not what *we* do, it is what God *has done* and what God *does for us* that takes us into his presence.

If you want to have God in your life—the Christian God—you come to Jesus and ask him to save you. He alone brings you into the presence of the Father, both now and at the end of this life.

Key thought: Jesus died for us, to bring us back to God.

We humbly thank you, Father, that you have made it possible for us to come back to you. We now receive your provision of forgiveness through Jesus Christ our Saviour. Amen.

God Is For Real: What God does for us – 2

'When Jesus landed and saw a large crowd, he had compassion on them and healed their sick.'
        —Matthew 14:14

Scripture reading: Acts 16:22–34

The first thing God does for us is to provide the way for us to be reconciled to himself—the way of salvation. Secondly, he restores his Kingdom to us—the Kingdom which was lost when mankind became separated from God through disobedience (see Genesis 3:23,24). Jesus said to his disciples: 'Do not be afraid, little flock, for your Father has been pleased to give you the kingdom' (Luke 12:32).

This fact is not well understood, even by those who appreciate the meaning of reconciliation with God. We need to understand it however, because it is very important to people who come to a Healing Service, and who have some sort of a need. This is why they are seeking God. They want to know what kind of help God is able, and wants, to give.

What does this 'Kingdom' mean? First of all, the Kingdom includes the reality of divine healing. Jesus said: 'preach this message: "The kingdom of heaven is near." Heal the sick' (Matthew 10:7,8). God has given us the Kingdom, of which healing is a part. The Kingdom is the perfection of God's blessing which includes healing for our minds, our bodies and our circumstances.

People with a need—some kind of sickness, hang-up or addiction— it may be something which they have not even admitted to anyone else, want to know if God can help them. I say that this is exactly what the Christian God offers to do.

Key thought: The Kingdom of God has been restored to us and it includes healing.

Father, we would draw upon your promise of healing which is ours because of what Jesus did and because it is part of your provision for us. We do this now. In Jesus' name. Amen.

God Is For Real: What God does for us – 3

'" ...do not worry about your life, what you will eat or drink; or about your body, what you will wear."' —Matthew 6:25

Scripture reading: 1 Kings 17:1–16

Not only does the Kingdom provide divine healing, but the Bible makes it quite clear that it also includes the material things which we need in life; it even refers to the things we eat and the clothes we wear. Christian people are rather sensitive about this. They like to think that their religion is spiritual. However, there is no need to be sensitive. Jesus told his disciples that if they made the Kingdom of God and his righteousness their priority, all their material needs would be met as well: '"But seek first his kingdom and his righteousness, and all these things will be given to you as well."' (Matthew 6:33).

The Kingdom of God includes healing and the Kingdom of God includes the things which we eat and the things which we wear and, Jesus said, the Father *wants to give us the Kingdom* (see Luke 12:32).

I share these very simple thoughts with you. I believe that there is a lot for us to really think about—so that we get this very clear in our hearts, our minds and our prayers. We need to know what God wants us to have and that, if you come to God, he will give you these things. He gives you a way to himself because of Jesus; he gives you healing for your mind, your body and your circumstances, and he gives the material things you need. That's Christianity in a nutshell.

Key thought: God wants to provide our everyday needs.

Thank you, Father, that you have made provision for our every need. We draw on that provision now. Thank you Father; thank you Jesus; thank you Holy Spirit. Amen.

God Is For Real: How to do it – 1

'Peter replied, "Repent and be baptised, every one of you, in the name of Jesus Christ so that your sins may be forgiven. And you will receive the gift of the Holy Spirit."'

—Acts 2:38

Scripture reading: Acts 2:22–41

There is nothing more needful than that our experience of God be real, not only at one time in our lives but day by day, as we pray for healing or whatever else is our need and our prayer.

It is not enough to know what God offers us; we must actually draw on it if it is going to work for us. Peter said that those who want to find God must repent, must believe on Christ, must be baptised, and must receive the Holy Spirit.

A good deal of very good instruction is given to people in church as to how they can believe on, or receive, the Lord Jesus Christ. If I were to put that in its simplest form I would say that it means that we accept Christ into our own lives, so that we put our trust and our confidence in him as the One who saves us and brings us back to the Father. Those who are Christians know that what made it work for them was their *acceptance* of Christ; there was a time when they did not accept him, and then there was the time when they did.

This is faith. It is believing that God is doing something and, as a result, you experience it. It is believing that God is going to become real in your life, and as a result of believing that, he does become real in your life. You accept Christ.

Key thought: Accepting Christ means that we put our trust and confidence in him.

Thank you, Father God, for your love in giving your one and only Son, Jesus, to be our Saviour. Thank you, Lord Jesus, for dying for us so that we may be forgiven, healed and saved. Amen.

God Is For Real: How to do it – 2

'to all who received him, to those who believed in his name, he gave the right to become children of God'   —John 1:12

Scripture reading: Matthew 15:21–28

If you know how to accept Christ and you have done this, then you know how to accept healing; you know how to find it 'for real' because the way of doing it is exactly the same. The point is you are praying the Prayer of Faith on each occasion. The Prayer of Faith is the same in principle whether it be to believe or accept Christ, or to believe or accept healing.

Let us look at the Prayer of Faith in relationship to healing. When a person comes to the Healing Service, they are usually in need of healing. That's why they come! If you are to have the healing of God, you must realise that it is available, then you must accept it and believe you have it. You make a decision, you exercise faith, you accept it for yourself, you make it real for yourself.

The difficulty is that people can go through this procedure as far as healing is concerned, but they are not healed. I will tell you the reason, keeping it in its simplest form.

Follow me closely; I am sharing with you something which is as important as far as the reality of healing is concerned as I have ever shared. If you accept Christ by faith, you say that he is yours even though you may not immediately feel, or be, any different. We say to people, 'Don't take any notice of your feelings; take notice of your faith. You affirm by faith that he is yours and, as you continue to do that by faith, saying that you have been brought back to God, then increasingly that will be your real experience'.

Key thought: God's promises are reality.

Help us, Holy Spirit, to believe the Word of God.

God Is For Real: How to do it – 3

'I have put my hope in your word.'   —Psalm 119:147

Scripture reading: Psalm 119:145–152

So very often people say that they accept healing—'I've prayed the Prayer of Faith'—but what they are really adding is: 'but I'm still sick'. I can sympathise with them because that might be the reality that they see and have; they still think 'sick'; they still talk 'sick'; they still fear 'sick'—and they are planning to go to the doctor the next time. It is not as easy to exercise faith about healing as it might at first sound, because if you are to exercise faith you have to start to live in terms of the healing and not in terms of the sickness!

I will give you a way to assess whether or not you have accepted healing and are exercising faith for healing. When you think about the matter for which you are exercising 'faith for healing'—the lump in your side, the pain in your head, or whatever are the symptoms—either for yourself or for another person, what is your heart reaction, your immediate reaction? Is it: 'I'm sick' or 'Dear me, there it is again—oh, it's hurting'? Is your reaction fear: 'Oh, dear me, I wonder what it might be? I must go to the doctor or the chemist'? Dear friends, I have to tell you that, if this is your heart reaction, you are not being healed and you will never be healed as long as that is your reaction to the problem. You are like those who say they accept Christ, but still say: 'I'm lost', because that's what they feel.

On the other hand, if you have disciplined yourself so that your heart reaction is to believe, by faith, for your healing, you are being healed.

Key thought: Our heart reaction to our problem is important.

Father, help us to believe your Word for our healing, and not rely on our feelings. Through Jesus our Lord. Amen.

God Is For Real: How to do it – 4

'…be strong in the grace that is in Christ Jesus.'   —2 Timothy 2:1

Scripture reading: 2 Timothy 2:1–13

If you have disciplined yourself so that, when you think of the problem, your heart reaction is to believe that you have healing, then you are exercising faith; you have accepted healing and you are being healed! You will find it real as far as you are concerned.

It isn't only about healing; it is about anything for which you are exercising the Prayer of Faith. It is so easy, it is so natural, it is so inevitable to be in bondage to the problem. Sometimes I hear people talking about the Church in very critical terms, and I realise that, however much they might protest about faith, they are not exercising faith about the Church. They are just being critical. Whatever it is, you must have the heart reaction whereby your heart sings by faith that God is working, and healing, and changing, and making all things new.

Don't be worried, don't be discouraged so that you feel: 'Oh, I can never make it work out'. It is important to know what you must *not* do, and what you must do. You move from one point to the other by realising what you need to do in disciplining yourself, so that you do it more and more.

If you really want God—a relationship with God—you believe on Christ, you accept him by faith in your heart. So it is with healing. If you want God's healing, you accept it by faith and increasingly you must come to the point where that is your heart reaction to the situation on every occasion.

Key thought: We need to discipline our minds to exercise faith.

Help us, Holy Spirit, to be disciplined so that we receive the promised blessing.

I'm Glad You Asked Me That:

How can I pray and really mean it?

'"Until now you have not asked for anything in my name. Ask and you will receive, and your joy will be complete."' —John 16:24

Scripture reading: Luke 18:35–43

How can I pray and really mean it? The question comes from someone who is sincere and who wants to pray from the heart. My answer is simple.

In Mark Chapter 11, our Lord Jesus tells us to pray about our desires. He says: '"What things soever ye desire, when ye pray, believe that ye receive them"' (v.24 KJV). When we are praying about desires, we will pray from the heart, and Jesus said this is how we are to begin to pray.

He also said that we are to believe we have received our desires, so that we 'do not doubt in our heart' (see Mark 11:23) — we are to affirm by faith that we have received our desires. We are to believe that our desires are being met and provided for by God.

We might well ask: 'What if our desires are not all that God wants us to have?'. Again, the answer is simple. One of the hallmarks of Christian prayer is that there is a sense of development. God leads us from point to point. He gives light enough for one step at a time and, if we are believing that we have received our desires, he is being enabled to reveal those desires to us more perfectly, if that is our need.

How can I pray and really mean it? Follow the instructions of our Lord Jesus Christ in Mark's Gospel.

Key thought: If we begin with our desires, believing we have received them, God will make other things clear to us, if need be.

Thank you, Father, that we can confidently ask you for what we need, knowing that you will only give us what is good. Help us to bring our heart's desires to you, our loving Father.

I'm Glad You Asked Me That: How can I distinguish
between God's will and self-will?

'I seek you with all my heart; do not let me stray from your commands.'
—Psalm 119:10

Scripture reading: Psalm 119:1–16

Complementing what I have said about believing we receive our
desires, it is of paramount importance, if we are to understand God's
will, that we know about the promises of God. Peter says: 'he has given
us his very great and precious promises, so that through them you may
participate in the divine nature and escape the corruption in the world
caused by evil desires' (2 Peter 1:4). These are the things that God has
covenanted to give us. This is what the New Testament is all about.

Paul says: 'For no matter how many promises God has made, they
are "Yes" in Christ' (2 Corinthians 1:20). That means the promises of
God reveal to us the will of God. And then, in another verse in the New
Testament it says: 'This mystery is that through the gospel the Gentiles
are heirs together with Israel, members together of one body, and sharers
together in the promise in Christ Jesus' (Ephesians 3:6).

God has made us promises; they reveal his will, and he wants us to
draw on them. That is what the New Testament says and it is my own
basic teaching about God's will in prayer.

You can know the difference between God's will and self-will if
you search the Scriptures so that you have the promises of God at your
fingertips. It is safe to say you can't go wrong in prayer if you know the
promises of God and believe you receive them.

Key thought: The will of God is revealed in Scripture in the promises
he has made.

*Your will, Father, is perfect and our only safe place. Help us to look for
your commandments and promises in Scripture so that we draw upon
them for your purposes in our lives. Through Christ our Lord. Amen.*

I'm Glad You Asked Me That: Am I being presumptuous by thanking God for healing? – 1

' ... *faith comes from hearing the message, and the message is heard through the word of Christ.*'   —Romans 10:17

Scripture reading: Romans 4:16–25

In principle, you are not being presumptuous by thanking God for healing, because there is a clear and definite promise of God that the Prayer of Faith will heal the sick (see James 5:14,15). There is more than one promise; it is a continuing theme throughout the New Testament. Indeed, if you are to exercise faith about a promise of God it means that you are thanking God that the promise is being fulfilled in your life.

Having said this, I want to say something else, because balance is always the vital thing in understanding and applying Scripture. We don't go into a sickness situation and automatically pray for healing. We need to take other things into account. As faith is what we are responsible for—Jesus said: 'according to your faith be it unto you'—we need to realise our limitations.

To give an example, during the week we were visited by five severely handicapped children; I think it would be most unwise to just blithely invoke a promise of healing with such people where the mountain is so big and faith is so small. I say this so that it is taken into account and so we make wise and balanced decisions in what we do.

Key Thought: It is not presumptuous to thank God for healing, because he promises to heal in response to faith.

Dear Father, thank you for your promise of healing, and thank you for your assurance that our small faith can grow so that you can use us to move mountains. Increase our faith, Lord, and glorify your holy name in and through us. Amen.

I'm Glad You Asked Me That: Am I being presumptuous by thanking God for healing? – 2

' " I have given them your word" '   —John 17:14

Scripture reading: John 17:1–19

Only today I was invited to speak on the phone to a lady who rang from Orange. She first contacted us three years ago when she was in the Royal Prince Alfred Hospital, Sydney. She had multiple cancers; she desired healing and she prayed to that end. As she became more informed, she realised that there was a promise of healing and, as her faith grew, she began to thank God for healing. She emphasised with me on the phone today that it has been a progressive experience. She said to me, 'First the blade ... (see Mark 4:28,29).

Now, after three years, she has just rung me from Orange to say that, finally, she has been completely cleared by her medical advisers. She had cancer in the bone marrow and her doctor now says, 'Your bone marrow is as good as mine!'

Her medical advisers said to her: 'We are perplexed. We don't understand why other people who have the same condition as you, and who receive the same medical treatment, don't do as well as you have done. Do you have an explanation?'. And she said, 'Yes, I have. I've learned how to pray'. And I was delighted when she told me that they accepted her explanation and her testimony.

Key thought: In principle, you are not being presumptuous by thanking God for healing; healing is a promise of God.

Our Loving Father, we thank you that we can begin with our desires. We thank you that you have made promises which reveal your will and we praise your name that, in principle, this means we are to thank you that your promise is being fulfilled in our lives. Through Jesus Christ our Lord. Amen.

Every Christian is a Minister – 1

'Now you are the body of Christ, and each one of you is a part of it.'
— 1 Corinthians 12:27

Scripture reading: Acts 6:1–10

Tonight[1] I would like to say something about what we are seeking to do at this time in our congregation. I remind you that our lay elders themselves recommended that they, as a group, go into abeyance; subsequently, this was confirmed, nearly unanimously, by our congregational meeting. The idea is to give every member of the congregation an opportunity to take up his or her own personal ministry. There is a tendency—and we are not free from it—of leaving ministry to those 'out front'. This new arrangement is not in place of having leadership, and leadership must not be in the place of everybody having a ministry. Let us get right the congregational part whereby everybody exercises a ministry; then we will get right the leadership part which should complement the ministry which every single person has, and is exercising.

It has been suggested by several well-meaning people—I don't resent the suggestion, for I welcome everything that is said sincerely—that the method of laying on of hands that we are now using, whereby anyone here can lay on hands, is wrong. They quote James 5:14: 'Is any one of you sick? He should call the elders of the church …'.

I want to say tonight, from the Scriptures, that what we are doing by allowing anyone to lay on hands is as right as it can possibly be. Until you come to this passage in James' Epistle, every illustration of healing in the New Testament is done by individuals acting just because they are Christians. The appointment and ministry of Stephen, the deacon, illustrates this.

Key thought: There are many instances in the New Testament where healings are performed by ordinary Christians.

Holy Spirit, help us to be ready for whatever ministry you want to use us for, so that others may be blessed.

[1] 23rd May 1973

Every Christian is a Minister – 2

'Stephen, a man full of God's grace and power, did great wonders and miraculous signs among the people … they could not stand up against his wisdom or the Spirit by which he spoke' — Acts 6: 8,10

Scripture reading: Acts 8:1–8

Stephen was someone set apart as a deacon. The job of deacons was to wait on tables and to be responsible for the social needs — the economic needs of the Christians. That is what they were commissioned to do — nothing more; it was in order to free the apostles for their primary work of prayer and the ministry of the Word.

I do not doubt that all the deacons were loyal and active in what they were told to do, but two of those men — Stephen and Philip (there could well be others who are not mentioned) — as well as performing their task of waiting on tables, exercised ministries of preaching the Word and of healing.

These were ordinary Christians who exercised remarkable ministries of witnessing and healing. They did not have a gift of healing. Their qualifications were that they were full of the Holy Spirit and wisdom.

Anyone who is a Christian can stretch forth his or her hand to heal; anyone who is a Christian can witness for Christ and preach the gospel. These are the twin things which Jesus Christ did and the twin things which he commissioned the disciples to do as well.

We have to take the New Testament as a whole. It is good that we have pastoral guidelines as to how the healing ministry should be exercised in the Church, such as in James 5, vv14 and 15, but this must not be urged to the point of excluding what is otherwise said in the New Testament.

Key thought: Our qualification for service is to be full of the Holy Spirit.

Help us, Father, to keep ourselves clean and pure in your sight so that we can be filled with your Spirit.

Every Christian is a Minister – 3

'But we have this treasure in jars of clay to show that this all-surpassing power is from God and not from us.' — 2 Corinthians 4:7

Scripture reading: Luke 19:11–26

Someone asked me: 'How can we be given a ministry?'. I will tell you. Do something by faith, for God. I repeat—by faith. Faith is believing it before you see it; you may feel nothing; you may see no result—you are doing it by faith. As you share a word of witness about Jesus Christ, or lay on hands in the Healing Service or at some other time—as you do something, God will give you a ministry. It may not come all at once and it may take time, but, if you are acting in faith, God will give you a ministry because he has promised to do so.

If, on the other hand, you are doing nothing but are waiting for something to 'come out of the blue' before you act, nothing will ever happen. Faith always has to precede sight, and faith is not only what you say—it is what you do. We are giving everyone in the Healing Service an opportunity to exercise faith and, as you do, God will increasingly give you a ministry.

I think this is a note of great encouragement. I trust that it will enable us all to go further so that we are all ministers.

Should you be one who has already been given a ministry then you should be concerned to go further, for God has more for everyone than they already have. If you have not got a ministry at all, begin now by faith and you will be in the great tradition of the New Testament, for Jesus sent them all out to teach and to heal.

Key thought: Do something for God, by faith.

Use me, Father, to be your means of blessing others. For Jesus' sake, and for your glory. Amen.

Preparation to Lay On Hands

'Do not be hasty in the laying on of hands, and do not share in the sins of others. Keep yourself pure.'   —1 Timothy 5:22

Scripture reading: 1 John 2:1–11

Do not take the laying on of hands lightly, for if in any way a person ministers unworthily he might well find the devil attacks him, which is what happened to the sons of Sceva (see Acts 19:13–16). Unless we are protected by the Spirit of God and the shield of faith 'with which you can extinguish all the flaming arrows of the evil one' (Ephesians 6:16) we may well find that we are the ones who suffer.

The first thing we must get right if we are to lay on hands effectively is that *we must like people*. It is not difficult to like those with whom you have things in common—anyone can do that; the real need is to like the people who are sent across your path, with their particular circumstances, their hang-ups, and themselves as personalities.

The next point involves our 'walk with Christ' and the need to be filled with the Holy Spirit so that the power of God is present to heal. We have to be right with God and with one another if we are going to be protected by God and used by him. So I can only suggest that, as we prepare ourselves to lay on hands, we open ourselves up to God so that the Holy Spirit might show us if anything needs to be made right. Then, as we repent, we can be in the position where God can protect us and use us, and others will be blessed.

Key thought: We need to spend time in preparation for the ministry of laying on of hands.

Help us, Father, to be faithful in preparing ourselves to be clean channels for your blessing to others. Through Jesus Christ our Lord.

The Battle of Faith – 1

'"say to this mountain, 'Go, throw yourself into the sea'"

—Matthew 21:21

Scripture reading: Matthew 16:13–20

What is the battle of faith? The first point I want to make is that, so very often, even with people who believe in the Prayer of Faith, we do not do anything about our problems, or those of other people. We are so used to them that it doesn't really register that we can, or ought, to do something about them. We never come to the point of realising that God can do something about these situations if only we prayed the Prayer of Faith—'whatever you ask for in prayer, believe that you have received it, and it will be yours' (Mark 11:24). This is not just to do with healing but it is to do with any kind of circumstance at all.

If we are to exercise the Prayer of Faith this is what we are going to do—we are going to cast that mountain into the sea! This is what we should do in prayer. This is exactly the same as when Jesus said in Matthew 16:19, 'Whatever you bind on earth will be bound in heaven'. Or, to use another scriptural way of putting it, it is casting out, or rebuking, Satan.

We need to realise that our Lord Jesus Christ used pictures with an exact meaning in mind. The 'mountain' indicates something big. The problems which concern us are, very often, big. They are big because they are of long standing; they are big because they do not respond to human resources; they are big because they are big in our minds. Christ says that we are to say to the mountain 'be cast into the sea'.

Key thought: The Prayer of Faith means that we are casting the 'mountain' into the sea.

Thank you, Father, that you have provided the means for us to overcome our problems. Through Jesus our Lord. Amen.

The Battle of Faith – 2

'You will tread our sins underfoot and hurl all our iniquities into the depths of the sea.'   — Micah 7:19

Scripture reading: Hebrews 10:19–25, 35

When we claim forgiveness from God for our sins, they are put behind God's back. It is as though we had never sinned. Dear friends, that is exactly the kind of experience we can have when we cast the mountain of difficulty into the sea. It can be to us as though it had never been. It is loosed. It is put behind us. It is put behind God. This is the first thing we are to do in prayer.

I've said before, and I say again—the only instruction given in the New Testament as to what we are to do by way of continuing in prayer is in Colossians 4:2, 'Devote yourselves to prayer, being watchful and thankful'. This completely knocks on the head the sub-Christian way of praying which is asking, asking, asking. We've made up so many things about prayer which are not in the Bible that it is no wonder our prayers are not answered.

By faith, we cast the mountain into the sea. Our only concern after that is to remain watchful and thankful in our prayers. In practice it might not be that the mountain disappears immediately. That is no fault of God's. It will disappear at once if our faith is complete—if we do not doubt in our hearts—but we know that, so often, our faith is not like that. So often, the mountain is big and our faith is small. It might well be that the answer is progressive and the Bible makes adequate provision for that.

Key thought: The Prayer of Faith is not 'asking, asking, asking'. It is believing the mountain has been removed.

Help us, Father, to continue to watch and to give thanks that the mountain is being moved. Through Jesus, our Lord. Amen.

The Battle of Faith – 3

'And he will stand, for the Lord is able to make him stand.'—Romans 14:4

Scripture reading: Ephesians 6:10–18

As far as our mental attitude is concerned, as far as our prayer attitude is concerned, the mountain has been cast into the sea and it is as though it no longer exists. Our only concern, our only prayer, our only need is to watch in the same with thanksgiving. That which God begins, he performs. But we are very human; we are very fallen. There is a conflict between what we are believing for and our doubts and fears. That is the 'battle of faith'.

The battle is to realise these alternatives. The battle is to increasingly seek to leave behind one's acceptance of that mountain of difficulty, and to accept the Kingdom reality and blessing of God.

One thing may help: the battle is won progressively. If you realise what the issues are you will find that God will increasingly enable you to count, or to reckon, that the mountain is cast into the sea, and he will enable you to increasingly believe that the Kingdom of God is within you in the situation for which you are praying. It is no disgrace, it is no sin, to wage the battle of faith. That's being a pilgrim.

Hallelujah! Friends, you will wage the battle all the days of this earthly pilgrimage—at least, that's my testimony so far. So let us wage the battle of faith. I believe that it is a holy battle. I believe that it is the battle of the Lord. So, if you are waging the battle of faith, take heart and draw upon God's strength.

Key thought: As we fight the battle of faith God strengthens us and builds our faith.

Thank you, Father, that your Word is true. Thank you for your grace and strength as we fight the battle of faith and believe that the mountain is cast into the sea.

A Review of My Teaching on the Healing Ministry:

What you must know – 1

'O Lord, you have searched me and you know me'   —Psalm 139:1

Scripture reading: Hebrews 11:1–7

What you must know, as far as the Healing Ministry is concerned is, first of all, that you must not affirm your problem. You are to face your difficulties, but you are not to react to them by making them the content of your mind. We all have faith, and your faith is what you affirm, and if you are affirming your problem, that is your 'faith'. If you are affirming your problem, if you have 'faith' for your difficulty, the problem will continue and, because it continues, it will get worse.

An important part of my own daily prayer time is in facing up to those areas where I am only affirming the problem, and in switching over so that I am affirming the answer provided by God. I affirm the answer with theological faith, meaning it is what I hope for; it is not what I see.

The second thing I want to say is that we need to realise that the problems we have are the result of our wrong thinking. I find in my counselling relationship with people that they have been affirming their difficulties for so long they no longer know what are the original causes. They now have presenting problems, that is, the things which are worrying them at the moment. Part of my counselling work is to help them see how the problem they now have has come from earlier experiences. It is no good trying to fix up the present unless you fix up the causative factors in the past. The Healing Ministry is very much concerned with doing this.

Key thought: Faith is what we affirm. We must affirm the answer provided by God.

Forgive us, Father, for our unbelief and negative thinking. Help us as we seek now to turn away from the problem and to keep our eyes fixed on you for the answer. Through Christ our Lord. Amen.

A Review of My Teaching on the Healing Ministry:

What you must know – 2

'Whoever gives heed to instruction prospers, and blessed is he who trusts in the LORD.'
—Proverbs 16:20

Scripture reading: Proverbs 15:16–33

If you react to your circumstances so that you are subjected to prolonged stress, eventually your immune system will be affected and, when your immune system is suppressed, this is when sickness comes.

Now we need to be truly diagnostic in our understanding of sickness. Your sickness is not simply the problem you have now. It is the result of your immune system being suppressed because of stress situations which have their origins in the past—and, of course, there are present areas of stress as well.

If you have a sickness, don't just go for the pills or the potions. Ask yourself: 'Why is my immune system suppressed? What am I worried about? Where has my thinking gone wrong?' and you will find, nine times out of ten, that you will get answers in those areas that are vital for you to understand. Do I make myself clear? We need to see where we have gone wrong in our thinking. When the stress is relieved and you are drawing on God's help instead of bemoaning your situation (through such attitudes as resentment or fear), your immune system will become strong again, and the disease will recede.

That is what happens as far as my experience goes, and I am quoting medical opinion as well; though not every medical doctor would agree. Insofar as it applies, you need to react to what is otherwise stress so that you are depending on God more.

Key thought: Stress can lead to the suppression of the immune system and result in sickness.

Holy Spirit, reveal to us what it is in the past which may have led to our present problems. For Jesus' sake. Amen.

A Review of My Teaching on the Healing Ministry:

What you must know – 3

'Do you not know that your body is a temple of the Holy Spirit, who is in you, whom you have received from God?'   — 1 Corinthians 6:19

Scripture reading: 2 Peter 2:4–12

The third thing we must know about healing is that God provides his perfect blessing for our situation. He provides newness; he provides wholeness; he provides healing; he provides forgiveness; he provides healing of the past, as well as the present. The important point I want to make is that God, because of Jesus, provides perfect blessing and healing for everyone according to their need. That is what you need to know as well, for unless you are clear that God has the help, you are not going to get far in altering your situation. God not only enables the normal healing processes of the body to be made fully active, but he can come in with a whole new ball game, which is provided under the Kingdom of God.

So there are three things to remember: Do not affirm your problem — you will only keep it going; Understand your situation in its earlier factors and the things which have suppressed your immune system leading to your ailments; Then remember, not least, that God has provided his perfect blessing under the Kingdom of God, and you need to know it is there.

Now, if you have difficulty in working through these things that I am sharing with you, do not be discouraged, do not give up. If you set your heart to understand and chasten yourself before the Lord your God, he will come and he will make these things clear to you by his grace and by his power, for only when God makes them real will they be real to you.

Key thought: God has provided the answer to our need, through Jesus Christ.

We praise and thank you, Father, for your provision of the way out of our difficulties. Thank you for hope and healing through Jesus our Lord.

A Review of My Teaching on the Healing Ministry:

What you need do – 1

'the power of the Lord was present for him to heal the sick.'—Luke 5:17

Scripture reading: Luke 5:17–26

There is only one thing you have to do to be healed. Jesus said: 'Have faith'. Faith means that you believe you receive the answer to your prayer so you do not doubt. Provided you do that unwaveringly, then you are doing what you need to do. But, if you are anxious about your problem situation or if you begin to strive in prayer, then you are not exercising faith that does not doubt; it will all collapse like a house of cards. I have been saying over a long period of time that, where this is the case, you have to look for another way in which to exercise faith; it is this other way that I want to explain now.

What I want to say in particular is that the perfection of God's blessing is available. Because Jesus has taken away the sin of the world and we are to be dead to sin, and because the Kingdom has been restored and we are to be alive to the Kingdom, it means that the perfection of God is available to us.

The word 'perfection' might not communicate all we need to know and understand. It is the perfection which is God that is available, and, as Paul says in Ephesians, part of God's provision is that we are to be filled with all the fullness of God (see Ephesians 3:19). God himself, because of Christ, and by the Holy Spirit, is so available that we are to be filled, the Bible says, with God.

Key thought: Another way in which to exercise faith is to be filled with God himself.

We are so thankful, Father, that Jesus has taken away the sin of the world and we have been brought into your Kingdom. Fill us, Father, Son and Holy Spirit.

A Review of My Teaching on the Healing Ministry:

What you need do – 2

'We proclaim him ... so that we may present everyone perfect in Christ.
—Colossians 1:28

Scripture reading: Colossians 1:3–14

There is no sickness or imperfection of any kind in God. Those things are unknown to God. It does not matter what your problem is—it is unknown to God, in the sense that it is not a part of God. It comes from the sin of the world. God is perfect. Let us realise this. The Bible says our body (the part that needs healing)—is a temple of the Holy Spirit. Our body is to be filled with the Spirit of God and there is no sickness, no imperfection, no infirmity, no problem, in God.

Just realise that God wants to fill you with himself. He is perfection, and in him there is no kind of darkness or problem or difficulty or infirmity whatsoever. What you need do is to know that, and rest in it. Again, you can start striving if you are not careful, but you don't have to. Just know what is available and, as you rest in him, you are drawing on healing.

If you are really going to do this in a way that is going to move the mountain, whether you are doing it for yourself or believing it for someone else, you have to take out of your mind any and every thought of the problem. When you think of the person for whom you are believing, or when you are addressing the Prayer of Faith to yourself, discipline your mind so that instinctively, completely and invariably, you see the person, or yourself, as filled with all the fullness of God.

Key thought: We are to be filled with all the fullness of God.

Thank you, Father, that there is no darkness in you, and that, through Christ, we have been brought out of darkness into your glorious light.

A Review of My Teaching on the Healing Ministry:

What you need do – 3

'Then Jesus told him, "Because you have seen me, you have believed; blessed are those who have not seen and yet have believed."'

—John 20:29

Scripture reading: John 20:19–31

When you think again of the person for whom you are believing, don't let your mind tell you: 'Oh dear me, I have not been believing this for that person for some time. What has been happening?'. Rather, discipline your mind to react by saying: 'I have accepted this for the person at this other time. God has been working in them in the intervening period'.

I met a member of the congregation in the chapel after the Service one night recently. He had just received anointing, and said to me: 'I am going to have a pre-operative check with my surgeon tomorrow for a cataract operation'. So I said: 'I will believe that God is blessing the doctor, and the surgical procedure'. And I also said to him: 'Why don't we just accept the perfection of God for your eye, so it is that which we accept?'. He gladly agreed and, there and then in the chapel, we had a quiet, simple prayer together when this was what we accepted—not the cataract or the impending operation. We were both able to rest in it. When the doctor examined him the following day, he said, 'There is something wrong. You haven't got this eye condition at all. It's not there. I can't explain it!'.

Isn't that wonderful? Isn't it simple? Isn't it conclusive? God is perfect, and he provides that you be filled with all his fullness, so there is nothing else there—and that is healing.

Key thought: We can draw on God's perfection for our need, and rest in it.

O Father, we thank you that you provide us with your fullness, and you are perfection, and we draw upon that now—your perfection, and your perfection only. In Jesus' name. Amen.

A Review of My Teaching on the Healing Ministry:

What you expect – 1

'O you who hear prayer, to you all men will come.'   —Psalm 65:2

Scripture reading: Matthew 6:1–8

The first thing you can expect from the Healing Ministry is that you will gain an understanding of how you can pray meaningfully and effectively in your real-life situation so that God is enabled to answer prayer.

I well remember, earlier in my experience of the Healing Ministry, going to a parish church and talking about the Prayer of Faith. A church warden came to me after the service and said: 'Mr Glennon, we don't even think our prayers are going to be answered. We open our mouths, and out come words'. Of course, people might be quite hurt and surprised by that statement. I can only say that I, myself, did not know how to pray so that God would answer prayer, especially where it concerned my emotional needs and the fear I had, and the problems that dogged my steps.

I did not know that fear brought about what you fear or that you have to react to your fear by affirming the promised answer of God. I did not know that you have to believe that you have received the answer of God so that you did not doubt in your heart. I did not know that you had to believe it before you had it, so you were not saying, 'it isn't working' but, instead, 'Thank you Father, by faith'.

The most I was told in my ordinary church life about the problems of life was something like this: 'My grace is sufficient for you' (2 Corinthians 12:9). I am not in any way deprecating that, but it did not stop me having a breakdown because I did not know how to pray more effectively.

Key thought: We need to learn how to pray meaningfully and effectively.

Teach us, Father, to so pray that our prayers will be powerful and effective.

A Review of My Teaching on the Healing Ministry:

What you expect – 2

'"But we want to hear what your views are, for we know that people everywhere are talking against this sect."' — Acts 28:22

Scripture reading: Acts 24

The second thing you can expect from the teaching and practice of the Healing Ministry is that your walk with the Lord will become a pilgrimage. I was converted as a youth in a meaningful way. Ever since then I have been able to say— 'Nothing in my hand I bring. Simply to thy cross I cling'. But, as I look back to that time, I would have to say this as well; meaningful as my experience of Christ was, it was also a fact that it did not alter, it never increased, it did not develop. I suppose that applies to many of us; we are not going forward.

If we are always going further in our walk with the Lord, we will always have a testimony that is up-to-date and is different from what happened yesterday or last week or last year.

When I first began the Healing Ministry a friend said something to me that I have never forgotten. He said: 'Don't take up a credal position'. By that he meant 'don't take up something that is never going to change. Always be going further forward'. It is not that God changes, but God is so infinite that we are ever going further forward into what God is and what God provides. That, too, is something you can expect from your involvement in the Healing Ministry or with teaching that is like that of the Healing Ministry. You are always going further forward in your understanding and your experience of God—Father, Son and Holy Spirit.

Key thought: Being a Christian means we grow in our love and knowledge of God.

Father, help us draw closer to you each day and know your power and presence in our lives, now. In Jesus' name we ask it. Amen.

A Review of My Teaching on the Healing Ministry:

What you expect – 3

'"The thief comes only to steal and kill and destroy; I have come that they may have life, and have it to the full."'   —John 10:10

Scripture reading: Luke 4:14–21

The third thing that you can expect from drawing on the teaching of the Healing Ministry is that you will have healing in spirit, mind, body and circumstance.

The ultimate reason why I am involved in the Healing Ministry is because, as far as my experience goes, I have seen more people converted to Christ through the Healing Ministry than in any other way. I have seen more people healed through the Healing Ministry, and I have seen more people find a deeper walk in the Spirit.

Let me give three illustrations. There is nothing exceptional about them; they just happen to be the testimonies which have come to my attention at the present time. The first is from a man in the congregation who told me: 'Through the Healing Service I have been led to Christ'. And I said to him: 'This will make a lot of difference'. He replied: 'It has made *all* the difference!'. The second relates to a young woman suffering from anorexia nervosa—as a result of prayer she is gradually resuming her normal weight and appearance; and someone else came to me last week and said, 'My prayer life has been transformed as a result of putting into practice the teaching that is given week after week at the Healing Service'.

I think it is quite enough to say that a person who draws on the insights I have shared with you will learn how to pray meaningfully and effectively. They will be ever going further forward in their experience of God, and drawing on healing and wholeness.

Key thought: Healing of the whole person, and a deepening spiritual life is to be expected when we come for healing.

We thank and praise you, our Father, for the blessing you pour out on us as we come to you for healing.

What God Told Me To Do – 1

'The eyes of the Lord are on the righteous and his ears are attentive to their cry'

—Psalm 34:15

Scripture reading: Romans 8:26–30

When I came to the Cathedral in 1955 it was only as a temporary arrangement. Archbishop Mowll wanted me to do a Social Work course at the university. So I came to the Cathedral as a place where I could do a minimum amount of work as a clergyman, and be able to do this full-time course. Before I had finished the course I had become the Precentor of the Cathedral and, with the strain of completing my university course, and being the Precentor of the Cathedral, which is a full-time job in itself, it was all too much for me, and I had what is loosely called a 'breakdown'. No-one knows what a breakdown is like unless they have experienced it—sufficient for me to say, it was horrific.

When I had absolutely nowhere else to turn, I had an experience of God which changed my life. The Holy Spirit said to me, 'You are to learn to depend on me more'. What God revealed to me was this: it was not going to be 'God helping me with my problems', but 'my problems helping me with God'. I was to learn to depend on God more. I was to learn to trust, not in myself but in God.

I now knew what to do and, each day, I would put my problems behind me. I would see God in front of me, and I would depend on God more. I persevered with this so that I ever increased in my experience of God, and my problems ever continued to disappear until, finally, they disappeared completely. That is what true healing is like. The problems are cast into the sea; they are put behind God's back. It is as though they never were.

Key thought: Our problems should be behind us and our eyes on God.

Father, help us to learn to depend on you and not on ourselves. For Jesus' sake. Amen.

What God Told Me To Do – 2

'At that time we were completely overwhelmed … Yet we believe now that we had this experience of coming to the end of our tether that we might learn to trust, not in ourselves, but in God Who can raise the dead.'
                                               —2 Corinthians 1:8,9 (Phillips)

Scripture reading: 1 Timothy 2:1–8

Out of the blue, people started coming to me with their problems. I could only tell them what I had learned, which was that my problems were to help me depend on God more. I found that what I shared with them worked just as effectively for them as it did for me.

About twelve months after I had begun the Healing Ministry in the Cathedral some young people in the congregation felt guided to go out and work for God in other places. I was very, very impressed with what they were doing, so much so that I said to God that I would go too—I would do whatever he told me to do. Again I was spoken to by the Holy Spirit. He said, 'You are to learn how to pray'. That is the purpose to which God has been pleased to call me.

I am sharing with you, not only my own call, but what I find to be a blessing to us all. Let your problems enable you to trust, not in yourself but in God, and make it a way of life. It is simple. It is straightforward. You will have to persevere, but it will work for you in the same way as I have found it worked for me and for many, many others. God bless you.

Key thought: Learning to trust in God and learning to pray can be our way of life.

Our loving Father, speak to us all we pray and say, 'Learn how to pray. Learn to depend on me more'. Let us learn to trust, not in ourselves, but in God who can raise the dead. Father, we make this our prayer and our purpose now and always. Amen, Amen, Amen.

Resources

Copies of this book may be obtained by contacting Zillah Williams.
Phone: 02 6254 3089
email: zillahwilliams@gmail.com

Further teaching by Canon Jim Glennon, including a 'Kingdom Ministry Outreach' pack'*, is available from The Healing Ministry Centre (Golden Grove).

The Healing Ministry Centre
Golden Grove Ltd
5 Forbes Street
Newtown
NSW   2042
Australia
Phone: (02) 9557 1642
Fax: (02) 9557 1412
Email: centre@healingministrysydney.org

* The pack includes an introductory DVD, two CDs and a catalogue of available resources for church or home use.
Also available at www.canonjimglennon.com